The Newquay Branch and its Branches

Plate 1. There can be few surviving branch lines in the UK to rival the variety of scenery to be found along the 20¾-mile permanent way between Par and Newquay. From the south Cornish coast at Par the line runs beside the old Par Canal before climbing the lush Luxulyan Valley at 1 in 37. This is followed by a few miles of china clay country around Goonbarrow and Bugle before the wild expanses of Goss Moor are encountered. There follows a run through rolling farmland to the north Cornish coast at Newquay. Although the branch survived the Beeching purge, passenger services struggle to make ends meet, particularly off season. In many ways this photograph is an epitome of the 1989 scene at Bugle. Class 122 "bubble" car No. 55003 leaves the weed-covered platforms of Bugle with the 12.45 Newquay to Par of 13th June 1989. In the foreground is the near-derelict Carbis Wharf branch which saw its last train some ten weeks after this photograph was taken. *JV*

Plate 3. *(Right)* In order to provide sufficient rolling stock for the mass exodus (and influx) of passengers from Newquay on summer Saturdays in the 1950s, some long-distance empty stock workings were necessary on preceding Fridays. Heading for the hills and Newquay along the Middleway to St Blazey Gate section, beside the River Par and the old Par to Ponts Mill canal, with the 12.05 pm FO Paddington to Newquay ecs on 8th July 1955 are 'Hall' class 4-6-2 No. 5972 *Olton Hall* and 5700 class 0-6-0 pannier tank No. 7715. In the days of steam all but the shortest local passenger trains were double-headed and sometimes a banker was also provided as far as Luxulyan. *R. C. Riley*

Plate 2. Crossing over the main A30 road in the wilderness of Goss Moor, between Roche and St Dennis Junction on 21st April 1983, is Class 37 No. 37272 heading one of the very infrequent spoil trains to visit St Dennis tip. The empty 'Turbot' wagons are returning to Tavistock Junction, to the east of Plymouth. The Class 37 was replaced by a Class 47 locomotive at Goonbarrow Junction. The flowering gorse in the foreground contrasts with the distant china clay workings of Wheal Remfry and Virginia Clay Works. *JV*

The Newquay Branch and its Branches

John Vaughan

Oxford Publishing Co.

Plate 4. A wonderful view of the approaches to Newquay station prior to 1904. During 1903/04 the original 1873/74 Cornwall Minerals Railway signal box (left) and engine shed were replaced and the station and track layout substantially changed to cope with more traffic, including that generated by the opening of the Newquay to Chacewater line throughout, in January 1905. In this view an ancient Dean 2-4-0T of the 1400 series (not to be confused with the well-known Collett 0-4-2T design of 1932) and five 4-wheeled vehicles leave Trenance Viaduct and roll into Newquay from Par in the early morning sunlight. *Woolf/Greenham Collection*

A FOULIS–OPC Railway Book

British Library Cataloguing in Publication Data
Vaughan, J. A. M. (John Austin Morley) *1943-*
The Newquay branches.
1. Cornwall. Newquay. Railway services, history
I. Title
385.0942372

ISBN 0-86093-470-5

Library of Congress catalog card number
90-84483

Published by:
Haynes Publishing Group
Sparkford, Near Yeovil, Somerset, BA22 7JJ

Haynes Publications Inc.
861 Lawrence Drive, Newbury Park, California 91320, USA

Printed by: J. H. Haynes & Co. Ltd
Typeset in Times Medium Roman 9/10pt.

Dedication

This book is dedicated to my father, Harold Malcolm Vaughan, who, sadly, passed away during its preparation.

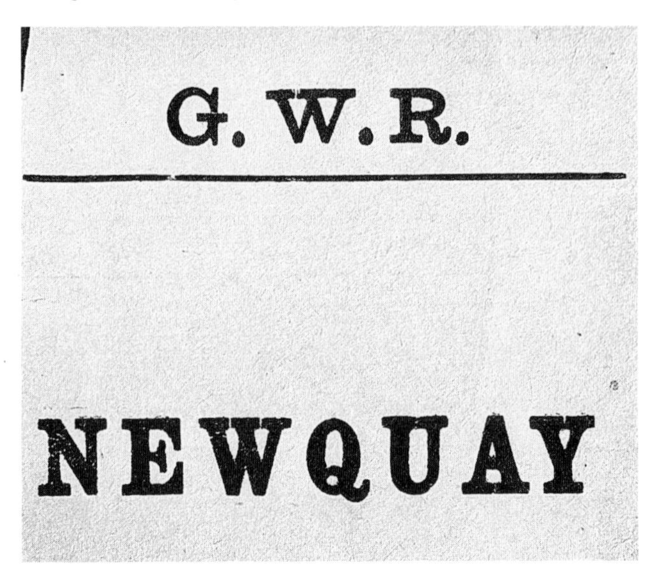

Plate 5. Some of the luggage on the above train could have been carrying this type of GWR label. *JV Collection*

Contents

	Page
Introduction	7
1 The Treffry Tramways	9
2 Cornwall Minerals Railway	16
3 The Great Western Railway	27
4 BR Steam in the 1950s	36
5 Fowey to St Blazey	41
6 The Port of Par	50
7 Par – Change for Newquay	55
8 St Blazey	61
9 Middleway to Ponts Mill	71
10 Luxulyan Valley to Goonbarrow Junction	79
11 The Goonbarrow Branch	96
12 Goonbarrow Junction to Bugle	101
13 The Wheal Rose Branch	106
14 Carbis Wharf	108
15 Bugle to St Dennis Junction	117
16 Newquay & Cornwall Junction Railway	124
17 Gothers Tramway	149
18 The Retew Branch	151
19 St Dennis Junction to Tolcarn Junction	158
20 Chacewater to Newquay and Treamble	164
21 Tolcarn Junction to Newquay	176
22 Newquay Harbour Branch	183
23 New Route to Newquay	187
Timetables	188
Signal Boxes	190
Miscellaneous and Gradient Profile	191
Acknowledgements	192
Bibliography	192

Plate 6. A magnificent spectacle on 8th August 1956 as a gleaming 'Castle' class 4-6-0 No. 5098 *Clifford Castle* proudly heading the "Cornish Riviera" pounds up the 1 in 60 from Par with the 'down' working. It was 50 years before this photograph was taken, in May 1906, when the first through coaches worked between Paddington and Newquay. The Newquay branch is the last in Cornwall to still receive through workings from London, the Midlands and the North on summer Saturdays. *Les Elsey*

SCHEMATIC DIAGRAM OF LINES INCLUDED (NOT AA TO BB)

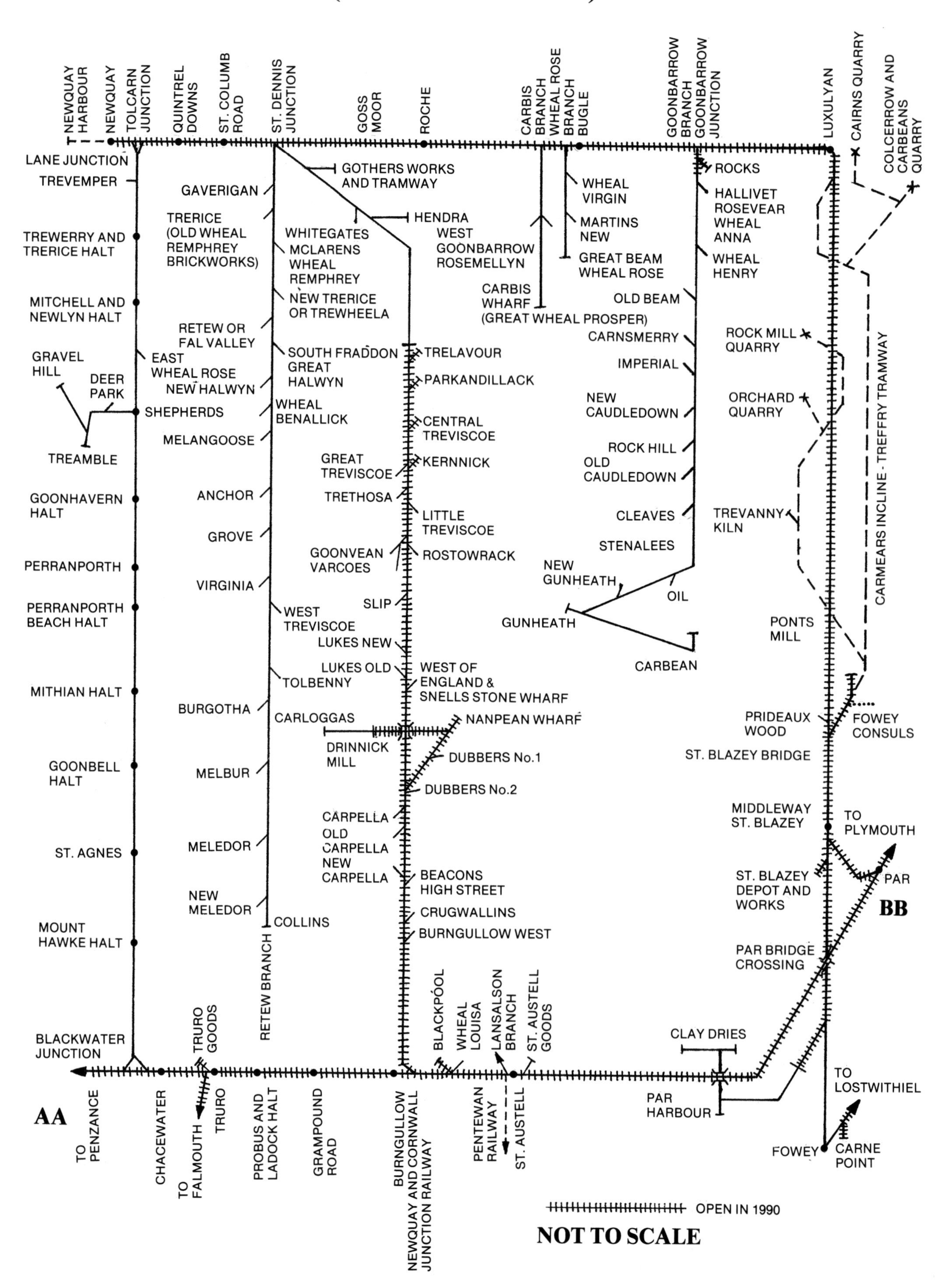

Introduction

The preparation of this book has been a classic example of a labour of love. When writing the book, it occurred to me that there can be few 25-mile stretches of railway line on the British Rail network which, in terms of diverse items of interest and changes in topography, can compare with the Fowey to Newquay route and its many tributaries. Also, although books have been written with references to the line, to my knowledge none have been published which describe all of the lines mentioned within these pages, and those which have appeared virtually ignore the past 30 years, which in many ways has been the period of greatest change.

This book covers in excess of 150 years of railway history. From the exciting days of Joseph Thomas Treffry who built tramways, canals and harbours, to the era of the Cornwall Minerals Railway and the entrepreneur William Richardson Roebuck, this volume traces the developments of those early days. Then the Great Western Railway came on to the scene and they operated some of the lines featured for over 70 years. After Nationalisation, British Railways took over the quaint old show but gradually steam petered out and many of the lines and sidings were closed (although it has to be mentioned that at least two of the line closures featured within took place in 1880 and 1887). This volume not only describes the diesel era but addresses the likely events of the 1990s, including the possible re-routing of passenger trains to Newquay and closure of part of the original route.

The Newquay Branch and its Branches is not just about trains. The entire area is rich in viaducts and tunnels, mines and pits, harbours and jetties, tramways and railways, inclines and engine houses, rivers and leats, monuments and remains, signal boxes and ground frames, railwaymen and passengers, railway companies and owners. It is, of course, not possible to satisfy all tastes. Even with a substantial 200-page document, such as the Cornish Archaeological Society's highly recommended tome on just the two miles of the Luxulyan Valley, one realises that content is all a question of balance. I have included some maps, timetables and notices and there are references to many items of signalling, but the book has not been filled with track plans and drawings which are readily available in publications dedicated to the subject. Inclusion of these would have resulted in removal of many of the unique photographs contained herein.

The photographs themselves span a period of 125 years with horse-drawn wagons contrasting with the IC125 High Speed Train units. Amazingly, over parts of the branch the 1841 alignment is exactly the same as that in use today. In many ways, despite many thousands of words, it is the photographs which show the splendid scenery, the wide range of motive power (ancient and modern), "then and now" scenes by way of comparison and, of course, views which, due to line closure or demolition, are no longer attainable, that are all-important. Sadly, despite extensive research, very few photographs of trains in action on some of the remote lines and sidings have been unearthed. Only a handful of unique or classic photographs which have been previously published appear within these pages.

Above all else it is the topography of the lines covered which is so fascinating. Treffry's goal of linking the south and north coasts of Cornwall was eventually achieved, which produced a remarkable journey for the rail traveller. From the port of Fowey passengers left behind the estuary of one of Cornwall's more important rivers and climbed through the granite cutting to Pinnock Tunnel, Cornwall's longest. The descent through rolling farm land ended up on the sandy beach at Par before continuing past Par Harbour and on to the major railway centre of St Blazey. This is the first point of note after leaving Par on today's branch line. After a trip beside the River Par and abandoned Par Canal the line climbs past Ponts Mill and up a ruling gradient of 1 in 40 for two miles through the mature deciduous trees of the magnificent Luxulyan Valley. At the top of the lush valley, with its many secrets from an industrial past including the Treffry Viaduct, are outcrops of granite which was once quarried in the area. After passing Luxulyan station china clay country comes into view and the run to the still active Goonbarrow Junction and the near-derelict Bugle station is fascinating. After reaching the 600 ft summit just beyond Roche station, the line crosses the wild and desolate Goss Moor with little foliage except for gorse and heather. Past St Dennis Junction and on to St Columb Road and Quintrel Downs the line twists and turns, through rural rolling countryside towards Newquay. After passing a series of ungated crossings and traversing the fine masonry viaduct across the Trenance Valley the seaside town with its superb beaches, splendid cliffs and ancient harbour is reached. Even in the 1990s the remarkable 20¾-mile journey from Par still takes 50 minutes at an average speed of 24.9 mph!

The obscure Goonbarrow, Wheal Rose, Carbis and Retew china clay lines had their own unique topography and the surviving line from Burngullow to Parkandillack is equally attractive, but in a bizarre way, as the track negotiates the clay tips of yesterday and today. The area of Hensbarrow Downs is unique in the United Kingdom and many have referred to it as a "moonscape". The long abandoned line from Chacewater to Newquay and its Treamble branch had the rural atmosphere of a typical GWR branch line, partly attributable to its seven wayside halts. Add to this harbour lines, obscure tramways and clay driers and it is clear the survey area is like no other, a fact hopefully emphasised by the 300 photographs.

I may sometimes claim to be a photographer of railways, but a railway historian I am not. However, in the preparation of this volume it has been necessary at times to be a combination of historian, researcher and collator. With some of the longer legal documents, such as deeds and Acts of Parliament, the role has been one of editor. I give full credit to all the high quality work contained in the books and documents mentioned in the bibliography. Also I am indebted to the dozens of contributors who have been generous with their time and assistance in supplying information, documentation and illustrations. They are all mentioned on page 192. However, I pay special tribute to Maurice Dart of St Austell who shares my interest in these railway by-ways for all of his help.

As a non-resident of Cornwall I regard it to have been a privilege to have prepared another railway book on the Royal Duchy, which I visit at least four times a year. Prior to 1850 my ancestors were Cornish and I hope this may prevent the "up-country" label from becoming too large! It is my sincere wish that you enjoy this volume as much as I have enjoyed its preparation.

John A. M. Vaughan
Goring by Sea,
West Sussex

FOWEY HARBOUR.

1 The Treffry Tramways

Most of the lines featured in this volume owe their existence to a greater or lesser degree to Joseph Austen Treffry. Born in 1782 as Joseph Treffry Austen, the son of Joseph Austen of Plymouth and Susanna Ann Treffry, the young Treffry inherited the entire Treffry Estates when his uncle, William Esco Treffry, who was the only male heir, died. The seat of the family was at Place, near Fowey and it was to Fowey that his attentions were drawn once he had completed his college training.

In 1811 he started building a new quay at Fowey which was finally completed in August 1813. He subsequently conducted a detailed survey of Fowey to determine its full scope for development to rival the port of Charlestown, south of St Austell, where most of the products from the pits and mines were shipped. Treffry also had major interests in the vast Fowey Consuls mines at Tywardreath, as well as innumerable iron and copper mines and clay pits within a 15-mile radius of Fowey. In 1823 Austen changed his name by deed poll to his wife's family name of Treffry, who had been landowners in the area since the Norman conquest.

Although the output from the various mines and pits varied as some became worked out, while others had yet to have major lodes discovered, market forces were all important. Cornwall's minerals were infamous for their volatility with years of prosperity which would be followed by market crashes and mass closures. The problem with many early mines and pits was that their profitability was so marginal that even a small reduction in market price resulted in losses. Part of the total cost of production was transport, which in the early 19th century was primitive. Teams of horses drawing 3-ton capacity wagons over poor quality roads and tracks was the norm. Accordingly, the resourceful Treffry turned his attention to canals, railways and docks.

One of Treffry's obsessions was to link the north and south coasts of Cornwall, which in the area of Par and St Austell, was a distance of a little over twenty miles. As early as 1815 he sponsored a survey to examine the possibilities of building a canal from Padstow to Fowey but this was found to be impracticable. An early attempt to build a railway from Fowey Consuls to Fowey had been dashed by the refusal of the influential Rashleigh family to allow building on their land, and attempts to secure special rates from the same family who also owned Charlestown Harbour, proved abortive. Thus Treffry focused his attentions on Par as a possible outlet for the output from his mines.

By 1828 Treffry had his plans for the proposed Par Harbour drawn up. He had rejected the idea of inner locks due to the windy and often inclement Cornish weather and instead, his designs showed a completely artificial tidal harbour. The entire complex would take ten years to build, starting with a jetty which could be used in the interim, followed by the dredging of the bay where the harbour was to be and the construction of a 1,200 ft long breakwater. This would enclose a vast 35-acre area for the harbour. Much stone was shipped from Treffry's Clift Quarry near Pentewan via Pentewan harbour, was owned by the Hawkins family.

Major clay merchants in the shape of John Lovering and Robert Martin showed some interest in using Par as an outlet due primarily to the monopoly position enjoyed by Charlestown and the often silt-bound Pentewan. The rivals made counter-proposals including a railway from the Pentewan Railway railhead (opened as a narrow gauge line in 1829 with wagons horse-drawn) into the clay-producing areas. By 1833 work on Par Harbour had sufficiently advanced for the port to receive its first commercial vessels. Copper ore from Fowey Consuls was brought down to the area around Ponts Mill some two miles from the harbour site, and Treffry considered building a canal to link Ponts Mill and the new harbour. In the Middle Ages the sea had lapped gently against the hills around Ponts Mill but centuries of mining had produced thousands of tons of spoil and waste, and by 1700 the sea shore was about 1½ miles further south, near the site of the present Par station. Further silting-up left the shore line where it is today, at Par Beach.

In the latter part of 1833 the Par Canal project commenced with the draining of the salt marshes below Ponts Mill. The canal was to be 6 ft deep at Par, 8 ft at Ponts Mill and 12 ft wide. By 1835 the work was complete with an incline plane at Ponts Mill bringing down ore from Fowey Consuls, which were in full production at that time. In the reverse direction coal was brought into the area to fuel the large steam pumping engines. For many years Treffry had pioneered the use of water power for his stationary engines which arrived on site via leats designed for the purpose. However, it was in conjunction with William West of St Blazey that a huge 80-inch engine was designed and the secret specification was passed to the famous Harvey's Foundry at Hayle to construct. In tests it produced the best performance of any engine in the County of Cornwall and resulted in fame for West and enabled him to construct his own foundry at St Blazey. The large engine house for the 80-inch engine was constructed by Captain Puckey.

During the construction of the canal the river had to be diverted and the canal built on its original course. On 11th June 1838 two canal boats were ordered from Charles Moore for £21 10s each and five years later two more cost £17 each. The incline plane to Fowey Consuls was half a mile long at a gradient of 1 in 9. Part of its course to Penpillick was through an 840 ft granite-lined 9 ft by 9 ft tunnel, which had two ventilation shafts. The double-track incline was narrow gauge and cost £2,819 to install. A second incline plane, costing £630, was constructed from the canal boat loading wharf by St

Plate 7. *(Opposite page top)* Joseph Austen Treffry was an aristocratic industrialist and, it is said, "a man before his time". Born in 1782 as Joseph Treffry Austen he inherited the vast Treffry Estates which included many prosperous mines, farms and harbours. Par Harbour was already part of the estate when, in 1838, Treffry purchased Newquay Harbour and associated land for £7,000. He then set about linking the north and south coasts by canal and tramway to serve his mineral interests. Previously, all transportation had been by horse and cart, such as this 3-ton load at Single Rose Clay Pit. The products of the air dry (left) and pan dry (right) were conveyed in either casks (barrels) or in jute sacks. All of Treffry's tramways provided for only horse-drawn wagons. *Royal Institution of Cornwall*

Plate 8. *(Left)* Whereas Par Harbour was largely man-made by the construction of a long, 1,200 ft breakwater and was essentially tidal, the Port of Fowey offered deep-water, non-tidal facilities. However, it was to be 1869 before the town was approached by the broad gauge Lostwithiel & Fowey Railway (which terminated about a mile short of Fowey) and 1874 before the Cornwall Minerals Railway opened their line from St Blazey. This view shows the busy harbour in Edwardian times (see also Plate 17). *JV Collection*

Blazey Bridge Crossing to a point on Tregaskes Burrows, near the Porcupine Inn. A third incline was later built and at the higher level most parts of the Fowey Consuls complex were connected by tramways. During the excavations for the canal a mediaeval bridge dating back to *circa* 1350 was discovered and not far from Ponts Mill an even older prehistoric clapper bridge was unearthed.

Treffry showed to the world, and to the irritation of some of the well-estabished landowners, that his "building agenda" was far from complete and in 1835 he issued a public statement letting it be known that it was his intention to build a railway or tramway from Par to Newquay, beginning with the section from Par to Mollinis, near Bugle. In the meantime, the Treffry empire had extended with acquisitions including Par Consuls, shipping interests, granite quarries in the upper Luxulyan Valley and assorted clay works on Hensbarrow Downs as well as the land to build the proposed tramway. There was plenty of conflict with, *inter alia*, the Turnpike Road Committees. By 1836 the workforce of the combined Fowey Consuls/Lanescott Mine complex totalled 1,680 persons, including 308 women and 315 children.

The first stage of the Treffry Tramway system was a disaster and after 18 months of effort an attempt to beat the terrain was abandoned in failure. It is not known to this day whether the contractor was out of his depth or whether Treffry had overstretched himself in taking on just too much. Treffry called upon William Pease who was to be Treffry's steward, as well as being a landowner in his own right, to specify a new route and to supervise personally the construction of the tramway. Another significant development at this time was the acquisition in 1838, by Treffry from Richard Lomax, of the whole of the Newquay Harbour complex and associated land. Lomax had improved Newquay in 1833 and the acquisition was a vital ingredient to Treffry's coast-to-coast plans. He also built a large lead smelting plant at Par. Eventually, this smelter was to have a most enormous stack which was a staggering 270 ft high, 27 ft in diameter at the base and 9 ft at the top. It was brick built and was a landmark for years, before being felled in 1907, after fissures in the brickwork appeared.

Having acquired Newquay Harbour, Treffry commenced discussions with Sir Christopher Hawkins, owner of Pentewan Harbour and an extensive mine and land owner. Treffry offered Hawkins use of Newquay Harbour and the Par smelter and proposed a tramway from the renowned Hawkins-owned East Wheal Rose mine near Newlyn. This tramway would, of course, link up with the Par to Newquay tramway and provide access to either port.

In 1837 both the surveying and quantity surveying had been completed for the Ponts Mill to (initially) Colcerrow Quarry. The diary of William Pease in May 1837 shows the cost of the rails and block "sleepers" for the 2,840 ft long incline, and the 6,000 ft line from the head of the incline plane to Colcerrow Quarry:

Incline:

	£	s	d
Rails 1,893 yards at 50 lb = 42¼ tons at £8 10s per ton	359	2	6
Saddles 1,893 at 12 lb = 10 tons 3 cwt at £8 per ton	81	4	0
Nails 55 lb to 100 = 18½ cwt at 17s	15	14	6
Wedges 75 lb to 100 = 25½ cwt at 15s	19	2	6
Blocks 1,893 for rails at 6d each	47	6	6
Blocks 122 for friction rollers at 6d each	3	1	0
Frames, shieves, brasses, stands brought the grand total to	£627	16	0

Incline to Colcerrow:

	£	s	d
Rails 4,000 yards at 50 lb = 89½ tons at £8 10s per ton	760	15	0
Saddles 4,000 yards at 12 lb = 21½ tons at £8 per ton	172	0	0
Total	£932	15	0

The incline plane from Ponts Mill would climb 300 ft in 2,840 ft; a gradient of about 1 in 9. The line would be on the eastern side of the valley and wagons would be hauled up and down the single line by power generated by a large waterwheel. Construction included a series of leats at the upper levels which were 3 ft wide and 15–18 inches deep. The use of the steep Carmears Incline precluded the future use of locomotives, but nevertheless the objective of reaching the granite quarries was achieved. Par Harbour became fully operational in 1840 and the first stage of the Treffry Tramway to Colcerrow Quarry was opened in 1841. The "T"-section rails which were fixed to granite sleepers weighed 42 and 56 lb per yard.

In order to reach Mollinis, near Bugle, by the continuation of the tramway, it was necessary to cross from one side on the Luxulyan Valley to the other at a level about 100 ft above the valley floor. From the top of Carmears Incline the tramway had run along a ridge of the hill on generally level ground, but to cross the valley a grand viaduct was planned. Again, it was Treffry and Pease who contributed to the 98 ft high, 648 ft long structure comprising ten arches of 40 ft each. It was constructed of granite moorstone and granite blocks

Plate 9. *(Top left)* A canal from Ponts Mill to Par was built in 1833 to transport primarily ore from the mighty Fowey Consuls Mine. In 1835 Treffry issued a public statement giving his intentions to build a tramway from Par to Newquay, beginning with the section from Par to Mollinis (Bugle). The route was designed to avoid steep gradients and the deep Luxulyan Valley was to be spanned by a viaduct. However, from the top of the valley to Ponts Mill an incline plane would be necessary. This opened to Colcerrow Quarry in 1841. The entire tramway to Bugle was opened in 1844. In this spring 1985 view of the Carmears Incline the granite block sleepers of the 1 in 9 (mean) route are clearly visible, even though the line was closed with the opening of the Cornwall Minerals Railway locomotive-hauled line up the Luxulyan Valley in 1874. *JV*

Plate 10. *(Top right)* The power for the incline plane was provided by a large water wheel; the water being provided by purpose-built leats. After closure of the incline the 30 ft water wheel, which was installed in a wheel pit capable of taking a 50 ft wheel, was removed and replaced by a 40 ft wheel upon the opening of Wheelpit China Stone Mill in about 1890 at the same site. The product of Wheelpit was conveyed in slurry form by a 6-inch pipeline to Ponts Mill. The works ceased operations in 1908 and the wheel was broken up for scrap during the Second World War but never taken away. The remains were photographed during a hike in 1985. *JV*

Plate 11. *(Left)* Historians agree that the ultimate monument to Treffry's numerous achievements is the Treffry Viaduct/Aqueduct towards the top end of the Luxulyan Valley. Built between 1839 and 1842, the structure is 650 ft long, 98 ft high with ten arches, each with a span of 40 ft. It contains some 200,000 cubic feet of granite. The 5-6 ton blocks came from Treffry's own quarries at Colcerrow and Carbeans and were conveyed to the site by tramway. This 1989 view was taken through a telephoto lens looking south from the site of the tramway to Cairns Quarry. Note the Treffry family crest in the centre. The Newquay branch passes under the right-hand arch. *JV*

Plate 12. One of the earliest of Treffry's tramways was the standard gauge line to Colcerrow Quarry at the north end of the Luxulyan Valley. From 1841 granite was conveyed by horse-drawn wagon to the top of the Carmears Incline. In 1855 an extension branch line to Gatty's Bridge and Cairns Quarry was opened. This line ran to the north-east of Luxulyan village, but by 1880 it had closed. After much "bramble bashing", these granite sleepers, which formed part of the old trackbed well over 100 years ago, were photographed on 10th June 1989. *JV*

weighing 5 to 6 tons each from Treffry's own quarries. The splendid structure took three years to build at a cost of £6,708. It doubled as an aqueduct and carried water beneath the granite slabs which supported the tramway. The water fed the leats on the eastern side of the valley. The tramway continued through Luxulyan village and across open farm land to Mollinis. The terminus was accessible to the principal china clay pits and also to a number of tin mines including Ballarat, Black Pepper, Hallew, Mollinis and Wheal Elcum. The chief civil engineer for the tramway was James Meadows Rendel.

The primary outgoing traffic on the tramway was copper ore, china clay, china stone, lead ore, granite and building stone to Par and incoming, coal, timber and lime for agricultural use. An entry in the *West Briton* newspaper in August 1843 referred to the Ponts Mill to Mollinis tramway as "nearing completion". This caused consternation to the shareholders of the Charlestown Harbour Company and they, supported by the Directors of the Cornwall China Stone & Clay Company, proposed the building of a railway from Nanpean and St Dennis to link up with the Pentewan Railway terminus at St Austell. However, as with earlier schemes, this came to nothing because by the time the proposers lodged their intentions by application to Parliament, Treffry had announced that he was about to commence construction of the line he had mentioned some years earlier, to link Newquay with his Ponts Mill to Mollinis tramway, with a branch down to St Dennis and Hendra Hill. This would later be extended through the heart of clay country to Treviscoe and St Stephen in Brannel. Although the proposers of the "rival" line tried to summon support from wealthy local landowners, little interest was shown. As if to rub salt in the wounds Treffry acquired by lease, both Hendra and Trelavour china clay pits in 1844, which would later be served by his planned tramway. Although many railway history books show the Bugle to Ponts Mill tramway opening on 18th May 1847, all the evidence shows it was opened at the beginning of 1844; according to the Pease diaries and the *West Briton*. Certainly the incline, viaduct and tramway were ready by then.

When the Ponts Mill to Mollinis standard gauge tramway opened throughout Treffry, Pease, Rendel and local dignitaries rode the whole length of the line with cable and horse power. The tramway soon settled down and achieved its objectives in conveying minerals out and fuel and fertilisers in.

Again, it is the 1845 diary of William Pease which gives insight into the carriage charges for iron ore and china clay from Bugle to Par by the ton:

Horse from Bugle to top of Incline Plane = $3\frac{3}{4}$ miles at $1\frac{1}{2}$d per mile	$5\frac{1}{4}$d
Machine man	$\frac{3}{4}$d
Man with wagons	$\frac{3}{4}$d
Discharging wagons in boats	1d
Boatage to Par, man and horse	1d
Discharging boat at Par	2d
Shipping	$\frac{1}{2}$d
Other	$\frac{3}{4}$d
Wear and tear on railway and canal	1s 1d
Wharfage at Par	4d
Total for iron ore	2s 5d
Extra for china clay	3d
Total for china clay	2s 8d
	(just over 13p)

While all of this building and acquisition activity was going on, Treffry held a number of other public and business positions. He had once been Sheriff of Cornwall, which contrasted with his directorship of the Cornwall Railway and which was enhanced in 1844 when he was appointed Chairman. It had obviously occurred to Treffry that a main line from one end of Cornwall to the other could only enhance the transportation system he had built. Isambard Kingdom Brunel later worked on behalf of the Cornwall Railway Company in building the main line and obviously Brunel met Treffry. It is interesting to ponder what discussions they may have had regarding the gauge of railways, with Treffry showing considerable foresight with his standard gauge lines and Brunel with his white elephant broad gauge.

Work had, by 1844, started in earnest on the tramway from Newquay to East Wheal Rose with the line to St Dennis and Hendra also making progress. As stated in Section 22, the Newquay Harbour line also commenced with a steep cable-hauled incline, and there was also a significant valley to span; the Trenance Valley just outside of Newquay. A 530-yard tunnel was necessary at Toldish, near Ruthvoes, which was reached by the railway builders in 1846. Ruthvoes is very near the site of the current St Dennis Junction. In the summer of 1846 Treffry was taken ill and was obliged to manage his complex affairs from his home at Place, assisted by his able steward

Plate 13. The Treffry Tramway to Mollinis terminated at a point *near* the Bugle Inn at Bugle. Similarly, the Cornwall Minerals Railway plans for converting the tramway to a railway to a point *near* the end of the said tramway at Bugle. Thus it is difficult to define exactly where the tramway terminated. The south loading dock at Bugle station site has been suggested but so has the old air clay dry at Wheal Virgin, seen here in June 1989. The dry still had rails in evidence in the mid-1960s – effectively a spur off the short Wheal Rose branch. *JV*

Plate 14. Not only did Treffry own mines, pits and quarries in the Par to Bugle area but pits at Hendra Hill and Dreamer's Delight, a pit near Retew Downs, were in his possession by the mid-1840s. As part of his desire to link the north and south coasts and to improve transportation, tramways from Newquay to St Dennis and Hendra, and to the significant East Wheal Rose Mine, owned by the Hawkins Estate, were constructed. Work started at Newquay Harbour in 1845 but it was 1849 before the lines were open. All traffic was horse drawn. In this remarkable view of what is now Newquay's main street, taken well before the turn of the century, six empty clay wagons are drawn by horses towards what is now Newquay station. *Woolf/Greenham Collection*

Pease. In 1847, despite Treffry's personal circumstances, he re-opened two lead and silver mines near Newquay and, following the bankruptcy of Edward Bullman of Leeds, he acquired his assets, including two pits at Parkandillack, close to Hendra and Trelavour.

In February 1849 the tramway between Newquay Harbour and East Wheal Rose was in operation and the line to St Dennis and Hendra Crazey followed in June 1849. Only an incline up to the clay works on Hendra Downs remained to be built. Treffry had also given thought to extending his earlier tramway from Ponts Mill to Mollinis, down to Par Harbour to save the transhipment to barge for the two-mile journey by canal to Par. In all, the tramways from Newquay had taken five years to construct. It was, of course, still in his mind to link Mollinis with the St Dennis line, but by 1849 it was not his top priority, especially as the year 1848 had seen a downturn in the china clay industry with major producers agreeing to quotas to avoid over-production. Treffry's last venture was the launch of the West of England Clay Company in January 1850. He was to be a co-partner and shareholder but three days before the lease was due to be signed Treffry died of pneumonia. He was 68 years old.

Treffry was a remarkable person by all accounts. He was a man of exceptional energy and imagination. He had interests in virtually every one of Cornwall's great industries. He was a man of great vision and was once described as "a man before his time, considerate, kind and humane". There was a massive turnout at his funeral and it is said that virtually every man, woman and child for miles around attended. After his death his estate went into chancery and there were few significant events for nearly seven years. It was Dr Edward Willcocks, a Treffry on his mother's side, who was Joseph Austen Treffry's mother's sister, who took over the family's affairs as best he could. He was inclined to be more academic than practical but he was nevertheless determined to learn more about mines, ports and railways. His doctorate in Civil Law was of limited use to him, although with the help of his cousin's former associates he survived. Only William Pease had defected – to the aristocratic Fortescue family.

On 16th May 1850 the good doctor had changed his name by deed poll to Dr Edward Willcocks Treffry. In the following years the original tramway was extended in 1855 from Ponts Mill to Par and, early in 1852, the Hendra Incline from Hendra Crazey to Hendra Downs had also been completed. The production of Fowey Consuls had started falling and Dr Edward sold both land and clay pit holdings, although the pits in question were producing only a few hundred tons of china clay per annum. Even Hendra was producing only 1,000 tons of china clay and 1,500 tons of china stone per annum; not much more than two or three modern train loads! These were bad times as the price of copper ore plummeted as imports from Chile, Bolivia and Peru flooded the market. From 15,254 tons of copper ore produced by Fowey Consuls in 1836 only 3,804 tons were yielded in 1860.

Edward had had little time to continue the tramway schemes and funds were not as readily available as they had been some twenty years previously. However, during 1864, Edward was approached by a group of china clay producers to provide the missing Mollinis to St Dennis Junction tramway link and to join the Hendra Downs line with the main Cornwall Railway at Burngullow, Penzance having been linked with Plymouth by rail in 1859 with the opening of the Royal Albert Bridge over the River Tamar. Edward became an official of the newly formed Newquay and Cornwall Junction Railway and the story of that line appears in Section 16. By the mid to late 1860s there was another depression in the prices of minerals, especially tin, and this impacted other minerals. In July 1867 the unthinkable happened and the great Fowey Consuls mine closed down, never to be reopened.

The tramways soldiered on, but in a survey report written in 1860, commissioned with a view to introducing locomotives between Newquay and Hendra, it was reported that the permanent way was less than substantial, the track was a modest 42 lb to the linear yard, viaducts and tunnels were unsatisfactory for locomotives and that points and crossings upon it were of an inferior description. The report concluded that the tramway was fit only for horse-drawn wagons and much work would be needed for locomotives to be able to use the lines. By 1870 the Treffry Tramway system was one of only two horse-drawn systems in the county (the other being the Pentewan which was converted for locomotive use in 1874) and was becoming increasingly archaic. It was thus perhaps timely when, in 1870, one W. R. Roebuck of London arrived in Cornwall with the objective of investing some of his spare capital in Cornish Railways.

Roebuck started meaningful negotiations with the Treffry Estate Trustees during 1872, and he was involved with Edward in discussing the possibilities of leasing both the Par to Mollinis and Newquay to Hendra sections of the Treffry Tramways. Terms were eventually agreed and Roebuck formed the Cornwall Minerals Railway Company to lease the lines, purchase additional land to allow the expansion and link-up of tramway lines and convert all lines to railways, capable of taking locomotive-hauled trains. Thus ended the era of the Treffry tramways with perhaps the greatest monument to the pioneer Joseph Austen Treffry being the Treffry Viaduct, with its now listed status hopefully ensuring all-time future preservation.

Plate 15. Just outside Newquay the Trenance Valley had to be crossed. To save time and money a flimsy 147-yard long viaduct was built, as seen in this remarkable pre-1870 picture. It had 18 granite pillars supporting a complex wooden structure comprising 25 arches, each with a span of 25 ft. The structure was 58 ft high and could support only small horse-drawn wagons. It was opened in January 1849 and was replaced in 1873 in anticipation of the coming of the locomotives of the Cornwall Minerals Railway. It was locally known as "the spider". *Woolf/ Greenham Collection*

2 Cornwall Minerals Railway

William Richardson Roebuck was far more than a casual investor. He clearly had a strategy which included not only the acquisition of minor railway lines in Cornwall but majority holdings in certain mines and pits. He had significant amounts of money to invest and it apparently took little time for him to contact all of the great property and investment holding Cornish families, such as Treffry, Hawkins, Carlyon, Robartes, Fortesque, Edgecumbe, Falmouth, Arundell and others. He soon became principal stakeholder in a number of enterprises including the Cornish Consolidated Iron Mines Corporation which was incorporated in 1872 to extract, process and ship iron ore from the mines in the Perran Lode, mentioned in the Chacewater to Newquay section.

Confirmed on 21st February 1872 was an agreement between the trustees of the Treffry Estate, Reverend Edward John Treffry, his son Charles Ebenezer Treffry and William Richardson Roebuck, whereby a lease for a term of 60 years was agreed to be granted of the said railways or tramways, to the said William Richardson Roebuck and his assigns. There followed some hectic activity as Roebuck tied together a number of "loose ends" so that an Act of Parliament could be drafted to authorise the construction of railways in the County of Cornwall, to be called the Cornwall Minerals Railway, and the amalgamation therewith of the New Quay & Cornwall Junction Railway, and other undertakings connected therewith.

Roebuck had not only to deal with land acquisition but he had to consider who would engineer the lines, who to employ as contractor, the cost of actual construction and the supply of locomotives, rolling stock and relative infrastructure items. It should be mentioned that Roebuck formed a limited company, the Cornwall Minerals Railway & Harbour Company and obtained a Board of Trade certificate under the Railways Construction Facilities Act of 1864, authorising the company to improve existing lines and make certain new railways in the area. However, the House of Lords negatived the certificate so that the company was obliged to go to Parliament for an Act of Incorporation in the normal way, which was passed on 21st July 1873. The Act described the existing system as "railways or tramways stretching, with some interruptions, from New Quay on the north west, to Par Harbour on the south east, on the lands of the Treffry Estates, and which are mainly used for the conveyance of minerals to the New Quay Harbour and to Par Harbour". The primary purpose of the Act was to convert the Treffry Tramway lines and permanent way to a standard capable of being worked by locomotives, rather than horses, and to link up the "missing" section between Bugle (Mollinis) and St Dennis Junction (Bodmin Road Junction) and between Drinnick Mill and Hendra, near St Dennis. A new line of four miles was proposed from Par (St Blazey) to the docks at Fowey. In addition to upgrading and linking there would also need to be some diversions, namely a route up the Luxulyan Valley to avoid the Carmears Incline (which would obviously be impossible for locomotives) and the narrow and low tunnel at Toldish, near Ruthvoes. There would be heavy earthworks in places, particularly Luxulyan, and new viaducts would be needed in the valley and also at Trenance, Newquay, where the old wooden-topped structure was incapable of taking the weight of locomotive and train. The 1873 Act also detailed the many road overbridges which would be necessary.

Broadly, the CMR company was authorised to "alter and improve the line from Par Lead Smelting Works to Ponts Mill and the line from the village of Luxulion (*sic*) to Mollinis at Bugle". These lines were to be linked by a new $2\frac{1}{2}$-mile long line on the western side of the Luxulyan Valley which would pass under the 98 ft high Treffry Viaduct, which carried the existing tramway. A new line across the bleak Goss Moor would link Bugle with Bodmin Road (St Dennis) Junction. Branches from Bugle to Carbus (*sic*), from Bodmin Road Junction to Melangoose Mill (the Retew branch), and from about half a mile short of East Wheal Rose to Treamble, were also included in the Act. Another link was that from Hendra Crazey to the New Quay & Cornwall Junction Railway at Drinnick Mill, the latter to be mixed gauge. The tramway from Hendra to Newquay and the line from East Wheal Rose to Treloggan Junction (later Newquay and eventually Tolcarn Junction) would also be upgraded. The engineer for the CMR work was W. H. Thomas and the contractor was Sir Morton Peto. West & Sons of St Blazey were heavily involved with the building, including iron bridge girders and supports cast in their St Blazey foundry.

Roebuck was able to deploy considerable manpower on the project and working in three large separate groups the work was carried out expeditiously. In addition to the aforementioned viaducts there were other obstacles to rapid progress, such as the 1,173-yard Pinnock Tunnel between Par and Fowey, to become the longest tunnel in Cornwall, and the blast through granite for the cutting, and the 50-yard tunnel at Luxulyan. There was also a significant railway buildings programme with a locomotive works and unusual roundhouse and turntable combination at St Blazey, as well as assorted goods sheds and, slightly later, passenger stations.

By February 1874 it was reported at the second general meeting of the Cornwall Minerals Railway that progress in the previous six months had been very satisfactory, from Fowey to Treamble. The wharfs and jetties at Fowey were in a "forward state" and the earthworks between Fowey and Pinnock Tunnel were almost complete, with permanent way and ballasting commenced. There were 100 linear yards of the tunnel to complete, but at the western end the permanent way from the tunnel down to Polmear, near Par Sands, had been completed with the track *in situ*. Some girders were required for a railway bridge over a road at Polmear. The crossing of the canal and river at Par had all been completed but there were problems with the red brick built St Blazey depot where there had been delays in the supply of materials.

The most difficult section was from Ponts Mill to Luxulyan and it was recognised from the start of the works that this would present the greatest challenge. It was anticipated in February 1874 that the two granite cuttings above Ponts Mill would take a further five to six weeks to complete and above that there was much work to be done on the viaducts, including the riveting of the girders (there is a fine photograph of this work on page 17). Between the northern end of Ponts Mill Viaduct and Rock Mill Viaduct there was a 40 ft deep gap in the embankment, which it was estimated would take some six weeks to fill. A further granite cutting at Rock Mill would require three to four weeks to complete, as would the large cutting at Luxulyan village. Otherwise progress on this difficult section was satisfactory.

From Luxulyan to Bugle the tramway had been reconstructed and the permanent way had been laid and ballasted.

The two public road overbridges at Luxulyan and Bowling Green were behind schedule, but Sir Morton Peto was confident that they would be finished at the same time as the rest of the work. The long stretch of new line between Bugle and St Dennis (then Bodmin Road) Junction was progressing well except the sizeable embankment which carried the railway over the main road on Goss Moor which still required a staggering 13,000 cubic yards of material to complete the same. Five miles of permanent way between Newquay and St Dennis Junction had been laid as had the upgraded line from East Wheal Rose to Newquay. Over bridges seemed to be the main problem with those at White Cross, Halloon (St Columb Road) and Goss Moor, and on the East Wheal Rose line those at Benny Mill and Matha incomplete.

Of the remaining sections of line the situation was mixed. The link-up with the Newquay & Cornwall Junction Railway, between Hendra and Drinnick Mill, was "rapidly approaching completion" but this conflicted with the Retew branch where work was not progressing well, due to the late possession of land. Surprisingly, work on the one-mile Carbis branch had not started, or "ground had not been broken" in report terminology. There was some work of importance outstanding on the Treamble line in respect of cuttings at Fiddler's Green and Rejourra. Bearing in mind the manual nature of the workings CMR progress was phenomenal. A contractor's steam locomotive was used on the Treamble extension and the railway company came in for local criticism, especially from the Methodist church, for carrying out work on the Sabbath. Not all of the manpower was found from local sources and large numbers of Irish navvies invaded the area.

Leading up to the opening a new jetty at Newquay was being completed and the new masonry piers of Trenance Viaduct now had their fine West & Sons iron girders providing support for the trains which would soon be running over them. An engine shed and turntable at Newquay were in the final stages of construction. Also a dozen or so of the 18 0-6-0 tank locomotives ordered from Sharp, Stewart & Company of Manchester had been delivered, along with a few dozen of the 400 goods vehicles which were to convey the minerals to the ports. A light locomotive traversed the line from Fowey to Newquay on 27th April 1874. A Board of Trade inspection of the lines took place on 15th May 1874 but an operating certificate was not granted as there was still some work outstanding. This included point detection work, the line having been provided with Russell's instruments, block telegraph and semaphore signals. Stevens's facing point indicators were used and the signalling was largely controlled from a series of CMR-designed signal boxes.

Following a busy few weeks, which not only included

Plate 16. Arguably the most significant find in the research for this volume is this superb 1873 view of Rock Mill Viaduct under construction in the Luxulyan Valley. The horse and single wagon, typical of the Treffry tramways of the era, are situated on the "valley floor" standard gauge line built between 1868 and 1870 from Ponts Mill to Rock Mill and Orchard Quarries, the stone from which was probably used in construction. Note the primitive way of lifting the granite blocks. The CMR line was opened on 1st May 1874 and today, Class 37s still rumble over the viaduct with clay trains! *Maurice Dart Collection*

Sunday working but various inducements such as free beer, the final work was completed. Again, there were complaints from the local community as it was reported that between Goss Moor and Halloon 50 to 60 navvies were employed and a steam locomotive was kept constantly running, bringing in ballast to assist track laying, all on a Sunday! The problem was that while the Cornish railway workers lived within the local community, the Irish navvies lived in tents beside the line and it is not unreasonable to assume that other than working on the track or drinking the CMR-supplied beer, there was not much to do in some of the remoter areas.

The Cornwall Minerals Railway was opened to traffic on 1st June 1874, just 11 months after the CMR Act was passed. The only item of non-compliance by the CMR had been their failure, in accordance with the CMR Act, to lay rails to both narrow (standard) and broad gauge between Drinnick Mill to St Dennis Junction. This had been noted by P. J. Margary, the Engineer of the Cornwall Railway, who reported the fact to his board, whereupon the CR instructed their solicitors to call upon the CMR to do so. This led to the institution of Chancery Proceedings in 1875, but having no defence to the action the CMR then laid the rails but in such a fashion that they were not usable.

The CMR General Manager, J. C. Richardson, flagged away the first train from Par (the present St Blazey). The guard was probably John Rice who had once worked on the Bristol & Exeter Railway as well as on the Treffry tramways. There were some curious workings in those early days of operation, especially on the branches before there were sufficient sidings. The locomotive would start in the middle of the train, dropping some of the rear trucks at certain points while gathering more wagons at the front of the formation and pushing them on to the end of the journey. On its return the engine would pick up the then laden trucks at the front of the return formation and simultaneously propel and haul to the original starting point.

Station Masters were appointed, despite the absence of passenger trains. They were located at Fowey, St Blazey, Luxulyan (then known as Bridges), Bugle, Roche (then Holywell, later Victoria), St Columb Road (then Halloon) and Newquay; the latter doubling as Harbour Master. There were resident railway representatives at Retew and Treamble. In addition, the CMR employed a significant number of drivers, firemen, shunters, guards, cleaners, fitters, porters and crossing keepers.

In August 1874 a tolls poster was produced which showed quite disparate rates for certain commodities over the various parts of the CMR. For example, upon the railways authorised by the CMR Act of 1973, metals, minerals, clays, wrought and cast iron, tiles, timber, lime, limestone, culm, coal, oarweed, dung, compost and manure, building stone, road stone, granite and iron ore were charged at 3d per ton mile, whereas grain, corn, flour, meal, potatoes, hay, straw, seeds, vetches, peas and salt were charged at 6d per ton mile. Upon the Newquay Railway and the East Wheal Rose branch, under the Treffry's Estate (Newquay Railway) Act of 1857, copper, tin and lead ore, other ores, wrought and cast iron, bricks, tiles, slates and timber were charged at 5d per ton mile, whereas lime, culm, coal, oarweed, dung, compost, various stone traffic, clay

Plate 17. Many of these early Cornish views feature horse traction. Not only were horses used on all of Treffry's pre-CMR tramways but they were used for shunting in many works and ports. In this early view of Fowey three schooners are being loaded with china clay. On the wharf nearest the camera two wagons are being unloaded by hand, while a solitary horse waits to haul the empties to the tiny single-wagon turntable, sidings and the "main" branch. More loaded wagons are just visible in the foreground. *JV Collection*

Plate 18. This is yet another very early (pre-1877) photograph showing No. 17 of the CMR, one of the original 0-6-0T locomotives built by Sharp, Stewart during 1873/74, just south of St Blazey depot. When the GWR took over responsibility for running the CMR in 1877 No. 17 was returned to the builders with two others in part payment of debts. In any event, all retained locomotives were renumbered by the GWR in 1877. No. 17 became the Lynn & Fakenham Railway's No. 1 *Melton Constable.* *Clinker Collection*

Plate 19. The original 18 Sharp, Stewart locomotives were designed to work in pairs "back to back" with one crew manning both engines "Fairlie style". The GWR retained nine of the originals but rebuilt them as 0-6-0 saddle tanks, and removed the names of the four locomotives which had carried them.

In this early Edwardian view, the former CMR No. 2 *Lord Robartes* had been converted in 1883 to GWR No. 1393 and is seen posing near Goonbarrow. It is likely the hand-written name *The Lion* was negative doctoring, rather than official naming. The engine lasted until 1936. *C. Batchelor Collection*

Plate 20. The last locomotive purchased by the CMR was an 0-6-0ST named *Goonbarrow* which worked the branch of the same name from its 1893 opening date. As No. 1388 it was absorbed into GWR stock in 1896. Another 0-6-0ST to work the line was this 1876-built Manning, Wardle locomotive. It was sold to Colonel Stephens for use on the Kent & East Sussex Railway in 1914 and renamed *Hesperus.* The name *Ringing Rock* later appeared on the Colonel's Selsey Tramway in West Sussex. The photograph dates to *circa* 1904 and clearly shows the GWR No. 1380 and the nameplate. *C. Batchelor Collection*

and sand were only 4d. Grain, corn, flour, meal, potatoes, hay and straw, etc., were, as with the new CMR lines, also 6d per ton mile. Upon the Newquay & Cornwall Junction Railway the rates were much less, being a mere three half-pence (1½d) per ton mile for dung, manure, oarweed, sand, coals, culm, coke, charcoal, etc., 2d for bricks, tiles, slates, all ores, various irons and 3d – half of that sum charged on the other lines – for sugar, grain, corn, flour, china clay and china stone, timber, etc. Two interesting additions to the long list were carriages not being adapted and used for travelling on a railway and not weighing more than one ton, 3¼d per mile and all goods which passed over or along the incline plane to Newquay Harbour, Pier, Wharfs or works adjoining the same, 2d per ton *in addition* to the above tolls.

Roebuck was a little unlucky with the timing of his railway and mining ventures. Even while the lines were being built or upgraded there were storm clouds looming as Cornwall headed for another of its spectacular crashes in the price the mine and pit owners were able to get for their products. In particular the iron ore boom in the Perran Lode (and elsewhere) crumbled as cheap sources of the mineral were found in southern Europe and South America. Having spent a fortune on the railway (just the 18 locomotives had cost £43,200) and having acquired eight steam cargo vessels, in addition to mining investments, pressure began to mount. In 1874 mines closed with such rapidity that by the end of the year only seven of the 25 iron mines remained open.

The Treamble branch had been extended by over a mile to Gravel Hill in 1874 with the consent of the landowner but without parliamentary sanction and this stretch of line was immediately affected as the iron ore traffic was reduced to a trickle. The guarantee of fixed amounts of iron ore had been a chief factor in the formation of the CMR. In an attempt to save something from the near ruins, Roebuck invested in new hydraulic tipping frames at Fowey for the handling of china clay, but nobody could do anything about the iron mines' closures. To make matters worse there had been an over-production of china clay between the years 1870 and 1873 and the prominent owners were obliged to regulate their output by mutual consent. The railway sued the Cornish Consolidated Iron Mines Corporation for failing to honour their contracts, but predictably the company went into bankruptcy. By 1875 Roebuck was in serious financial difficulties and the unfortunate Sir Morton Peto, the contractor who had invested heavily in the company, was by then completely ruined financially. China clay production slumped during 1875 and 1876 to the lowest level for many years.

The CMR made a despairing attempt to augment their income by inaugurating a passenger train service between Fowey and Newquay. The coaches for this traffic were small 4-wheeled carriages built at Bristol. The whole of the passenger rolling stock ever owned by the CMR comprised three third-class and three composite coaches. It seems the coaches may have been once owned by the Midland Railway. The initial timetable showed trains leaving Newquay at 6.45 am and

Plate 21. This view of 39 staff of the Cornwall Minerals Railway dates back to 1874 and shows a set piece at St Blazey station. Also visible is one of the original Sharp, Stewart locomotives. The fine Plymouth bricks were later rendered – compare with Plate 89. When opened in 1876 the station was called Par, but once the connection between the CMR and the GWR was opened in January 1879 the "main line" Par station retained its name but this station became St Blazey. It closed finally in 1925 but the buildings lasted a further 45 years plus. *Royal Institution of Cornwall*

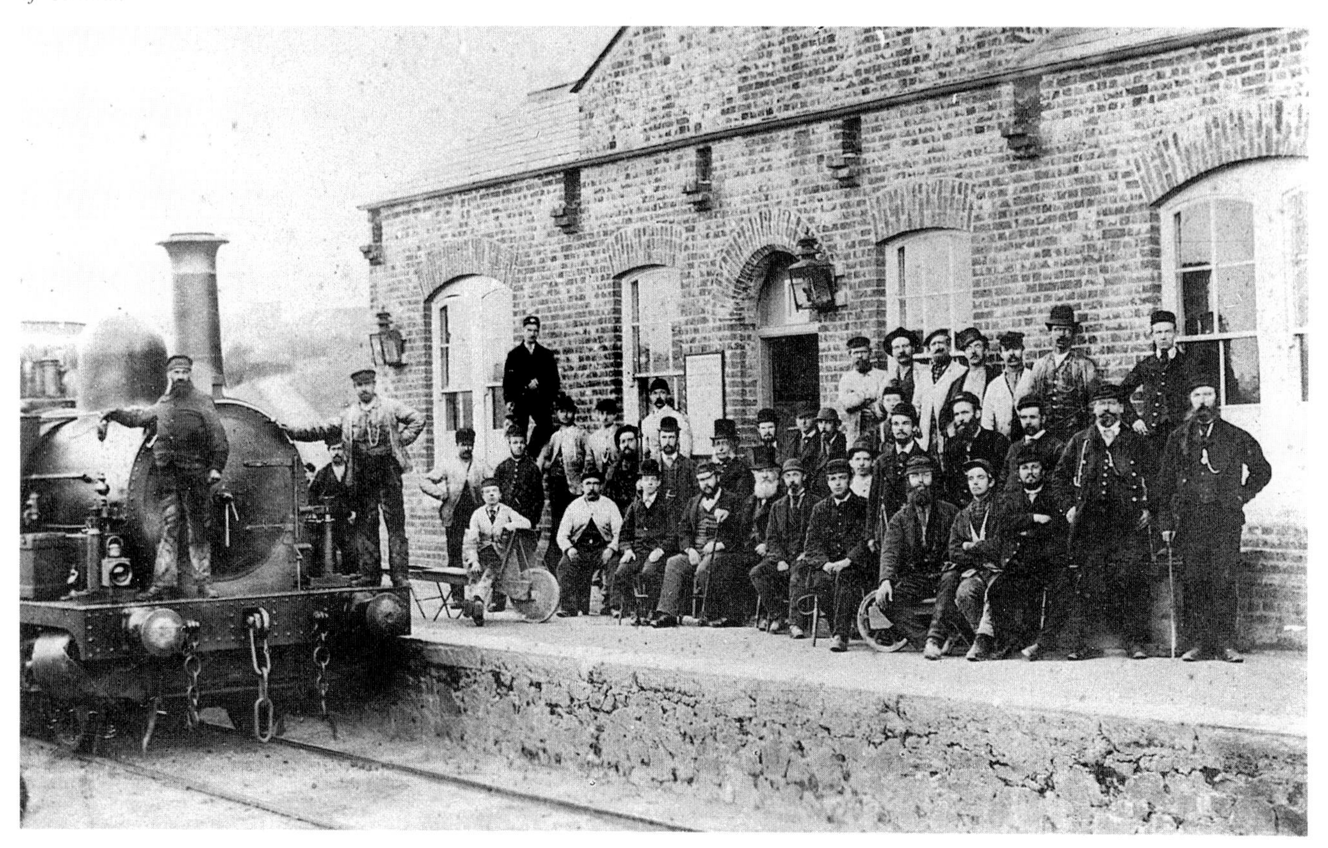

Plate 22. St Blazey station and depot from Middleway about 1890. The photograph was worth including despite its poor quality because it shows the platforms and passing loop, the original CMR signal box (left background – closed 1908), the point rodding from Middleway signal box and the complete lack of sidings in what is now the 'down' yard (although many sidings later located on the right have recently been removed). A Dean 2-4-0T and some rigid 6-wheelers wait to depart for Newquay. The river is white with clay waste. *JV Collection*

4.15 pm arriving at Fowey – about 26 miles away – at 8.20 am and 5.50 pm. The trains returned from Fowey at 8.45 am and 7.15 pm, arriving at Newquay at 10.20 am and 9.30 pm. A horse-drawn connecting coach service was provided between Halloon (St Columb Road) and Wadebridge and between Par (CMR) and Par (GWR).

The first passenger train from Fowey to Newquay put on a brave face, visibly ignoring the depression. It was decorated with flowers and greenery. Mr Richardson, the General Manager, rode the train as did both the Truro Town and St Blazey Volunteer Bands. There were festivities at every intermediate station. School children lined the platform at Roche

Plate 23. This October 1903 photograph shows the high timber footbridge which spanned the single track at Middleway Crossing. The locals, including many children, have gathered presumably to see the aftermath of a rainstorm with the water in the River Par and the old Ponts Mill to Par canal about to overflow. Note the single gate over the line, controlled by the Middleway signalman. The bridge was removed in the 1930s. *L. T. George Collection*

Plate 24. This old and faded photograph taken towards the end of Queen Victoria's reign shows the original Cornwall Minerals Railway signal box at Luxulyan. It was located on the north side of the line at the east end of the station. The GWR 0-6-0ST poses just at the start of the siding – before the island platform was constructed in 1910. The signalman leans out of his box, the driver has an oil can in hand, the shunter his shunting pole, while the fireman stands on top of the rail. The road bridge in the background survives. *C. Batchelor Collection*

Plate 25. Although far from being technically perfect this turn-of-the-century photograph, taken from a clay tip just west of Imperial Clay Works, shows a pair of GWR saddle tanks descending carefully past Carnsmerry towards Goonbarrow Junction on the Goonbarrow branch. The village in the left background is Bugle. The "raw" state of the countryside in these early days is most noticeable. The train comprises 14 wagons and a GWR brake van. Note the little tramway in the central foreground. *Maurice Dart Collection*

Plate 26. This photograph, taken in 1989, shows the main cast-iron bridge support for the 8-ton restricted Carbis Bridge which carries the Bugle to Roche road over the Carbis Wharf branch near its terminal point at Great Wheal Prosper Clay Kiln. It is testimony to the fact that the beam was cast by West & Sons at their St Blazey Foundry in 1873, the year before the branch was formally opened. Sadly the line closed in August 1989. *JV*

(Victoria) and there were major celebrations at St Columb Major! All civil dignitaries were on hand at Newquay and both coastguards and lifeboatmen presented arms. The bands played the National Anthem and there was a grand procession to Prouts Hotel for a civic dinner. The GM of the railway predicted that Newquay would soon become one of the best watering places (seaside resorts) in the Kingdom. On 14th July 1876 the first excursion was run in connection with the United Methodist Church of St Blazey. Upward of 200 availed themselves of the trip which included public tea at Newquay.

During 1877 and into 1878 there were still but two trains per day between Fowey and Newquay. By 1878 the Sunday service which had provided one train each way had been withdrawn. The minerals situation continued to decline with, in 1877 and 1878, New Pembroke, Restinnins and Treffry's Regulus or Treffry Consuls all closing. Several of the smaller china clay pits also closed. Even Treffry's successor, Dr Edward Willcocks Treffry, was unloading his clay pit interests as he offloaded his lease on the Bloomdale pit to William Varcoe & Sons. Edward Treffry died in 1880 from which date the Treffry family affairs were managed by the Treffry Estates Company. With finances now well strained Roebuck approached the Great Western Railway in April 1877 in an attempt to launch a rescue package. By an agreement dated 30th April 1877, sanctioned by Parliament on 10th August 1877, the GWR undertook to work the line for a term of 999 years dating from 1st July 1877, subject to certain conditions and stipulations. In fact the agreement did not come into operation until 1st October 1877 owing to certain obligations having to be fulfilled before the agreement became binding upon the GWR.

The GWR was to receive 53.11 per cent of the gross receipts, with a guaranteed minimum. The GWR guaranteed to the CMR a minimum net income of £15,000, £16,000 and £17,000 for the first three years, increasing each year by £250 until the sum of £18,500 was reached. Again, there were a number of clauses and provisos. The lines handed over to the GWR and as specified in the agreement were as follows:

	Miles	Chains
The Par & Fowey Railway, from Fowey to the junction with the Newquay Railway.	16	39
The Newquay Railway, from St Dennis to Newquay.	10	63
The Newquay & Cornwall Junction Railway from Burngullow to the junction with the Newquay Railway.	5	25
The Retew Branch from the Newquay Railway.	2	5
The Carbis Branch from the Par Railway.	1	0
The East Wheal Rose and Gravel Hill Branches.	9	75
	45	47

As mentioned in Section 17, the Gothers Tramway opened from Gothers to Domellick in 1879. Slowly but surely there were signs that the economy was improving, although the iron ore industry was never to recover, as demonstrated by the lifting of the Gravel Hill extension, which had been disused for some time, in 1888. Another important development in the history of the CMR was the construction in January 1879 of a double-track loop between Par (CMR) and Par main line (GWR) station. From 1st January 1879 Par (CMR) was renamed St Blazey. It was possible for passengers travelling from the CMR lines to book through to any GWR station and vice versa. Between 1879 and 1892 there was, of course, a break of gauge at Par main line and passengers were obliged to change trains at the then junction station. All freight had to be transferred between trains and a large transfer goods shed was provided for the purpose.

In March 1885 the CMR enrolled a Scheme of Arrangement with its creditors involving the issue of additional stock and exchanging other stock. In the 1885 CMR report the Directors stated in reference to the above scheme that "the control of the affairs of the company is thus restored to the hands of the Board, and the Directors are now in a position to give their attention, with advantage, to all matters relating to the development of traffic". The accounts received from the GWR for the six months ended 31st December 1885 showed total gross receipts of £16,406 compared with £15,046 for the previous six months; an increase of 9 per cent. Between the years of 1875 and 1885 china clay and china stone production doubled, which contributed to a modest revival in the fortunes of the CMR. Bradshaw's Timetable for November 1888 shows there were four 'down' and five 'up' trains between Fowey and St Blazey and three through trains in each direction between Par and St Blazey to Newquay. This increased to five trains each way per day between Par/St Blazey and Newquay in 1893, the year after cessation of the broad gauge. This change in GWR track gauge policy affected not only the interchange at Par but also at Drinnick Mill on the N&CJR section, where there had been a change of gauge since 1874.

Additional revenues flowed in, and true to their word, the Directors of the CMR made plans to increase traffic to such an extent that, even though the GWR were operating their established lines, they still found the resources to undertake three major schemes. With a capital of £24,000 construction of a $3\frac{1}{2}$-mile branch line from Roskear Sidings (now Goonbarrow Junction) near Bugle to Carbean started in 1890. Built over difficult terrain the heavily graded, tightly curved line was opened to freight traffic in October 1893 and at the same time a further half-mile branch line from Bugle to Martins Goonbarrow and the Great Beam clay kilns was opened throughout, a spur to Wheal Virgin possibly having been opened at an earlier date. This was known as the Wheal Rose branch – not to be confused with the original Treffry Tramway and CMR East Wheal Rose branch. The Goonbarrow branch was worked independently by the CMR, with its own locomotive, from 1893 until 1st July 1896 when the whole of the Cornwall Minerals Railway was purchased by the GWR and absorbed into their system. The CMR was then dissolved. The final CMR scheme was taking control of the old abandoned rival Lostwithiel & Fowey Railway. The line had been opened in June 1869 as a broad gauge freight line from Lostwithiel to Carne Point, a mile or so short of Fowey. It succumbed to CMR competition once the latter's direct line to Fowey was opened in 1874. The CMR undercut the rates of the L&FR and when, in 1880, heavy repairs were needed to the broad gauge bridges on the branch, it was forced to close. The line reopened as a standard gauge branch line, extended to link up with the CMR St Blazey to Fowey line on 16th September 1895. Thus at this time Fowey enjoyed two passenger routes. It had not been the competition only which had resulted in the closure of the original Lostwithiel & Fowey Railway, but also the decline in the china clay industry, which had, of course, also impacted the CMR. In its early years the broad gauge line carried 27,000 to 29,000 tons of clay but from 27,000 tons in 1874 it plummeted to less than 8,000 tons in 1879. The line was to have the last laugh as, following complete closure of the CMR line to Fowey in 1968, it is now the only rail route to Fowey.

In the 1870s and 1880s there had been a number of schemes to link the CMR lines to other railways and with various rival lines. The most promising was arguably the Cornwall Minerals and Bodmin & Wadebridge Junction scheme of August 1873, which would have seen Ruthern Bridge on the Bodmin and Wadebridge line, later owned by the London & South Western Railway, linked with the CMR near Roche.

The locomotive engineer of the Cornwall Minerals Railway was Francis Trevithick and, as aforementioned, the headquarters and main works and locomotive depot was at St Blazey. For the forthcoming opening and operation of the CMR he designed a 30-ton 0-6-0 tank locomotive with outside cylinders. The engineering firm of Sharp, Stewart & Company built 18 examples of the locomotive based on Trevithick's plans. The CMR locomotives were numbered consecutively from 1 to 18 and carried the following builder's numbers: 2350 to 2361 and 2368 to 2373, but as can be seen from the chart which follows, CMR running numbers were not applied consecutively. Four of the engines were named but as delivered locomotive No. 1 unfortunately carried a nameplate misspelling the family name 'Treffry'. The names were: No. 1 *Treffrey*, No. 2 *Lord Robartes*, No. 5 *Fowey* and No. 6 *Newquay*.

The locomotives were not particularly powerful for the heavily graded lines they were to work upon, but it was the intention for them to run in pairs, footplate-to-footplate. There were no coal bunkers and coal was inconveniently carried on top of the side water tanks. The backplate had a gap in the middle which was designed to allow the crew to move with ease from one footplate to the other. In this context the locomotives resembled a Fairlie type of operation when coupled in the usual way. Even the locomotive roundhouse at St Blazey had nine roads, each capable of taking two of the 0-6-0 tanks. The CMR livery was said to be a dark reddish brown with yellow and black lining, although it is possible the locomotives were black. Not only was St Blazey depot designed to take all 18 locomotives but the turntable was also tailor-made and able to take two coupled tanks at the same time, in other words a pair in normal operating mode. The specification of the locomotives was as follows:

Sloping outside cylinders (2)	$16\frac{1}{4}$ in by 20 in
Wheel diameter	3 ft 6 in
Boiler length	8 ft 2 in
Boiler diameter	4 ft $\frac{3}{8}$ in
Tubes – number and diameter	195 × $1\frac{3}{4}$ in
Boiler pressure	140 lb per sq in
Grate area	10.8 sq ft
Heating surface tubes and firebox	752.8 and 70.7 sq ft
Weight loaded – leading axle	10 tons 7 cwt
driving axle	10 tons 17 cwt
trailing axle	9 tons 12 cwt
Total	30 tons 16 cwt
Wheelbase	5 ft+6 ft

All of the locomotives had Allan straight link motion, this being standard Crewe practice and reflected the fact that Trevithick was the retired Locomotive Superintendent of the Northern Division of the London & North Western Railway.

Sadly, due to the decline in the china clay traffic shortly after the commencement of services, 18 locomotives were never required, and it is said that when the GWR took over the operation of the line in 1877 some of the locomotives had never been steamed. Consequently, half of the stock was returned to the builders, Sharp, Stewart & Company, for resale. Apparently, the CMR still owed the manufacturers money for the initial order and the return of the surplus stock cleared the debt. Nos 1 to 9 were taken into GWR stock and renumbered 1392 to 1400 – so these locomotives carried CMR numbers for only three years. Of Nos 10 to 18, Nos 11–14 and 18 were sold to the Lynn & Fakenham Railway, later the Eastern & Midlands Railway as tank engines, whereas Nos 15 to 17 were sold to the Lynn & Fakenham Railway with 4-wheeled tenders. Some of these were absorbed by the Midland & Great Northern Joint Railway. Four were later rebuilt as unsatisfactory 2-4-0 tender engines rather than their previous "tender tank" status. No. 10 was sold to the Colne Valley & Halstead Railway and, almost unbelievably, it survived until 1948 in the hands of South Hetton Colliery.

Nos 1 to 9 were rebuilt by the GWR in 1883/84 as saddle tanks with extended frames. The water capacity increased from 780 to 840 gallons and the weight increased by two tons overall. They had rear bunkers for carrying coal, an altogether more sensible arrangement. Also the crew were afforded more protection than hitherto, with a slightly extended cab. No. 1398 was sold to the Sharpness Dock Company as early as 1883 but in December 1912 No. 1400 took the number of 1398. Of the remaining eight locomotives six had new boilers fitted by Swindon Works in 1895 with a working pressure of 150 lb per sq in. These locomotives were generally reallocated at this time, although one stayed at St Blazey for a short while. A popular location for these CMR locomotives was Swindon where they could be seen shunting the wagon works. Nos 1393 and 1398 (original 1400) lasted until 1936 when they were scrapped. It is interesting to relate that in 1910 and in 1934 locomotives of the 1361 and 1366 classes of the GWR, built to replace the CMR locomotives, were of almost identical specification to the CMR machines, testimony indeed to the design of the originals.

The only other locomotive owned by the CMR was the example they used exclusively on the Goonbarrow branch, which the CMR opened and ran after the GWR assumed responsibility for running the rest of the CMR network. The branch opened in 1893 and the CMR built a locomotive shed at Stenalees. For this purpose they obtained an engine from Messrs Peckett & Sons of Bristol. Appropriately named *Goonbarrow* the 0-6-0 saddle tank weighed 27 tons with a coal capacity of $1\frac{1}{2}$ tons and a water capacity of 780 gallons. It had two 14 in by 20 in cylinders and 3 ft 7 in wheels. The boiler had 125 tubes of $1\frac{3}{4}$ inches diameter and the wheelbase was 10 ft. When the GWR absorbed the CMR in 1896 *Goonbarrow* was, perhaps surprisingly, taken into GWR stock and numbered 1388. It was sold in 1911 to the Cwm Ciwc Colliery, Llanharan, South Wales. The colliery closed in 1921 and all trace of the locomotive was then lost.

The CMR made a considerable impact on the railway map of Cornwall and both Treffry and Roebuck made significant contributions to both the mining and local communities. Perhaps the greatest debt is owed by Newquay itself because without the railway it would no doubt still be a small fishing port.

Plate 27. It has been suggested in the past that this late 1880's view of the Newquay terminus shows CMR 0-6-0T No. 7 before rebuilding by the GWR. However, close scrutiny shows the tank engine is in fact a 2-4-0 of the Great Western Railway. In any event, No. 7 was sold by the CMR/GWR in 1883. The buildings in the background in Station Road (now Cliff Road) survive today (see Plate 291) but shops have been built in front. This turntable was removed in 1904 when the station underwent extensive modification and enlargement. Note the gardens on the right and the loading bay on the left. *Woolf/Greenham Collection*

Plate 28. The wooden "spider" viaduct of the Treffry Tramways across the Trenance Valley at Newquay (see Plate 15) was replaced in 1872/73 by this more substantial structure. It was capable of supporting locomotives and, in fact, lasted until the late 1930s. On masonry piers the iron-work was supplied by West & Sons of St Blazey. In this historically significant Victorian photograph a CMR 0-6-0T locomotive hauls empty clay wagons from Newquay Harbour to St Dennis and Hendra. The viaduct was single track. *Woolf/Greenham Collection*

CMR No.	Name	Builder's No.	Building Date	GWR No.	Disposal
		(Sharp, Stewart)			
1	Treffrey	2350	1873	1392	Scrapped November 1906
2	Lord Robartes	2351	1873	1393	Scrapped March 1936
3		2352	1873	1394	Scrapped September 1933
4		2357	1873	1395	Scrapped March 1934
5	Fowey	2354	1873	1396	Scrapped March 1934
6	Newquay	2355	1873	1397	Scrapped December 1933
7		2356	1873	1398	Sold to Sharpness Docks in April 1883. Scrapped in 1924
8		2353	1873	1399	Scrapped March 1934
9		2359	1873	1400*	Scrapped October 1936
10		2358	1873		Sold to Colne Valley & Halstead Railway † Then South Hetton Colliery
11		2360	1874		Sold to Lynn & Fakenham Railway (later Eastern & Midlands Railway)
12		2361	1874		Sold to Lynn & Fakenham Railway (later Eastern & Midlands Railway)
13		2368	1874		Sold to Lynn & Fakenham Railway (later Eastern & Midlands Railway) Withdrawn 1898
14		2369	1874		Sold to Lynn & Fakenham Railway (later Eastern & Midlands Railway)
15		2370	1874		No. 3 *Blakeney* Sold to Lynn & Fakenham Railway (later Eastern & Midlands Railway)
16		2371	1874		No. 2 *Reepham* Sold to Lynn & Fakenham Railway (later Eastern & Midlands Railway)
17		2372	1874		No. 3 *Melton Constable* Sold to Lynn & Fakenham Railway (later Eastern & Midlands Railway)
18		2373	1874		Sold to Lynn & Fakenham Railway (later Eastern & Midlands Railway) Withdrawn 1898
		(Peckett)			
–	Goonbarrow	559	1893		Sold to Cwm Ciwc Colliery in September 1911 by GWR

* Renumbered 1398 by GWR in December 1912.

† Later named *Haverhill* – finally scrapped 1948.

Some of Nos 11-18 later absorbed by the M&GNJR.

Below left: 1878. Below: 1888 Bottom: 1910.

Cornwall Minerals Railway.

PENZANCE AND PLYMOUTH TO NEWQUAY AND FOWEY

	Week Days. 1	2	3	4	5	6	Sundays.	
	1 3 A.M.	1 2 3 A.M.		1 2 P.M.				
Penzance ...de.	...	6 25	...	3 50	...	...	...	..
Falmouth.........	...	7 15	...	4 35	...	...	...	...
Truro...............	...	7 48	...	5 15	...	...	...	...
Par ....ar.	...	8 32	...	5 57	...	...	...	...
				1 2 3				
Plymouth .....d.	...	6 50	...	3 20	..	...	...	...
Par ....ar.	...	8 31	...	5 0	...	...	...	...
		1 3 A.M.	1 3 P.M.	1 3 P.M.				
Fowey ....de.	8 0	8 45	5 25	7 15	...	...	...	...
Par ....ar.	8 15	9 0	5 40	7 30	...	...	...	...
Par (Saint Blazey) ......d.	...	9 5	...	8 15	...	...	...	...
Bridges............	...	9 20	...	8 30	...	...	...	...
Bugle...............	...	9 25	..	8 35	...	...	...	...
Victoria	...	9 35	...	8 45	...	...	...	...
Halloon (Saint Columb)	...	10 0	...	9 10	...	...	...	...
Newquay......a.	...	10 20	..	9 30	...	...	...	...

NEWQUAY AND FOWEY TO PENZANCE AND PLYMOUTH.

	Week Days. 1	2	3	4	5	6	Sundays. 1	2
	1 3 A.M.	1 3 A.M.	1 3 P.M.	1 3 P.M.				
Newquay.....de.	7 0	...	4 25	...	...	...	...	...
Halloon (Saint Columb)	7 21	...	4 46	...	...	...	...	...
Victoria	7 41	..	5 6	...	...	...	...	...
Bugle................	7 51	...	5 16	...	...	...	...	...
Bridges	7 57	...	5 22	...	...	...	...	...
Par (Saint Blazey .....ar.	8 15	...	5 40	...	...	...	...	...
	A.M.	A.M.	P.M.	P.M.				
Par ....de.	8 20	9 5	5 45	6 20	...	...	...	...
Fowey.........ar.	8 35	9 25	6 0	6 35	...	...	...	...
	1 2 3 A.M.		1 2 P.M.					
Par ....de.	8 31	...	7 50	...	...	...	...	...
Truro ....ar.	9 19	...	8 37	...	...	...	...	...
Falmouth.........	10 0	...	9 15	...	...	...	...	...
Penzance ...ar.	10 45	...	10 4	...	...	...	...	...

PAR, ST. BLAZEY, and NEWQUAY (1st and 3rd class).—Great Western.

Miles.	Down.	Week Days. mrn	mrn	aft	aft	aft
	Par ....dep.	6 5	9 15	1253	5 25	8 7
¾	St. Blazey.........	6 9	9 20	1 0	5 29	8 10
4¼	Luxulyan	a	9 32	1 13	5 39	8 22
6½	Bugle	....	9 41	1 19	5 44	8 30
8¾	Roche	6 34	9 47	1 28	5 51	8 36
14¼	St. Columb Road. ‡	7 0	10 0	1 42	6 5	8 49
20¾	Newquay † ... arr.	7 18	1015	1 55	6 20	9 5

Miles.	Up.	Week Days. mrn	mrn	aft	aft
	Newquay ......dep.	8 55	1115	1255	5 25
6¼	St. Columb Road ‡ ...	9 7	1128	1 11	5 39
12	Roche...............	9 22	1144	1 26	5 53
14½	Bugle	9 29	1151	1 33	6 0
16½	Luxulyan	9 36	1157	1 39	6 6
20¼	St. Blazey............	9 48	1211	1 52	6 20
20¾	Par 22, 27 ......arr.	9 50	1214	1 54	6 22

a Stops to set down from London on informing the Guard at Par.
† Station for St. Columb Minor (2 miles): also for Watergate Bay. ‡ Station for St. Columb Major (2½ miles).

PAR, ST. BLAZEY, and FOWEY (1st and 3rd class).—Great Western.

Miles.	Down.	Week Days. mrn	mrn	aft	aft	aft
	Par ....dep.	9 15	10 5	1253	5 25	6 55
¾	St. Blazey..........	9 20	1010	1 3	5 32	7 1
4¼	Fowey.........arr.	9 32	1023	1 15	5 44	7 13

Miles.	Up.	Week Days. mrn	mrn	aft	aft	aft
	Fowey........dep.	8 0	11 55	4 43	6 5	8 18
4	St. Blazey.........	8 15	12 11	4 58	6 20	8 35
4¾	Par 22, 27....arr.	8 17	12 14	5 0	6 22	8 37

LOSTWITHIEL, GOLANT, and FOWEY (1st and 3rd class).—Great Western.

Miles.	Down.	Week Days. mrn	mrn	aft	aft	aft
	Lostwithiel ...dep.	10 5	11 8	3 0	4 20	7 50
3¼	Golant.............	1015	1118	3 10	4 30	8 0
5¼	Fowey.........arr.	1020	1123	3 15	4 35	8 5

Miles.	Up.	Week Days. mrn	mrn	aft	aft	aft
	Fowey..............dep.	9 45	1027	1 55	3 50	6 5
1½	Golant	9 52	1034	2 2	3 57	6 12
5¼	Lostwithiel 22, 27 arr.	10 0	1042	2 10	4 5	6 20

CORNWALL MINERALS.—G. W. [Sec., H. Gibbs.

Miles from Par.	Paddington Sta.,	gov	mrn	mrn	gov
	4 London .dep	9 0	....	5 30	11¼b
	18 Exeter .. "	2 40	8 40	1158	4b10
	18 Plymouth "	6 50	11 0	2 40	6b5
	Par ....dep	8 40	1245	4 23	7 25
½	St. Blazey	8 45	1250	4 25	7 30
—	St. Blazey .dp	8 46	1251	4 29	7 31
4	Fowey ....arr	8 58	1 3	4 41	7 43
4	Bridges, fr Luxu-	8 56	1 1	....	7 41
6½	Bugle .....[lyan	9 2	1 7	....	7 47
8¾	Victoria*	9 9	1 14	....	7 54
14¼	St. Columb Road	9 23	1 29	....	8 8
20¾	Newquay ...arr	9 33	1 42	....	8 21

Up.	gov	mrn	aft	gov	gov
Newquay.dp	7 20	11 2	....	5 30	....
St. Columb R.	7 36	1118	....	5 46	....
Victoria (for	7 52	1134	....	6 2	....
Bugle [Roche)	7 59	1141	....	6 9	....
Bridges †....	8 5	1147	....	6 15	....
Fowey .dep	8 0	1142	3 50	6 10	8 20
St. Blazey a	8 12	1154	4 2	6 22	8 32
St. Blazey ..	8 20	12 2	4 7	6 30	8 40
Par 19, 18 ar	8 22	12 4	4 9	6 32	8 42
19 Plymth ar	1018	1 50	6 5	8 10	1026
19 Exeter . "	1240	3b50	9 26	1020	....
8 London . "	6 0	8b15	....	4 0	....

b 1&2 class. * Station for Roche; † for Luxulyan.

3 The Great Western Railway

After a mere three years of freight operation, and just over a year of running of the Fowey to Newquay passenger service, the GWR took on the actual operations of the Cornwall Minerals Railway lines from 1st October 1877, having accepted responsibility as sole lessee of the Cornwall Railway the previous year. Although the GWR influence was immediate, the change of gauges at Par from 1879, when the spur linking the CMR lines with the main line was constructed, prevented a total interchange of locomotives and rolling stock. Also the GWR had been very astute in the timing of the CMR deal. With the depression in the mining and china clay industries during 1877 their "acquisition" was negotiated at the right time when the officials of the CMR would have had little "clout" in upping the ante. In fact, although it cannot be positively established, there is no doubt the CMR were making losses and had debts, eg they had not paid in full for their Sharp, Stewart locomotives, and had it not been for the GWR there is every likelihood that the CMR would have been wound up.

As recorded in the CMR section, the GWR returned half of the CMR's locomotives to the builders for resale and gradually introduced their own classes of tank locomotives. Although the original second-hand CMR passenger coaches continued in service for some time, GWR rolling stock started to appear from the 1880s. After the conversion of the main line from broad to standard gauge in 1892 there was a migration of older GWR stock to the CMR lines, including 6-wheelers and later some splendid clerestory roofed bogie coaches. Gradually the GWR improved passenger services and the timetables of the late 19th century show a gradual increase in the number of passenger trains. The GWR were instrumental in a series of station name changes. Halloon was changed to St Columb Road in November 1878 and the following month Par (CMR) became St Blazey station. Holywell became Victoria and finally in November 1904 Roche, and Bridges was renamed Luxulyan in May 1905. Also, in earlier years, Bodmin Road Junction became St Dennis Junction and Newquay Junction, later Treloggan Junction, was renamed Tolcarn Junction.

Plate 29. Although this view has been published previously I have still to find a better photograph of the GWR station at Fowey in Edwardian times. Half-ton clay casks abound in a variety of GWR and private owner wagons while they wait for loading at the near-by docks. Examples of GWR 2-6-2T and 0-6-0ST can be seen in the station area. Nothing in this view now survives, save for the distant hills on the far (east) side of the River Fowey. *English China Clays*

Plate 30. This fascinating photograph showing the then common occurrence of flooding in the low-lying Par station area was taken in GWR days prior to 1907, but after the conversion to standard gauge in May 1892. During 1907 the 270 ft high stack of Par Smelting Works (visible in the background) – built in 1865 and which had a diameter of 27 ft at the base and 9 ft at the top – was felled due to fissures in the brickwork. The train on the main line is from Penzance and has some clerestory bogie coaches, while the Newquay branch formation includes three vintage 6-wheelers. *Royal Institution of Cornwall*

Plate 31. Before the trees took over, obscuring this view, a Prairie tank and an 0-6-0 pannier tank, double-head a St Dennis Junction to St Blazey china clay train into the unlined 50-yard Luxulyan Tunnel. The brakes on this unfitted train will be pinned down for the 1 in 37 descent. The photograph was taken on 9th June 1933. *L. T. George Collection*

Plate 32. There is much to absorb in this magnificent view of Bugle station in 1910. The GWR Dean 2-4-0T brings two 6-wheeled clerestory coaches, a bogie coach and a 4-wheeled van into the station, with a Par to Newquay working. In the foreground is a hand crane used for loading casks of china clay into freight wagons, while behind the last coach stands the original CMR signal box, the last to be replaced (with St Blazey Gate) in 1916. *L. T. George Collection*

Plate 33. This photograph of Bugle was taken on 1st June 1922, before an island platform was constructed. On the left are two clay wagons, a coal wagon and a flat wagon with some mining machinery thereon. Although in the same position, a heavier crane than that appearing in the 1910 photograph has been erected. The signals in front of the bridge indicate routings for Carbis and Newquay. The stacks belong to the long-abandoned Wheal Hope Kiln and East Goonbarrow. Their respective wharfs were on the Wheal Rose branch and a wagon is just visible to the left of the dark figure on the platform. *L. T. George Collection*

Plate 34. Another splendid view of Bugle in Edwardian times. A loaded 'up' clay train seems to be engineless (probably shunting on another siding), while on the left a single GWR wagon is being loaded with casks, and on the right, nine wagons are being loaded from the clay dry (of which this is the only known picture) on the Bugle loading dock. The wooden CMR signal box can also be seen. *JV Collection*

Plate 35. The GWR signal box was constructed to replace the CMR example in 1916. It was located on the south side of Mollinis Crossing (see Plate 156). Signalman Roberts poses for the photographer in happier days. The box assumed ground-frame status in 1964. Under the rationalisation scheme of 1973, signal boxes at Bugle, St Blazey Bridge Crossing and Tregoss on Goss Moor were all dispensed with. Not a trace of this fine structure now remains. *Maurice Dart Collection*

Quintrel Downs station (really a halt) was opened by the GWR in 1911.

Over the years the GWR made considerable investments in the various lines. As a result of the depression in the mining industry and the closure of most of the mines in the Perran Iron Ore lode, the Gravel Hill extension from Treamble had been lifted as early as 1888. It was the CMR company which, in what was almost a last act, opened the Goonbarrow branch in 1893 and in cooperation with the GWR the line from Lostwithiel to Fowey was reopened as a standard gauge branch on 16th September 1895. The GWR opened their Chacewater to Newquay line throughout in 1905 and in anticipation of this event a particularly large sum of money was spent on enlarging and modernising the Newquay terminus. In common practice with their main line contracts a W. H. Smith & Sons bookstall was opened at Newquay station in 1896. As mentioned in Section 21 of this volume, the 1905 changes included a new locomotive shed, abolition of the original end-of-platform turntable and the provision of additional platform accommodation. All of this work not only facilitated the branch trains and freight business but provided the potential for long-distance through trains, which commenced with through Paddington to Newquay coaches in May 1906. The journey from London took five minutes under eight hours at that time, compared with a best 1989 time of 4 hours and 27 minutes by High Speed Train.

This through coach working was to lead the way to a

Plate 36. Originally the troublesome railway bridge across the A30 road on Goss Moor was wooden. However, in 1930 the GWR set about replacing the structure with iron girders. The line was closed briefly and two massive steam cranes were moved into place to position the girders. The stone abutments were renovated and many locals from Roche village strolled down the road to witness the event. *Maurice Dart Collection*

burgeoning holiday trade which in later years, with high spots in the mid-1930s (and again under the auspices of BR in the mid-1950s), resulted in regular through train workings from many parts of the United Kingdom in the summer months and especially on summer Saturdays. Traffic became so heavy that the GWR laid long sections of double track along the erstwhile single-line Newquay branch, including Goonbarrow to Bugle in 1930, and from St Dennis Junction to Tregoss Moor in 1921. Tolcarn Junction to Newquay was doubled in two stages; 1940 and 1946 following the completion of the new masonry Trenance Viaduct. This operation was interrupted by the Second World War. There were innumerable other changes to the trackwork of the Newquay branch and branches including, for example, the reinstatement of the Tolcarn Junction east to south chord in 1931, extension of passing loops including that at St Columb Road also in 1931, modifications at Bugle in 1930/31, changes in configuration at Luxulyan in 1910, 1916 and 1936 and many, many more, most of which are incorporated in the relevant sections of the text.

Changes under the GWR were by no means confined to the main Newquay branch. Not a year passed without the railway opening, closing or modifying the scores of china clay driers served by the railway. Major events included the severing of the Burngullow to St Dennis Junction line from 1909 to 1922 at Carpella due to the Carpella Mining Company exercising its rights to extract minerals from the part of its land carrying the Newquay & Cornwall Junction Railway line, the closing of the Treamble branch from 1917 to 1926 (when the line was relaid and freight services recommenced) and the extension of the Retew branch from Melangoose Mill to Meledor Mill in 1912 to cater for the growing demands for china clay and china stone.

On the debit side the GWR kept their commercial heads and while they expanded facilities in a number of areas they also closed them. For example, the main line Burngullow station was closed on 14th September 1931 and after persevering with modest passenger traffic for many years, services between Fowey and St Blazey were withdrawn on 8th July 1925, although workmen's trains continued for a further nine years. The GWR also closed the Newquay Harbour branch finally during 1926, although traffic had been in decline for decades. In the very last days of the GWR the Shepherds to Treamble branch virtually closed. It was used by troop trains in the Second World War, although it seems that it was the summer of 1949 when the last train traversed the line. Gothers Tramway also closed during the GWR era in 1931 but this was attributable to the china clay company rather than the GWR.

As regards the many modifications which were introduced at the china clay driers and sidings during the 1877 to 1948 period, very few were financed by the GWR. There was a legal agreement between the representatives of the GWR and the relevant china clay company whenever sidings were lengthened, reconfigured, modified or lifted. Every agreement contained scores of regulations and stipulations about the movement of railway wagons, maintenance of the permanent way and fencing, access to the railway lines by non-railway employees, etc. There were also sections relating to the costing of works and it is clear that these estimates were highly detailed incorporating pounds, shillings and pence.

Although the CMR lines were not unsafe before the takeover by the GWR, standards were improved. This included not only comprehensive rulebooks but public notices and signs, station and yard lighting, the quality of track and the permanent way and perhaps above all, signalling. In fact between the years of 1877 and 1916 the GWR closed and replaced every one of the original CMR signal boxes. However, it must be said that even though the CMR worked on the train staff and ticket system combined with block telegraph, for which Russell's instruments were used, photographs show GWR influence at an early date, especially in the standard lower quadrant semaphore signal department.

An area of massive change during the years of the GWR was the development of the main ports of the CMR system, Fowey and Par. Originally developed by Treffry, both ports enjoyed a significant increase in traffic during the days of the GWR. In the main Fowey handled all the large ocean-going ships destined for cross-Atlantic or Baltic trade, whereas Par's main business was in coasters on domestic runs or to the nearer ports of mainland Europe. In particular, Fowey was developed by the GWR in the early days of the present century and they once owned 800 yards of jetty frontage. Details of the developments follow in relevant sections.

Whereas the loads handled at Fowey and Par dramatically increased, those at Newquay decreased. There was less scope for development of the harbour at Newquay, it was further away from the china clay producing areas, could handle only small vessels and, of course, all rail traffic had the ponderous and costly requirement of traversing the cable incline down to the harbour walls and jetties. However, whatever the GWR lacked in their ability to enhance the lot of the harbour, the company virtually transformed the town of Newquay and the railway was solely responsible for putting Newquay on the holiday resort map. From a population of just over 1,000 in 1870 Newquay grew to have almost 8,000 inhabitants in the 1921 census and nearly 10,000 by 1951 – in addition to the vast influx of summer visitors and "part-time" residents. Large amounts spent on publicity, added to a national population who, over the years had more and more disposable income, resulted in the addition of Newquay to the list of desirable watering places along the Cornish coastline. Despite rationalisation over the years this tradition will continue into the 1990s as Newquay continues to be the only Cornish branch line which continues to receive through trains from locations as diverse as Glasgow, Newcastle and London on summer Saturdays.

Although the lines and routes of the Treffry Tramways and the Cornwall Minerals Railway were finally absorbed into the substantial Great Western Railway from 1896, even with the influences of powerful General Managers, such as Sir Felix Pole and Sir James Milne, plus an illustrious list of Locomotive Superintendents and Chief Mechanical Engineers including Dean, Churchward, Collett and Hawksworth, these Cornish by-ways retained their unique atmosphere. Of course, there were changes over the decades but ironically it was under the auspices of British Railways and more recently British Rail which have produced the greatest change, with the end of steam, the closure of many lines and the extreme rationalisation of others. Remains from the days of the GWR are now hard to find with the closure of signal boxes and the removal of traditional pagoda huts on the minor stations. Year by year the infrastructure has been whittled away but at least for now, Goonbarrow, Par and St Blazey signal boxes survive and the listed buildings at St Blazey are also safe, although the main roundhouse is now sadly used as industrial units. There is still the odd manhole cover displaying the legend "GWR", the Newquay station building and 1946 signal box are still standing, although neither for its original purpose. Part of the original Quintrel Downs corrugated hut survives but with future changes, including the possible abandonment of the Goonbarrow Junction to St Dennis Junction via Bugle and Roche section, recollections of the GWR can only diminish.

Plate 37. Roche station once boasted a passing loop and a medium-sized goods yard on the 'up' side. The station was located at the summit of the line between Par and Newquay and in the summer months assisting locomotives were removed either here, or on the 'down' run, at Luxulyan. The loop was eventually removed, the goods yard closed and from 3rd January 1965 the signal box was also made redundant. Pictured here on 25th May 1922 the 'down' station shelter is much the same today. *L. T. George Collection*

Plate 38. St Columb Road station on the same day in 1922. While the freight locomotive shunts the goods yard on the 'down' side, china clay wagon No. 42849 is left stranded on the 'up' line. This station also had a passing loop and, as with Roche, the signal box was closed on 3rd January 1965. The GWR poster on the right advertises "Cheap Day", "Half Day" and "Market" tickets. The nearest village to the station is in fact Indian Queens. *L. T. George Collection*

Plate 39. The variously spelt Quintrel Downs station in fact resembled a typical GWR wayside halt, although few halts had as many as six oil lamps! The station was opened in 1911, although Quintrel Sidings had existed before that date. The pagoda hut seen here was later moved to the end of the platform. The signal and point levers in this cabin were later removed to the pagoda hut before automatic barriers were installed in 1981 (see Plate 254). *L. T. George Collection*

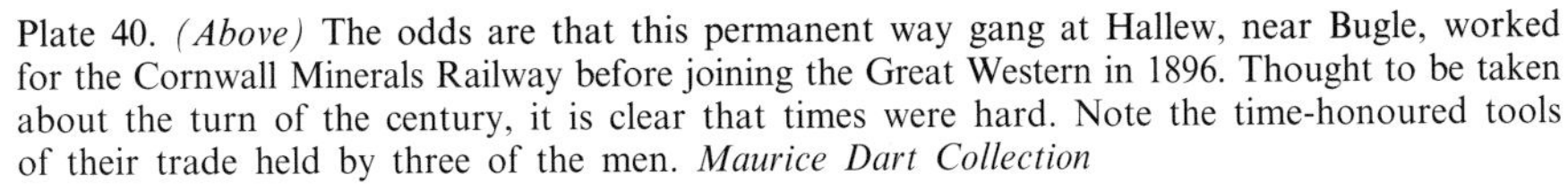

Plate 40. *(Above)* The odds are that this permanent way gang at Hallew, near Bugle, worked for the Cornwall Minerals Railway before joining the Great Western in 1896. Thought to be taken about the turn of the century, it is clear that times were hard. Note the time-honoured tools of their trade held by three of the men. *Maurice Dart Collection*

Plate 41. *(Right)* Resplendent in his Great Western Railway uniform is Mr Tallack, the Station Master at Bugle in 1912. He was succeeded by Mr Sowell. When one gazes at the overgrown platforms and scene of general dereliction at Bugle today, it is hard to believe the station ever justified such a senior post. *Maurice Dart Collection*

Plate 42. *(Below)* The "intermediate" CMR viaduct across the Trenance Valley at Newquay lasted from 1873 until 1938/39, when it was replaced by the present masonry viaduct. In this pre-First World War photograph one of the highly successful Churchward 4500 class 2-6-2T locomotives heads east away from Newquay with a remarkable collection of rolling stock. In addition to the two bogie clerestory coaches there are three 6-wheelers including one 4-compartment example, one 5-compartment type and another with four compartments and a guard's section. The area below is now built-up. *Woolf/Greenham Collection*

Plate 43. The line from Chacewater to Newquay was opened throughout in 1905. The line was quite busy in the summer months but as it served only two centres with any population, St Agnes with a population of just over 4,000 and Perranporth, the long months of winter saw few passengers. The GWR employed their interesting "railmotors" on the line and in this 1913 view of Newquay one of the cars leaves for Chacewater. Introduced in 1903, most were converted to auto trailers by 1935. *Woolf/Greenham Collection*

Plate 44. In this superbly animated scene hundreds of excursionists arrive at the Newquay terminus on a summer day in 1903. The photograph can be dated from the pre-1904 modifications, which included removal of the turntable from this location, but also from the poster which states "Great Western Railway 1903 Tourist Guide". The no doubt lengthy train has been powered by a pair of 0-6-0 saddle tanks. Note also the gasworks, right centre. *Woolf/Greenham Collection*

THE NEWQUAY BRANCH AND BRANCHES

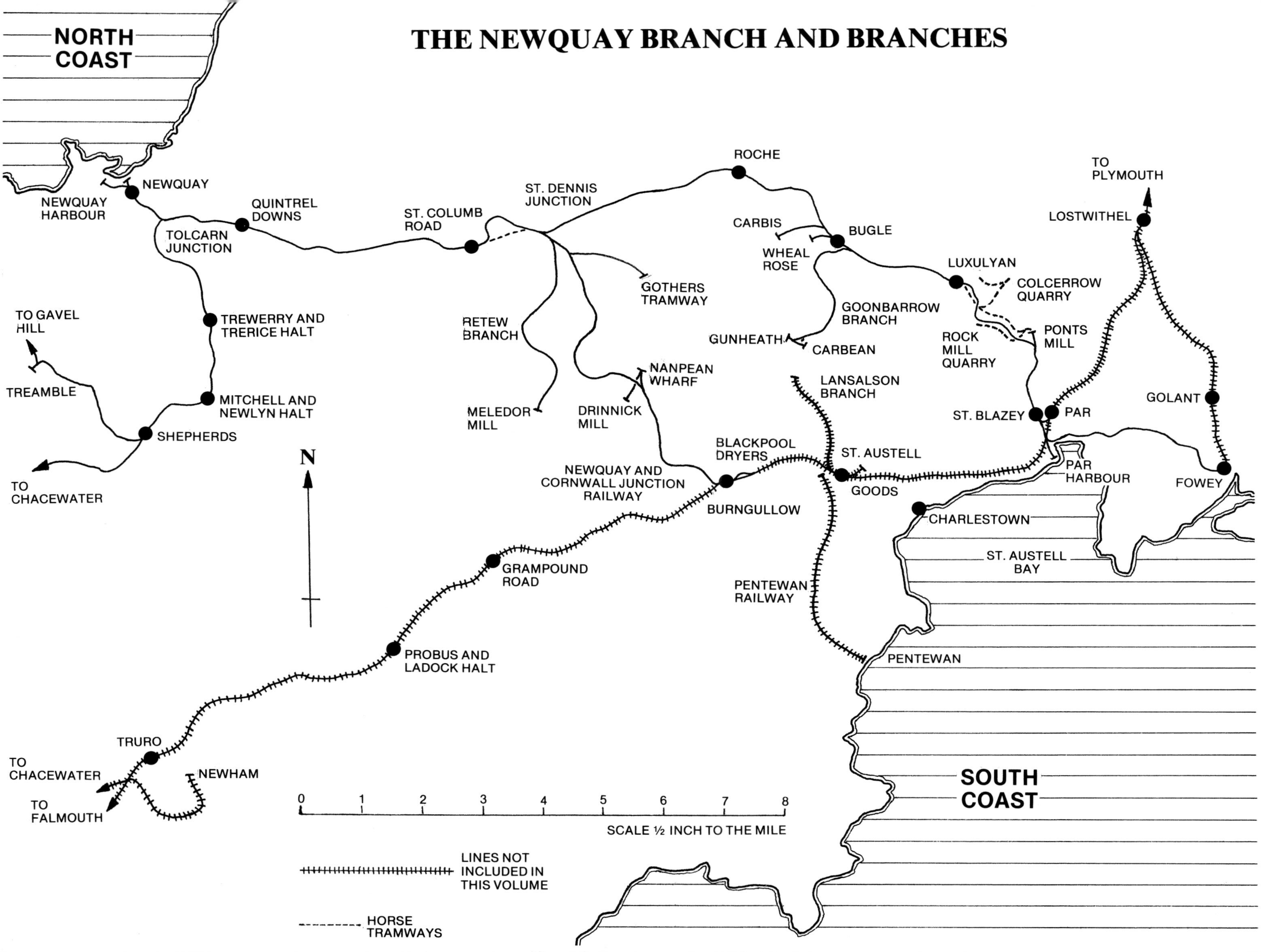

4 BR Steam in the 1950s

In the early 1950s the country was still recovering from the Second World War. There had been a handful of "new build" locomotives since 1941, when Hawksworth took over the role of Locomotive Superintendent and Chief Mechanical Engineer of the Great Western Railway from his illustrious predecessor Collett, but by and large this era of British Railways resembled the immediate pre-war period, albeit with a run-down railway infrastructure.

St Blazey had an allocation of some 35 locomotives in the mid-1950s but this was sometimes inflated by locomotives working long-distance freights and by certain main line passenger trains. There were a few pannier tanks surviving in the early 1950s from the 19th century, notably the 2021 class, and Churchward's 4500 and 4200 classes dating back to 1906 and 1910 respectively. Mainly the pattern of motive power utilisation was the small pannier tanks working the minor china clay lines and branches, the Prairies working branch passenger services and freight, the heavy tanks working the demanding Fowey line and a wide variety of 4-6-0s and on occasions the 6300 class Moguls working main line freights and frequently the summer Saturday trains to Newquay.

In total, the classes of steam locomotive which could be found at St Blazey and on the Newquay branch and branches were as follows: 0-4-2T 1400 class (which replaced the GWR 3500 class 'Metro' 2-4-0Ts), 0-6-0T 1366 class, 0-6-0PT 2181 class, 0-6-0PT 1600 class, 0-6-0PT 5700 class, 2-6-0 6300 class, 2-6-2T 4500 class, 2-6-2T 5100 class, 4-6-0 'Manor', 'Grange', 'Hall', 'County', 'Castle' classes, 2-8-0T 4200 class and 2-8-2T 7200 class. It must, however, be emphasised that not all of the above classes, for example 'Castles' and 'Counties', were allocated to 83E. BR Standard 4-6-0 4MTs sometimes worked to Newquay.

There were many restrictions for locomotives on the lines featured in this volume. For example, it was only the old 2021/2181 class of pannier tank and later the 1600 class which could work over the Goonbarrow branch, although very occasionally, with special authority, a Prairie could work over part of the branch. Other restrictions related to the maximum loading for a particular class of steam locomotive, for example on the steep climb from St Blazey to Pinnock Tunnel on the Fowey line, a 4200 or 7200 class heavy tank could handle twenty loaded wagons, whereas a smaller Prairie tank was restricted to twelve wagons.

Perhaps the most interesting contrast was on the formidable 1 in 37 climb up the picturesque Luxulyan Valley. An unaided 'Castle' could take 230 tons up the valley on the 'down' run to Newquay, whereas a 'Hall' or a 'Grange' could manage only 190 tons unassisted. A pair of 'Castles' was restricted to 450 tons which dropped to 410 tons if a 'Castle' was paired with a 'Manor', while a 'Castle', when banked by a Prairie tank was restricted to 320 tons. Apart from the smallest tank locomotives other passenger engines were allowed a trailing load of 180 tons. Trains exceeding 500 tons were once a regular sight on summer Saturdays where two 4-6-0s would double-head the train with a further banking locomotive at the rear (which would normally be detached at Luxulyan station – but sometimes Roche). Steam survived until 1962 after which time all coaling stages and water columns were removed and the early generation diesel-hydraulics took over for an era of short duration.

Plate 45. The following nine photographs show the wide variety of motive power which could be seen in action on the Newquay branch and its branches during the 1950s. The retention of so many ex-GWR steam locomotives into the 1950s made the 1948 Nationalisation easier for GWR fans to live with, and certainly the atmosphere of many lines changed little during the immediate post-war period. On 29th July 1958 a 1400 class 0-4-2T leaves Fowey station for the sidings after arriving with a train from Lostwithiel. No. 1419 was operating in "push–pull" mode with its auto trailer. *Peter Gray*

Plate 46. There were well over 800 5700 class 0-6-0 pannier tanks built and they could be seen throughout the ex-GWR system, including St Blazey. Rolling into the yard from Par on 20th July 1961 is No. 9655 with a mixed freight which includes not only ICI chemical tankers but a "not in common use" St Blazey GWR brake van. The semaphore signal gantry survives at the time of writing. *R. C. Riley*

Plate 47. Although St Blazey had mostly allocations of 0-6-0 and 2-6-2 tank locomotives, due to the many restrictions on the minor freight-only mineral sidings, a pair of either 2-8-0 or 2-8-2 tanks of the 4200 or 7200 classes were employed on heavy trains over the St Blazey to Fowey line. They occasionally worked through to St Dennis Junction. On 28th September 1957 it was one of the old 1910 Churchward 4200s which was photographed at St Blazey with a load for Fowey. No. 4206 would soon be blasting up the 1 in 36 to Pinnock Tunnel – bunker first to avoid crew asphyxiation. *Les Elsey*

Plate 48. One of the few post GWR steam locomotive builds were the Hawksworth 1600 class 0-6-0 pannier tanks of 1949, and in fact it would have been the 1950s before No. 1664 rolled out of Swindon Works. On 6th August 1956 the 41-ton locomotive was given an onerous job of hauling a long string of china clay empties up the Luxulyan Valley and on to St Dennis Junction. The diminutive machine is seen blasting through the rock cutting above Ponts Mill. *Les Elsey*

Plate 49. *(Left)* Above all else the Newquay branch will be remembered for its long-distance summer Saturday trains which could load up to 15 coaches, and which always required two, but sometimes three, locomotives. The Treffry Tramway alignment was never designed for 500-ton loads which is apparent both by curvature and gradient. On 9th July 1960 the 12.30 pm Newquay to Paddington was double-headed by a grubby 'Manor' 4-6-0 No. 7816 *Frilsham Manor* and 'Hall' 4-6-0 No. 6913 *Levens Hall*, photographed between Quintrel Downs and St Columb Road. *Peter Gray*

Plate 50. A typical Newquay branch train with one of the purposeful 4500 class 2-6-2T locomotives, No. 4552, making short work of the Luxulyan Valley with the three non-corridor BR coaches forming the 2.40 pm Par to Newquay on 9th July 1955. Note the 83E St Blazey shed plate and the large BR lion and wheel emblem. *R. C. Riley*

Plate 51. The 'Grange' class 4-6-0s were effectively 'Halls' with smaller driving wheels. They were particularly suited to the Cornish main line where a little more power was preferred to a little more speed. Having just crossed Goss Moor No. 6809 *Burghclere Grange* heads the 4.34 pm Newquay to Par. Roche will be the next stop. Note the tiny "Par" carriage board on the leading coach. *R. C. Riley*

Plate 52. Yet another GWR 4-6-0 express passenger locomotive class to be spotted on the Newquay branch on summer Saturdays was Hawksworth's 1000 'County' class. These two-cylinder machines had a high-pressure boiler and some were fitted with double chimneys. Photographed just west of St Dennis Junction, on the CMR alignment which avoided the Treffry Tramway, Toldish Tunnel section, on 9th July 1960 was No. 1002 *County of Berks* double-heading an overnight train from Manchester with 'Castle' class 4-6-0 No. 4095 *Harlech Castle* – super power at that time! *Peter Gray*

Plate 53. To many, 'Castles' and 'Kings' were the ultimate in GWR motive power, but as 'Kings' were not permitted to cross the Royal Albert Bridge into Cornwall the 'Castles' were the most prestigious class to be seen in the Royal Duchy. On 20th July 1954 an excursion from Exeter arrives at Newquay and passes the gasholder landmark (recently obliterated), behind a very clean No. 5021 *Whittington Castle.* The platform being used by the special has now been abandoned and the track lifted. *Les Elsey*

5 Fowey to St Blazey

Fowey and its natural deep-water harbour sprang to prominence in the early 14th century. In the early days it was an important centre for naval activities and in 1342 it was reported that Fowey had despatched 29 ships and crews, numbering 720 men, to take part in naval operations in Scotland and France. In mediaeval times Lostwithiel, the upriver ancient Capital of Cornwall, had begun to lose the tin trade as mining activities began to silt up the River Fowey at that point. Fowey was the beneficiary of Lostwithiel's problem. It was not until the mid-1850s, however, before Fowey really came into its own right as an important port, firstly for loads of timber, but following the opening of the Lostwithiel & Fowey Railway in 1869, and the Cornwall Minerals Railway in 1874, for large volumes of china clay, china stone and other mineral traffic.

The Lostwithiel & Fowey Railway ran from Lostwithiel to a point known as Carne Point, some distance north of the ancient town of Fowey. The broad gauge line hugged the western river bank of the river and consequently there were no problems with gradients. The line was worked by the Cornwall Railway – the company which also owned the Cornish main line east of Truro. The L&FR had ambitious plans for Fowey. They wanted to set up a Fowey Harbour Board on which the railway would be heavily represented. They wanted to build a line of quays from one end of the Carne Point river frontage to the other and to levy rates.

Long before the days of the Green Party there were local objections. Locals saw advantages only for the railway company and Lostwithiel in particular saw the prospect of their ancient rights being eroded. Above all else the huge cost of these developments, amounting to some £60,000, far exceeded the asset value of the company and accordingly there would be little security for those advancing money. Eventually, however, just three jetties were built which were sufficient for the railway company to commence trade and for them to convey nearly 29,000 tons of freight, primarily china clay, by 1872. The next two years saw the L&FR consolidate its

Plate 54. In 1968 the St Blazey to Fowey line was abandoned and converted into a private road for the exclusive use of English China Clay lorries. Consequently, from that date all rail-borne china clay traffic arrived at the docks via the line from Lostwithiel. The line was opened as a broad gauge route by the Lostwithiel & Fowey Railway in 1869 but closed again due to CMR competition and a lack of capital in 1880. The GWR reopened it as a standard gauge line in 1895. On 23rd July 1986 an ECC-acquired Class 08 shunter propels a string of "clay hoods" to the unloader at the dockside. *JV*

position, but in the meantime the Cornwall Minerals Railway was driving through its direct line from St Blazey to Fowey which offered direct access to the heart of china clay country and a through line to Newquay.

The opening of the CMR spelt disaster for the Lostwithiel and Fowey line. The possibilities of a route from the Par area had been on the cards for many years. Indeed, back in 1825 Joseph Thomas Treffry had proposed such a line to capitalise on the improvements he had set in motion at Fowey in 1811, when the building of a completely new quay at the harbour had commenced. Treffry had tried to capture some of Charlestown trade by publicly stating that Fowey was better than any other harbour in the west of England for wet and dry docks, on a scale suitable for merchantmen. However, Treffry knew that without a railway Fowey could not expand to the envisaged degree. However, in 1825 the Rashleigh family would not let him build a railway over their land and to detour around their land would have been too expensive. Treffry uttered, "I thought my idea of a railway was a sound one, but I have been prevented from carrying it out through the influence of a neighbouring country gentleman." It was thus nearly 50 years later that the CMR overcame these difficulties with the opening of their line on 1st June 1874.

Almost immediately the Lostwithiel & Fowey Railway tonnage dropped to only one-third of its 29,000-ton peak of 1873 and by 1879 it grossed less than 8,000 tons. The CMR had not entered the transportation fray without investing in its own infrastructure at Fowey. The CMR built three large jetties south of Carne Point, each ranging from 90 to 114 ft in length. Each jetty was served by double tracks which partially merged and were served by a single wagon turntable on the mainland sidings. Both horses and capstans were used in the movement of wagons on the jetties. During the mid-1870s there developed a battle between the L&FR and the CMR with each trying to undercut its competitor's rates. Whatever rate the Cornwall Railway and the L&FR came up with the CMR did better, and due to a combination of a disastrous reduction to 2s 2d per ton carriage for china clay from Burngullow to Fowey, which it could ill afford, followed by the Lostwithiel and Fowey line becoming unsafe, it closed from 31st December 1879. By then the L&FR simply did not have the money available to repair their line. The CMR had deliberately not linked with the L&FR – there being a gap between the two routes of about half a mile. The recession in the china clay industry in 1877/78 had not helped the L&FR in its fight. Ironically, after the closure of the L&FR, business boomed. Between the years 1885 and 1890 Fowey shipped the largest tonnage of china clay of any port in Cornwall due to vessels using the port having significantly increased in size, Fowey's ability to handle deep-draught ships, combined with a vigorous overseas export trade. During this period the "average tonnage" league made interesting reading: Fowey 110,000+, Par 85,000+, Charlestown 55,000+, Pentewan 20,000+ and Newquay 4,000+. Insignificant amounts were shipped from other Cornish ports.

With the involvement of the Great Western Railway the CMR reconstructed the Lostwithiel to Fowey line as a standard gauge branch in 1895. By then the GWR were not only operating the main line through Cornwall but from 1892 all GWR broad gauge lines were converted to standard gauge. With the opening of the "new" line in September 1895 came the joining of the former L&FR line with the CMR line; the entire route being in the hands of the GWR from July 1896 when they absorbed the CMR. The GWR invested a fortune in the Carne Point area, adding to the CMR jetties so that by the Edwardian era, seven jetties were in operation. Tonnages doubled and redoubled reaching a peak of nearly 600,000 tons before the First World War. Due to the loss of European markets the volumes had dropped to 400,000 by 1918.

The following decades produced plenty of technological innovation. The GWR installed mechanical devices to facilitate high-speed loading, they built a power station adjacent to the harbour and, in 1923, an eighth jetty was built. The second Carne Point signal box was closed in 1925 and another more modern signal box was opened on the river side of the sidings at the north end. For decades the scene did not change greatly, although when the passenger service between Fowey and St Blazey closed in 1925 the only access for rail travellers was via Lostwithiel. Before closure in 1925 there was but one train per day each way between St Blazey and Fowey. The station layout at Fowey was altered in 1936 and during the Second World War there was again a significant decline in traffic.

In 1950 jetties Nos 5 and 6 closed and in 1954 Carne Point signal box was abandoned. In 1962 the use of No. 7 jetty was reduced and in January 1965 the passenger service between Lostwithiel and Fowey was withdrawn. In the same year 900 vessels were loaded at Fowey. It was during the mid-1960s that negotiations between British Railways and the English China Clay Company commenced about the long-term future of Fowey. ECC had for some time perceived a need for good road access to Fowey Docks. The local roads were narrow and did not lend themselves to heavy use by 38-tonne lorries conveying china clay. On the other hand, BR was keen to enter into a long-term arrangement with ECC which guaranteed a minimum annual tonnage of china clay for transportation by rail. BR's steeply graded line from St Blazey ran past ECC's massive drying plant at Par Harbour and BR had access directly to Par Harbour and via Lostwithiel to Fowey. Accordingly, part of the overall "deal" was for BR to close their Fowey to St Blazey line and for this section to be converted into a private road for the exclusive use of ECC.

ECC leased the deep-water loading jetties from BR and the major Fowey Docks Development scheme ensued. There would be four modern operational jetties; three equipped for road and rail usage and a fourth for china clay slurry only. There would be a 22,000-ton bulk store and rapid loading equipment with a maximum capacity of 1,000 tons per hour. The old CMR railway line closed in October 1968 and work on the conversion to road began immediately. The 3.2-mile stretch for conversion had five bridges and 13 over-passes. Embankments had to be widened to provide a two-lane road and a new bridge had to be built over the Fowey Road at Polmear. The 1,173-yard tunnel presented special problems. The ventilation shafts had to be specially cleaned and after laying the road surface traffic lights had to be installed because the narrow tunnel could take only a single-lane road. Tunnel lighting was installed and six miles of concrete kerbing were laid. In total 18,000 tons of hard-core went into building the road and some 15,000 tons of tarmacadam, including surface coating, was used. Most of the concrete products were manufactured by the relevant Division of ECLP. Finally, during 1987/88, in anticipation of the end of the old vacuum-braked clay hood wagons, the old traverser and tipping equipment had to be modified and replaced to accommodate the new air-braked CDA wagons, which have a payload of nearly three times that of the old wooden-bodied wagons.

Whereas in the days of steam, Par Harbour had its own shunting locomotives, at Fowey it was normally the CMR/GWR/BR locomotive which headed a train to the docks which then performed the shunting duties. Horses were used

Plate 55. Over the years the docks at Fowey had been enlarged and developed by the GWR. There was at one time some 800 yards of jetty frontage for the shipment of china clay. However, the development of greatest significance occurred in 1968 when ECC took out a long-term lease on the docks from BR. This mid-1950s view does not vary greatly from the scene depicted in Plate 17. No. 1419 and its auto trailer pass by aloofly on a Fowey to Lostwithiel local. On the left is the steeply graded siding to the power station and on the right are the standard clay wagons before they were fitted with vacuum brakes. *C. H. A. Townley*

Plate 56. A busy scene at the west end of Fowey station. Resting in the 'down' bay is a 4500 class 2-6-2T, probably between turns on the Lostwithiel passenger service. Blasting away and trying to get a head start for the climb to Pinnock Tunnel, necessary even though the wagons are empty, is 4200 class 2-8-0 No. 4273. The lower quadrant signal has already been restored to danger. The signal box here was closed from 30th June 1968. *R. C. Riley*

Plate 57. In the early 1960s St Blazey was invaded by the first influx of diesel-hydraulic locomotives. Surprisingly, photographs of the D6300, Class 22 North British diesels on china clay lines are quite hard to come by. On 23rd July 1965 a pair of the 1,100 hp diesels working in multiple wait to leave Fowey for St Blazey, with clay empties initially bound for St Blazey. *George Hemmett*

Plate 58. *(Below)* Slow-moving Class 9 freight 9B25 passes the headshunt and descends into Fowey with a mixture of box vans and clay wagons on 22nd July 1960. Designated Class 42 'Warships', these 2,200 hp diesel-hydraulics were remarkably versatile with a useful power-to-weight ratio. No. D816 *Eclipse* is seen in green livery before yellow warning panels were added. *R. C. Riley*

Plate 59. The third of a trio of diesel-hydraulic photographs shows No. D816 *Eclipse* on its return journey from Fowey to St Blazey descending the 1 in 36 from Pinnock Tunnel. The train of clay empties is unfitted and despite the presence of the 78-ton diesel up front, the brakes on the wagons will be pinned down. The line opened in 1874 and closed in 1968, six years short of its centenary. *R. C. Riley*

on the jetties but at the sidings it was nearly always a tank locomotive which moved the goods wagons filled with their "white gold". This was not always the case when the heavier 2-8-0T and 2-8-2T types worked over to the docks from St Blazey. Their wagons would be shunted on certain of the sidings with whatever motive power was in the area. However, after the 1968 development plan ECC purchased some redundant ex-BR Class 10 Blackstone-engined diesel-electric shunters (Nos D3452, D3476 and D3497). Once BR's diesel brought their load into the Carne Point sidings it would be the ECC shunter which propelled the wagons onto the tipping/traversing equipment. These elderly shunters were replaced by ex-BR Class 08 shunter No. 08398 in 1987.

From St Blazey to Fowey steam locomotives would always work bunker first. The smoke and steam from a steam locomotive as it blasted up the 1 in 36 and through the narrow granite-lined Pinnock Tunnel would have asphyxiated a crew if operating in chimney-first mode. When returning from Fowey to St Blazey the locomotive would, of course, be chimney first and there was still the one-mile climb to Pinnock signal box, but beyond the box and through the tunnel the journey was downhill and in any event, on the return journey the wagons were empty which would have called for only a modest regulator opening.

The small 6-lever Pinnock signal box was opened on 8th January 1908 and after a short period of temporary closure it was finally closed in 1958. It is said that the box was re-erected at Par as a BR painters' shop. Trains used to stop at the east entrance to the tunnel on the down run to have their brakes pinned down. There was a further stop board at the west end of the tunnel. The tunnel was difficult to build, the rock being comprised entirely of granite. More importantly, the tunnel was the longest railway tunnel in the County of Cornwall at 1,173 yards. The single-line branch meandered down from Pinnock towards Par Sands through rolling farmland. At Par Sands trains again stopped to have their brakes picked up. In the reverse direction brakes were picked up at Fowey station.

Once across Par Sands, which still plays host to holidaymakers and caravaners, the branch converged towards the Par Harbour branch having curved northwards to pass under the main line. The approach to Par Bridge Crossing was controlled by the signals of Par Bridge Crossing signal box, which closed with the line to Fowey from 6th October 1968. The actual crossing survives and is used by a (normally) daily train to Par Harbour. Until recently removed, the train shunter operated the manual crossing gates. In its final years the St Blazey to Fowey line was operated by diesel-hydraulic locomotives of Classes 22, 42 and 43 and original 'Warship' types. From 1968 all china clay trains travelling from the Cornish clay driers to Fowey ran via Lostwithiel, necessitating a reversal for east-bound trains to reach their Carne Point destination.

Plate 60. The 1,173-yard Pinnock Tunnel on the St Blazey to Fowey line was the longest in Cornwall. Parts of the tunnel were unlined but in October 1968 ECC spent a considerable amount of money on partial lining, cleaning and restoring the ventilation shafts and installing a traffic control system on this single-track section of their private road. Other major items were the concrete road and extensive lighting. A Heavy Transport (ECC) Ltd Foden lorry travels where the tank engines once blasted. A 1980 photograph. *ECC International*

Plate 62. *(Above)* Pinnock Tunnel signal box, opened on 8th January 1908, served the purpose of providing an additional block section between St Blazey and Fowey. Although traffic was steady, rather than heavy over the line, the box was deemed to be superfluous and was closed from 12th January 1958. The building appears to have been used subsequently on the lineside near Par station. *Maurice Dart*

Plate 61. *(Left)* The westerly portal of Pinnock Tunnel on 5th May 1957 with a Pinnock Tunnel signal box signal located immediately behind a splendid stop board instructing drivers "ALL DOWN Goods & Mineral Trains Must STOP DEAD Here". Passenger services had been withdrawn from 8th July 1925, although workmen's trains ran until 1934. *Maurice Dart*

Plate 63. This is certainly not a Class 1 train and the crew have not bothered changing the headcode since some previous main line duty. In green livery with small yellow warning panel, Class 22 No. D6342 leaves Pinnock Tunnel with St Blazey-bound empties on 9th May 1963. Introduced in 1962 the locomotive was withdrawn just six years later. *Carey Batchelor*

STOP
BOC International Ltd

Plate 64. *(Top left)* On 9th July 1955 4200 class 2-8-0T No. 4247 clanks its way down the gradient into Par Sands with a long rake of empties from the docks at Fowey. The 2-8-0Ts could haul twenty loaded 13-ton clay wagons over the climb from St Blazey to Fowey, compared with the twelve-wagon capability of a 2-6-2 Prairie tank. This is also the "before" photograph in a before-and-after comparison – see below. *R. C. Riley*

Plate 65. *(Below left)* This picture was captured on film 34 years after the above view was recorded. The focal point is the building above the rear of the ECC International Ltd lorry – the same as that in front of the tank engine above. Although the scene is unmistakably the same, both foliage and buildings have increased – and the permanent way now seems to be wider than 4 ft $8\frac{1}{2}$ in! *JV*

Plate 66. Just south of St Blazey the line from Fowey joined the line from Par Harbour (right). The lines ran parallel past Par Bridge Crossing and signal box to St Blazey yard. The line on the right survives but the track being traversed by 4500 class No. 4526 was lifted in 1968. The bridge arches behind carry the main line from Plymouth to Penzance, which runs in a north/south direction at this point. Note that the short lower quadrant semaphore signal is "off" but the tall repeater is firmly "on". *Les Elsey*

6 The Port of Par

Once Treffry's plans to build a railway from the Par area to Fowey had been thwarted by local landowners, especially the Rashleigh family, his attentions turned to Par and the possibilities of building a harbour there. As detailed in the section on Treffry's Tramways, by 1828 plans had been drawn up for a completely artificial harbour occupying some 35 acres. The harbour would be tidal which would place some restrictions on access and the size of vessel using the port. Following the construction of a 1,200 ft long breakwater, sufficient progress had been made by 1833 for the port to receive its first commercial vessel. Shipments mainly comprised copper ore, granite and china clay, while incoming loads included coal, lime and sand; in fact any commodity which could not easily be transported overland – the main line railway from the other side of the Tamar not reaching Par until 1859.

As the business in copper ore and granite diminished, and following the opening of the canal from Ponts Mill to Par, and later the Treffry Tramway from Mollinis, near Bugle, china clay became all important. By 1855, 15,000 tons of china clay was shipped from Par; a figure which exactly doubled by 1860. By 1865, 44,000 tons of china clay were shipped and during 1870 the total had reached 52,000. Although there was overproduction leading to a depression in the china clay industry in 1876/77, by the late 1880s the Par Harbour tonnage in that commodity had risen to 85,000 tons per annum. At this time there was a large smelter at Par as well as a local brickworks. Completion of the Cornwall Minerals Railway lines brought their share of prosperity to the Port of Par, although for a year or two it seemed that there would be competition between Fowey and Par. The involvement of the Great Western Railway at both ports ensured a degree of equity but it was the nature of the two installations which ensured an identity; Fowey dealing with large ocean-going vessels and large long-haul loads, with Par taking coasters of a smaller size for domestic UK and cross-channel shipments.

Not all of the china clay shipped from Par came from a great distance. Just to the north of the harbour area there were a number of driers in the Par Moor complex which included Hensbarrow, Hallaze, Pentruff, Great Treverbyn, Ruddle Common and Carvear. Not all were rail served. However, the

Plate 67. A general view of the Port of Par from the hills above St Blazey. Par Sands are on the left and on the far side of St Austell Bay is the coastal hamlet of Polkerris. Three coasters can be seen in the tidal harbour and railway wagons can be seen on the left and in the middle foreground. There was once a complex railway network in the docks area but this is now reduced to two sidings. The photograph dates back to the mid-1950s. *JV Collection*

greatest impact on Par Harbour was undoubtedly the advances in pipeline technology. Gradually over the early decades of the 20th century china clay in slurry form was increasingly transported over several miles by mainly underground pipeline. As a result of this, English China Clays built a vast clay drying plant at Par Harbour and even today steam can be seen rising from the four tall modern stacks 24 hours a day, seven days a week. Clay is piped from a variety of clay works, some of which are eleven miles away. Only a modicum of clay now arrives by rail and the main purpose of the railway wagons which visit Par Harbour is to *collect* bagged china clay for transhipment up country or abroad.

The throughput of Par Harbour continued to steadily increase and by 1933 the annual total for china clay reached 100,000 tons per annum. In its first 100 years of operation Par had seen the transition from wooden 50-ton schooners to 2,000-ton coasters. It was after the Second World War that the large English China Clays Company took out a 999-year lease on the port and the company produced long-term plans for modernisation. Initially changes were minor but in 1961 large sums of money were spent modernising and enlarging the port. A total of ten berths were provided with the largest some 280 ft in length. All of the quays were concrete and modern loading equipment was provided. In 1964 ECC purchased the port outright. In 1965 a total of 1,500 vessels were loaded at Par Harbour. Since the conversion of the St Blazey to Fowey line from railway to private road, much of the dried china clay produced by the harbour plant is taken by lorry to Fowey where it is loaded onto the larger ships. However, Par still enjoys a lucrative trade with large tonnages leaving from the still-tidal harbour.

There were once two points of access to the not inconsiderable railway network within the confines of the harbour. There has always been the existing and surviving access direct from St Blazey but until 1965 there was also access from the main line to the west end of the harbour area. There was also one other line which left the harbour complex; a spur which ran under a very low bridge beneath the main line and across the coastal road which served the aforementioned clay driers. It was for this reason that Par Harbour required its own shunting locomotives, all with cut-down cabs.

Over the years these locomotives attracted some degree of notoriety. The most famous were a pair of Bagnall 0-4-0 saddle tanks; No. 2572 of 1937 *Judy* and No. 3058 of 1953 *Alfred*. Earlier locomotives included an old 1879-built 0-4-0ST called *Punch* (Manning, Wardle 713, rebuilt with a vertical boiler in 1936) and a 1927-built Sentinel (6520) called *Toby*. Other shunters appeared from time to time and in recent years one of the most important shunters was a specially adapted road-going Ford tractor. Since the early 1970s there have been no dedicated shunters in the harbour area and the only sign of railway motive power is when St Blazey's Class 08 shunter leaves wagons for loading on the surviving siding. A recent development was the arrival of a Southern Railway bogie utility van which acts as an ECC clubhouse for the company's railway enthusiasts.

In terms of railways the Par Harbour area is but a shadow of its former self. The little clay wagons no longer run along the quayside and the former locomotive shed is no longer used. However, despite rationalisation, the harbour area is at least rail connected – by a siding which runs from the south end of St Blazey depot across Par Bridge Crossing to the massive Cambrian China Clay store. Workings are approximately daily, Mondays to Fridays. Happily both *Alfred* and *Judy* have been preserved as reminders of Par Harbour's past.

Plate 68. For many years the rail system around Par Harbour had its own motive power. The necessity to have standard gauge locomotives with drastically cut-down cabs was due to the interchange of main line goods wagons, and a very low underbridge which took an extension of the harbour lines underneath the main line, to a string of clay dries located on the north side of the main line between Par Harbour and Par Moor. In 1969 Bagnall 0-4-0ST No. 3058 of 1953 *Alfred* was still at work. Note the tight curve and crossover. *Peter Gray*

Plate 69. *Alfred* in action in 1963 as the little 4-wheeler shunts eight loaded clay wagons within the dock complex. Over the years the docks enjoyed a variety of motive power, ranging from Sentinel locomotives to converted road-going tractors. Happily, *Alfred* and earlier sister locomotive *Judy* have both been preserved. *Carey Batchelor*

Plate 70. There are major china clay drying plants at Par Harbour. It is the terminal point of scores of pipelines which carry clay slurry from clay works throughout the Hensbarrow Downs area north of St Austell. Steam can be seen being emitted from four tall chimneys 24 hours per day, seven days per week. There is now little traffic carried by rail but sufficient for a daily visit by the St Blazey Class 08 shunter. On 21st July 1986 it was No. 08801 which dropped off three wagons at the exchange point. *JV*

Plate 71. The ECC employees' railway society saved Ashford-built bogie Southern Railway utility van No. S392 from the breaker's yard and had the vehicle transferred to a disused siding at Par Harbour for a model railway room/club house. In this view, looking north towards St Blazey, the present BR interchange point is on the right and an IC125 is passing on the main line over the Par Harbour branch in the background. *JV*

Plate 72. No time for fair-weather photographers here! In absolutely torrential rain, 350 hp Class 08 No. 08955 eases across Par Bridge Crossing with a wagon from Par Harbour on its daily working. The shunter opens the old crossing gates. Future inflation can be checked because on 14th March 1989 carrots at the greengrocers on the right were 10p per pound! *JV*

Plate 73. In the early 1970s a branch of the Great Western Society based at Didcot had a preservation outstation at Bodmin General station. Their prime exhibit was a 1361 class 0-6-0ST No. 1363. The attractive dock shunter trundles along the exchange sidings with an immaculate GWR coach during an open day at Par Harbour on 13th April 1974. It is interesting that the 1910-built 1361 class were almost identical to the old Cornwall Minerals Railway engines – even retaining their Allan straight link motion. *Les Elsey*

Plate 74. A 1988 view of the south end of St Blazey yard with Par Bridge Crossing in the distance. The locomotive is the unique Class 50/1 No. 50149 *Defiance* which, for 15 months, was fitted with Class 37 bogies, limited to 80 mph and allocated to the Freight Trainload Laira Pool before reverting to a "normal" 100 mph express passenger Class 50 in Network SouthEast livery. The two-tone grey locomotive prepares to leave the yard, on 3rd February 1988. *JV*

7 Par – Change for Newquay

"Par – change for Newquay" was for many years the message offered by the station signboards and, indeed, between the years of 1879, when the Cornwall Minerals Railway built a connecting loop from its own Par (later St Blazey) station to the main line Cornwall Railway Par station, and 1892 when the GWR (which subsumed the CR) abandoned its broad gauge, a change at Par for Newquay was unavoidable.

However, over the years this situation was to change. In the early years, even though the CMR services were operated by the GWR, the locomotives and rolling stock were closely associated with the CMR line from Fowey to Newquay. But with the growing importance of Newquay as a resort, and with a standard gauge main line and branch, a degree of interchange became inevitable. The GWR were operating through coaches from Paddington to Newquay from 1906 and within a few years through trains were routed to the north Cornish coast and its increasing holiday facilities. Eventually, trains from many parts of the UK worked through to Newquay in the summer months with summer Saturdays in particular being extremely busy.

Between the years of 1876 and the last day of 1878 there was no railway link between the CMR and the CR, only horse-drawn coaches. However, once open, passenger trains using the connecting spur adopted unusual patterns in connecting with workings both to and from Fowey and to and from Newquay; the former requiring a reversal at St Blazey (CMR). In the main, trains leaving Par were split at St Blazey with half travelling south for the twelve-minute journey to Fowey and the other half heading north for the 50-minute trip to Newquay. Trains would be joined at St Blazey in the opposite

Plate 75. Since the spur from the main line Par station to St Blazey station of the Cornwall Minerals Railway was opened in January 1879 it has always been a case of "change at Par for Newquay". There was, in any event, little choice until 1892 when the main line was converted to standard gauge which, theoretically, permitted through workings. Swinging off the main line at the north end of Par station with a Newcastle to Newquay SAGA special (senior citizens' holidays) is 'Peak' Class 46 No. 46012 (since scrapped) on 2nd June 1980. There are now through workings only on summer Saturdays, although a local Plymouth to Newquay dmu ran during 1988. *JV*

Plate 76. These views of Par show the rate of change over a period of 21 years – and there have been many more changes since the 1976 view. In this wonderful July 1955 view, all the ingredients of traditional railway infrastructure are visible, such as gas lamps, wooden signals, goods shed, station awnings, water columns, cattle dock, etc. Heading a mixed freight up the main line is 'Grange' class 4-6-0 No. 6821 *Leaton Grange*.
R. C. Riley

direction. A handful of trains ran to Fowey only and similarly (but especially in the Edwardian era) trains also ran only to Newquay. In fact, in the 1910 Bradshaw, the Par to Fowey and Par to Newquay timetables are shown separately, although it is obvious that some departures and arrivals were still "joint" trains. The traffic on the Par/St Blazey/Fowey line did not increase once the Lostwithiel to Fowey passenger service commenced in 1895, and by 1925 the receipts did not begin to pay for the cost of providing the service, which was withdrawn from July of that year. Workmen's trains continued to run, however, until 1934. St Blazey station closed from 21st September 1925, although it was used by workmen until 31st December 1934.

In later years it was not always necessary to change at Par for Newquay, even on a local train. Some trains started from Plymouth and ran through to Newquay. Even at the beginning of the 1988 summer timetable there were two through local trains from Newquay to Plymouth and one in the opposite direction. Conversely, in the 1968/69 working timetable, all Newquay branch services started and finished their journeys to Newquay and back at Bodmin Road station on the Cornish main line. Over the decades there were other starting points and combinations of working but by 1989 sanity had returned to the timetable which, except for summer Saturdays, contained the unequivocal message, "Par – change for Newquay", for each of the half-dozen branch trains per day, except the 19.32 from Par to Newquay which started its journey at Falmouth Docks!

Par station was opened on 4th May 1859. Although owned by the Cornwall Railway it was leased in turn to the Bristol & Exeter, South Devon and Great Western Railway companies. The station comprised a main stone-built station building and platform on the 'down' side and less permanent wooden buildings located on an island platform on the 'up' side. The standard gauge loop line to St Blazey and Newquay was opened from 1879 and, as aforementioned, Par's junction status came into its own when the broad gauge main line was abolished in 1892. Sidings were provided and on the 'up' side of the station there was a large goods shed which doubled as a transhipment shed prior to 1892.

The station provided a main line passing loop between 1859 and 15th October 1893 when the line to St Austell was doubled, and 19th December 1894 when the line to Milltown Viaduct, just above Lostwithiel, was also doubled. A signal box was, and still is, located at the south ('down') end of the 'up' platform. The platforms were lengthened in 1913 and the branch platform (north side of the island) was lengthened in 1924. There were later carriage sidings on both the 'up' and 'down' sides of the station and the 'down' siding, just outside of the station, was converted into a 'down' loop on 5th April 1943. There were a number of detailed changes to the overall track layout and sidings over the years including provision for a short-lived Freightliner terminal in 1968.

However, in 1974 there were drastic alterations at Par.

Various sidings and complicated slip points were removed and the entire layout was rationalised and simplified. The wooden goods shed was removed as were most of the 'up' side station buildings, leaving just a short awning with waiting shelter screen. The footbridge connecting the 'up' and 'down' platforms lost its roof. In the 1980s, following the closure of both St Austell and Burngullow signal boxes, an electronic signalling control panel was installed in the manual Par signal box which then interfaced with Lostwithiel, Truro and St Blazey. A small signalling and telecommunciations depot was established on the north ('up') side of the station area using, in part, old box van bodies for storage accommodation.

Although a shadow of its former self, Par is still, together with Lostwithiel, the busiest station in Cornwall. In addition to main and branch line passenger trains, china clay traffic from Goonbarrow to Carne Point, Fowey and the main line air-braked freights pass the station on their way to and from St Blazey yard. The morning and afternoon trains to Drinnick Mill and Parkandillack must reverse at Par, with the locomotive running round. Add to this the Mondays only fertiliser train from Truro to Ince and the postal and van trains in both 'up' and 'down' directions and at times the number of movements is impressive. In the evening the TPO postal still runs and late evening and early morning the sleepers still run between Paddington and Penzance. Other sundry workings can include engineers' ballast and spoil trains and ecs workings. There are also block trains such as the Burngullow to Irvine china clay slurry tanks. Late evening the "West Cornwall" freight to Truro and Ponsandane sometimes runs but much other traffic, such as the perishables and the Chacewater cement, now have a place only in the railway history books.

For the time being it is not only the sighting of these trains which is of interest but also the operation of semaphore signals which control all movements in the area. On summer Saturdays, when High Speed Trains run through to Newquay, it is fascinating to see a traditional GWR junction in full flight with extra trains not only to and from Newquay but to and from Penzance as well. From the enthusiasts' viewpoint it is unfortunate that, except for summer Saturdays, passenger trains normally comprise either IC125 units, Sprinters or diesel mechanical multiple units. From Par to St Blazey the line is double track but on arriving at St Blazey a train destined for Newquay, Goonbarrow or Ponts Mill will take the single-line token from the St Blazey signalman. The single line commences just beyond the old St Blazey station and continues through to Goonbarrow Junction.

Although Par continues to be important on the Cornish railway map, if the plans for re-routing the Newquay branch trains via St Austell and Burngullow come to fruition, main line trains will not stop at Par, due to the steep gradients either side of the station. Although Newquay branch trains will still start and terminate at Par it will definitely then be "St Austell – change for Newquay", thus ending over a century of tradition.

Plate 77. A rather bald comparison with Plate 76 is this May 1976 study of an 'up' inter-regional train from Penzance, double-headed by a Class 50 and a Class 47 working in tandem. This was the year when the use of headcode panels ceased and all were briefly turned to "0000". All of the items mentioned in the previous caption have been stripped out but in addition the telegraph poles and bullhead rail have also gone! However, a new signal has sprouted out of the platform as the island's 'up' starter. *JV*

Plate 78. Saturday, 3rd October 1987 was an appalling day weatherwise but it was the last summer Saturday of through locomotive-hauled trains from Newquay to distant locations. The following year IC125 units would fill the role. The "board" is off for No. 50041 *Bulwark* at the head of the 16.28 Newquay to Wolverhampton while No. 50009 *Conqueror* sweeps into Par with the 07.20 Glasgow to Penzance. *JV*

Plate 81. *(Top right)* Having arrived from Newquay with the 10.40 am departure on 18th May 1959 No. 5557 runs around its two coaches and prepares to couple-up for the return journey. Four railwaymen have time for a natter which adds to the leisurely atmosphere. This locomotive was one of the later and heavier 1927-built 4575 class – a development of the 4500 class. *M. Mensing*

Plate 79. Apparently railway photographers in 1955 roared around the countryside in split-screen Morris Minors. With Dick Riley's "charabanc" on the right, 'Grange' class No. 6869 *Resolven Grange* receives Prairie tank assistance (No. 4567) with the 9.36 am Newquay to Paddington of 9th July 1955. The island platform is still used by Newquay branch trains – and a large number of china clay trains! *R. C. Riley*

Plate 82. *(Bottom right)* The overbridge at Par has become a hackneyed photographic location over the years but it is, nevertheless, a super place to watch trains. Having come down from ECC Rocks Driers at Goonbarrow, new Railfreight liveried Class 37 No. 37673, with St Blazey "lizard" crest on the rear cabside, avoids the platform roads with 18 CDA china clay wagons in tow. It will need all of its 1,750 hp to haul its 900-tonne load up to Treverrin Tunnel on its way to Lostwithiel and Carne Point, Fowey. Photographed on 13th March 1989. *JV*

Plate 80. There have been rumours for some years that all semaphore signals in Cornwall would be replaced by a modern colour light system controlled from a single location at Par. More recently, the rumoured location is Plymouth. However, for the moment, these lower quadrants at Par survive. Once the lines covered in this volume were controlled by 30 signal boxes and innumerable ground frames but now only Par, St Blazey and Goonbarrow survive. On 23rd February 1982 suburban 3-car unit No. P317 will shortly be leaving for Newquay. *JV*

5557

Plate 83. The author travelled from Sussex to Cornwall overnight when he heard that snow had fallen in Cornwall on 18th January 1985, such is the comparative rarity of the event. Class 118 dmu Nos W51312 and W51327 forming a Newquay to Par working use the crossover on the double-track spur between St Blazey and Par, in order to reach the island platform on 19th January 1985. Within 24 hours the snow had melted. *JV*

Plate 84. It is difficult to imagine a more incongruous sight than Network SouthEast Class 47 No. 47583 *County of Hertfordshire* hauling withdrawn wooden-bodied "clay hoods" from St Blazey yard to Sharpness Docks for cutting up – but that is exactly what happened on 2nd February 1988. The formation has just started to negotiate the spur to the main line. *JV*

8 St Blazey

Being so near to Treffry's Par Harbour, a significant number of early mines, including the vast Fowey Consuls complex, and adjacent to the main Cornwall Railway line, there was perhaps an inevitability that the Cornwall Minerals Railway would site their Headquarters at St Blazey. Above all else, the original tramway from Mollinis, via the Carmears Incline in the Luxulyan Valley, ran past the site, parallel with the canal which, by the time the CMR started building, had been disused for two decades.

Built on 600 square yards of land to the west of the tramway, but to the north of the main line, the CMR Headquarters was a grand affair. Designed by the last of the great Victorian railway engineers, Sir Morton Peto, the buildings were classic in design and unusual for Cornwall in that they were built of red brick imported from the Plymouth area. The design included not only offices but a substantial works, with a high chimney for the blacksmiths' forges. In particular, the locomotive shed was unusual in that it was designed on a roundhouse and turntable principle with nine "roads", each capable of taking two CMR tank locomotives, ie the entire 1874 fleet. Other buildings included an erecting and repair shop (the works), a boiler house, a fitting shop and the aforementioned smithy.

Slightly to the north of the main buildings was a wagon shop and a goods shed. Early postcards show a further small engine house alongside the wagon shop. Beyond that was the brick-built Par station, which became St Blazey when the loop to Par main line station was opened in January 1879. In later years the brickwork of the station was rendered, as seen in the accompanying photographs. In addition to the many buildings there were a large number of sidings to the east, but mainly to the west of the wagon shop. Over the years there were many modifications to the St Blazey site including a passenger footbridge from the St Blazey road across the sidings to the station.

The GWR demolished the goods shed and replaced it with a loading wharf and crane, while at the south end of the yard a steeply inclined coaling stage was built. Coal wagons were propelled up the incline and unloaded into the bunkers and tenders of the steam locomotives below. At the south end the lines and sidings tapered into just two roads; one leading to Par Harbour and the other to Fowey. In the 1910s, 1920s and

Plate 85. Although not unique, the construction in 1873 of the Cornwall Minerals Railway locomotive depot at St Blazey on turntable and roundhouse principle was certainly unusual. Furthermore, the building and the adjoining works, offices and sheds were built of red brick rather than the customary stone. There were nine roads, each capable of taking two of the 18 Sharp, Stewart-built CMR locomotives. On 28th September 1957 only 2-6-2T No. 4584 is clearly visible. *Les Elsey*

Plate 86. In this very rare view at St Blazey one of the Sharp, Stewart 0-6-0Ts had just been converted to a saddle tank by the Great Western Railway. The conversions took place in 1883/84 and included lengthening the frames in order to provide a bunker and replacing the weatherboards with small cabs. Water capacity increased from 780 to 840 gallons and their weight increased by 2 tons. *JV Collection*

Plate 87. St Blazey depot and works on 23rd April 1956. In the background is the main works building, by then disused for its original purpose, while on the right is the roundhouse. On the left is the end of the coaling stage incline. The leading locomotives are 4500 class No. 4559 and 1600 class No. 1664. At this time St Blazey had an allocation of three dozen locomotives. *Maurice Dart*

Plate 88. The St Blazey coaling stage towards the end of the days of steam in 1962. On the right are locomotives of the 5700 class 0-6-0PT and 5100 class 2-6-2T. St Blazey was always the motive power operations centre for the Cornish china clay lines and branches, the drivers having comparatively few Class 1 turns. *Carey Batchelor*

1930s there were further sidings extensions including land to the north-west of the station, which itself closed in September 1925 when the passenger service to Fowey was withdrawn (except for workmen's trains which continued until December 1934).

Although the locomotive works ceased to be used for the purpose in the days of the GWR, it was from the 1960s onward which saw the start of significant rationalisation. Although British Railways could not demolish the listed buildings the original station building did meet its end in the early 1970s. Before that, in 1967, some four years after the end of steam in the area, the lines to the former works and the coaling stage, including the incline, were removed. The line to Fowey was closed and lifted in 1968 and by then little-used sidings were being removed. The sidings down to the large loading wharf, just inside the old entrance off the old St Blazey Road, were removed in the early 1980s and by that time many of the buildings were showing signs of minimum maintenance by BR. In fact the roof of the roundhouse and Supervisor's offices was unsafe. Consequently, in April 1987, the roundhouse was closed, after 113 years of operation.

Many of the sidings to the north-west of the old station were removed at this time and in 1988 work started on a major scheme, which saw completely new offices built north of the roundhouse but to the west of the wagon works. With the withdrawal of the "clay hood" wagons in February 1988 the wagon works was modernised and equipped to deal with modern air-braked, roller-bearing wagons of today's private owner and Railfreight fleet. The diesel fuelling point was moved from just south of the turntable to the east side of the wagon works building and a large number of sidings were removed. In 1989 the individual roads of the roundhouse were separated by breeze-block walls and each section was leased out as a small industrial unit. New power supplies were provided and the buildings, including the roof, made safe. Diesel locomotives continued to cross the turntable on their way to the wagon works for minor attention, such as fitting new brake blocks. The GWR signal box and a reasonable selection of lower quadrant semaphore signals have survived into the 1990s. The remains of the old St Blazey station platforms remain, although the edging and surface have crumbled with the passage of time. High floodlights now provide new lighting standards for the shunting yard in hours of darkness.

St Blazey has always been the hub of the operational wheel in terms of freight and china clay train operations. In terms of locomotive allocation, number of wagons controlled and the number of staff "on the books", St Blazey has shrunk from the halcyon days but it is, nevertheless, still the nerve centre of the railways of central Cornwall. The days of the paper-driven control system, which gave way to Telex after the Second World War is now computer-based with commensurate communications technology. The Area Manager now resides in Plymouth, Swindon is nominally in charge of

Plate 89. St Blazey station with the original brickwork rendered (see Plate 21) on 10th February 1961. It is hard to believe that the station was then still standing over 30 years after closure. The two tracks here are still occasionally used as a passing loop for 'up' and 'down' Newquay branch trains, although the odds are one of them will be a freight or a summer Saturday working. One of Churchward's 1911 Moguls of the 4300 class, No. 7335, prepares to leave with a freight for Tavistock Junction. *R. C. Riley*

Plate 90. A very sad week at St Blazey. After 113 years of continuous operation the roundhouse was last used on 24th April 1987. It is "bed time" on 22nd April 1987 as, one by one, St Blazey's allocation of Class 37s are put in their bays until the following day. Only the locomotives for the evening air-braked freights will stay in the yard. No. 37175 leaves the turntable to join Nos 37196 and 37207. *JV*

Plate 91. Posing in front of the listed 1873 CMR building is No. 37142 and ZVV wagon No. KB741623 on 15th October 1982. This locomotive was earmarked to receive the name *William Cookworthy*, the Plymouth apothecary who is credited with the discovery of china clay in Cornwall, but because of the external condition of the locomotive the honour fell to No. 37207 and later No. 37675. *JV*

Plate 92. St Blazey underwent considerable modifications during 1988/89, including the building of a new administrative block, wagon works extension and new fuelling point. At precisely 10.18 on 14th March 1989 Railfreight Class 37 No. 37031, which had just been refurbished by Plymouth Laira and was out "on test", gleams beside No. 08955 which is indulging in a little shunting. The fuelling point is on the right. *JV*

Plate 93. Photographs of the original A1A-A1A 2,000 hp, 117-ton 'Warships' on china clay duty are very hard to come by. However, by 1963 the class had already been relegated to secondary duties in the West Country. In clean green livery with small yellow warning panel, No. D600 *Active* stands at the head of a freight in St Blazey yard. The wagon works can be seen behind the locomotive. *Carey Batchelor*

Plate 94. Although the 204 hp Class 03s were successful in some environments, in common with other shunters they were built just as the BR traffic patterns changed and goods yards and wagonload freights disappeared from the scene. No. D2183 emerged from Swindon Works in March 1962 and by September 1968 it had been withdrawn. The diesel-mechanical 0-6-0 is seen at BZ (83E) in ex-works condition. *Carey Batchelor*

Plate 95. St Blazey signal box is one of the survivors which will continue to perform its mechanical marvels into the 1990s. Reversing into the yard at 20.10, having just arrived with Plymstock to Chacewater cement tankers on 15th April 1985, is "Hoover" Class 50 No. 50006 *Neptune* (now scrapped). BR lost this potentially lucrative contract on cost grounds in 1986, and the Blue Circle Cement depot at Chacewater has now closed completely. *JV*

Plate 96. A sight to behold in 1986 is a main line express taking to a single-track branch line with the driver of a 100 mph locomotive slowing to 5 mph to collect a single-line token. No. 50034 *Furious* is surrounded by vintage token catchers, signals and point levers as it passes St Blazey with the 07.25 Manchester to Newquay of 23rd August 1986. Note the speed restrictions; 20 mph on the 'down' and 15 mph on the 'up' road. *JV*

Plate 98. *(Right)* A morning and evening ritual which was fascinating to watch but hard work to perform, was getting 107-ton locomotives on and off shed. Already history is this shot of No. 37207 *William Cookworthy* being retired for the night on 2nd March 1984. Before the advent of "Driver Only" operation the guard on the left is obviously pushing hard! Each bay has now been converted into an individual factory unit. *JV*

Plate 97. The 'up' evening air-braked freight, due to depart BZ at 22.00 but often early, is normally marshalled by a train crew which signs off early evening. The formation then sits quietly at St Blazey until the new crew is ready and the road is clear. On 22nd April 1987 it was Railfreight Class 47 No. 47220 which was to head a lighter than usual load of 400 tonnes across the Tamar. *JV*

Plate 99. One of the most prestigious Chartex specials ever to work along the Newquay branch was the Railway Pictorial Publications Railtours (RPPR) "Penzance Pullman", which comprised eight first-class coaches, four restaurant cars and a brake coach. Part of its itinerary included a run from Par to St Dennis Junction and back with a photographic stop at Goonbarrow. With passengers having enjoyed on-train lunch, Nos 25155 and 37299 wait to leave Par loop on the 'down' run, 26th April 1980. *JV*

Plate 100. *(Below)* The view from St Blazey 'down' yard looking towards Middleway (see barrier in the distance). Class 37 No. 37674 has just passed BZ station and come to a halt with the afternoon Parkandillack to St Blazey ABS on 16th June 1989 and is about to reverse into the yard. The short distance between the 'down' starter and 'advanced' starter signals should be noted. The 'advanced' also protects Middleway Crossing. *JV*

Plate 101. The new scene at St Blazey with the roundhouse on the left abandoned, and a new "locoport" built in front of the wagon works, five Class 37s line up across the old turntable. They are No. 37674 in "old" Railfreight livery, Nos 37671 the new *Tre Pol and Pen* and 37670 in new Railfreight livery and Nos 37414 and 37412 (formerly *Loch Lomond*) in Highland Rail livery. A dmu is being refuelled. Photographed on Sunday, 11th June 1989. *JV*

control activities and the Tiger Railcar Leasing representative has a significant input into wagon control and clay company requirements. However, despite these influences, it is the St Blazey Supervisors, the Freight Manager and the railmen of St Blazey who really run the business. While there may be fewer clay loading points these days, requirements are constantly changing and it is a nightmare trying to supply wagons at a moment's notice, while at the same time ensuring train crews are able to work the trains, that a locomotive is available and that the logical order of operating can meet all requirements. There are scores of pitfalls ranging from crippled wagons to delays of ships in the Channel due to gales. Overall, there are other problems such as achieving volume targets and ensuring that all is well with the daily trains that work into and out of Cornwall, to locations as diverse as Switzerland and the West Highlands of Scotland.

The St Blazey train crews have worked diverse diagrams over the years. In days gone by workings varied from minor branch clay trains with small pannier tanks or diesel shunters to main line turns which, especially on summer Saturdays, included several Class 1 trains as far as Penzance in the "down" direction and Exeter "up" country. In the war years St Blazey drivers regularly worked beyond Exeter, on both passenger and freight workings. In more recent times 83E/BZ men worked Class 1 trains over the Newquay branch and on to Plymouth. They still work air-braked freights as far as Exeter Riverside and passenger turns on certain branch dmu services. In recent times most of the air-braked china clay trains are "Driver Only" – although a shunter is present on the branches, or as at Carne Point, Fowey or at Goonbarrow, "in residence". Operations at St Blazey are literally around the clock, although in recent times Sundays are a little quieter, especially in winter.

The classes of steam locomotive shedded at St Blazey were those as previously described in the section on BR Steam in the 1950s. However, it is worth repeating that some three dozen steam locomotives plus visitors have been replaced by nine Class 37 Co-Co diesel-electrics and a single Class 08 shunter. Following the introduction of further long-haul freight traffic during 1989, two additional Class 37s were added to the allocation, although all locomotives are strictly allocated to the new sector FTLL pool (Freight Trainload Laira). Invariably, as locomotives fail or are returned to works for attention, other Class 37s are drafted in but two locomotives now have distinctly Cornish names: No. 37671 *Tre Pol and Pen* and 37675 *William Cookworthy* (previously carried by Nos 37196 and 37207 respectively).

While there is an association between the china clay industry in Cornwall and the railways there will continue to be a St Blazey on the rail network, and while the Department of the Environment continues to list buildings, there will continue to be links with the old Cornwall Minerals Railway and their grand St Blazey Headquarters.

Plate 102. In 1833 a canal was built to convey minerals from Ponts Mill to a basin near Par Harbour. It was about two miles in length and the alignment can still be seen clearly. With the alignment on the left, single power car No. W55026 accelerates towards Middleway Crossing with the 07.50 Par to Newquay of 5th May 1989. Sadly, the 65-seater was more than adequate for the number of passengers. *JV*

Plate 103. When lengthy air-braked freights arrive at St Blazey they normally pull forward through the old station towards Middleway, with the longest trains straddling the crossing. After spending the afternoon of 21st October 1988 on the Drinnick Mill branch Class 50/1 No. 50149 *Defiance* brings 800 tonnes of china clay to a stand just short of Middleway. The iron bridge is the same as that seen in the Victorian photograph, Plate 22. *JV*

9 Middleway to Ponts Mill

Just to the north of St Blazey is Middleway Bridge Crossing which carries the St Blazey to Tywardreath road across the Newquay branch railway line and the River Par. It also crosses the alignment of the old Par Canal. The railway line is single track at this point and in the early years a ground frame and crossing keeper's cottage controlled the crossing. In GWR days a signal box was built on the 'down', or west side of the line to the south of the road. The small cabin was of interesting design because the point levers and signal wires had to span the River Par to reach the rods and pulleys adjacent to the track. Curiously, although traffic on the Newquay branch could never be described as busy, a substantial wooden pedestrian footbridge was built across the railway and river at this point. It was demolished in the 1930s, however, and was never replaced. It was a sad day in January 1981 when Middleway Bridge Crossing signal box closed; the gates were removed and automatic barriers with CCTV control from St Blazey signal box were installed.

The river, old canal and the railway run side by side to the north with trains passing along what almost appears to be a causeway. Semaphore signals abound, although St Blazey Bridge Crossing is now controlled by a colour light in the 'up' direction and a semaphore on the 'down' run. Again, there was once a signal box located on the 'down' side, north of the main A390 road it protected. After being physically moved 22 yards to the north in 1973, to accommodate barrier work and bridge widening, it finally closed on 30th September that year. There are the remains of some old disused lime kilns on the 'up' side of the line, and a few years ago a laundry with a splendid stone stack stood on the south-west corner of the crossing. Now there is only the audible warning signal of an approaching train and automatic barriers to interest the student of railways. The line continues beside the river and old canal alignment to reach Ponts Mill.

The entire Ponts Mill area is steeped in history. As stated in the Treffry Tramway section, the sea once reached this point before 400 years of mining activity produced enough silt and spoil to push the shoreline to where it is now, some two miles to the south. Activity in the area was arguably at its height in the mid-1850s when inclines brought down the substantial output of the Fowey Consuls to Ponts Mill for conveyance to the then new Par Harbour. Granite, ores and china clay were being carried down the Carmears Incline in the Luxulyan Valley from the pits around Bugle and the quarries at the top of the valley. Until 1855 all of this had to be transhipped from wagon to barge for the journey to the sea. Add to this local activity, milling and crushing, combined with the water from man-made leats and the River Par tumbling through, and the vast amount of manual labour involved, the scene must have been remarkable.

Nowadays the scene is considerably less frantic. At milepost 283 the main Newquay branch starts to climb steeply as it crosses the River Par. Just before the bridge is a ground frame

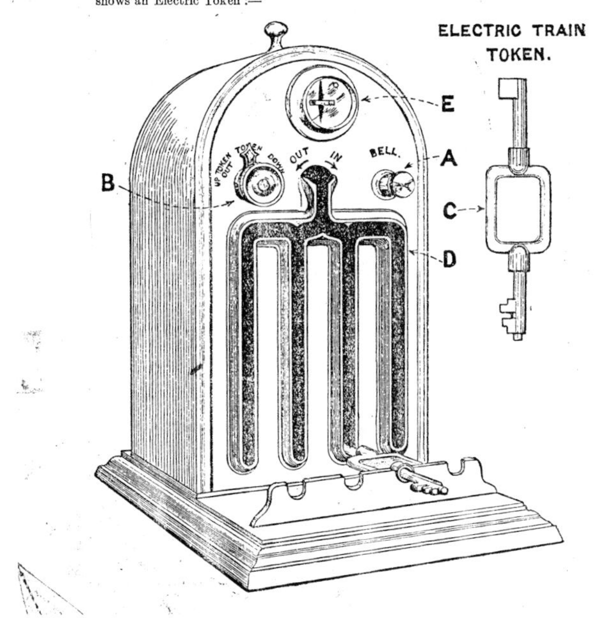

Private, and not for publication.

(Circular No. 3313)

GREAT WESTERN RAILWAY.

Introduction of Electric Token Instruments between St. Blazey Bridge, Pontsmill and Luxulyan.

Commencing on October 19th, 1914, the existing Electric Train Staff Instruments for working between St. Blazey Bridge and Luxulyan will be withdrawn, and the Line between these points will be worked on the Electric Token System, as described herein, with an intermediate instrument at Pontsmill.

The diagram shewn below represents the Electric Token instrument, when it is in its normal position, that is, when there is no train in the section, and also shows an Electric Token :—

Plate 104. By the length of the name one could be forgiven for thinking that Middleway Bridge Crossing Ground Frame was a location of some importance. In fact it was strategically placed but this did not save the structure from demolition in 1981 when CCTV cameras and automatic barriers took over. When photographed on 15th March 1980 the box had just been repainted! Note the control levers crossing the river on a timber beam. *JV*

Plate 105. A favourite location for railway photography is the causeway between Middleway Bridge and St Blazey Gate, due to the pleasant surroundings and the unrestricted view of the trains. In super lighting conditions at 13.13 on 17th March 1989, No. 37669 brings a Polybulk and a Tullis Russell clay wagon down from Goonbarrow to join the afternoon 15.45 Speedlink service from St Blazey to Gloucester. *JV*

Plate 106. This sparkling shot was taken on 6th August 1956 and shows a tired-looking 4500 class 2-6-2T No. 4505 double-heading a Drinnick Mill to St Blazey via St Dennis Junction train with a 5700 class 0-6-0PT of the 87XX series. A load of over 450 tons will be pushing the pair towards Middleway. The river in the foreground is milky white from clay works excavations. *Les Elsey*

which controls the siding down to the existing ECC Ponts Mill installation. The point levers are unlocked by the shunter travelling in the brake van on the local Ponts Mill china clay train working – normally worked by the St Blazey Class 08 which propels its train from St Blazey. The ground frame can only be operated in conjunction with telephone communication to the signal box. A control box at the ground frame contains token instrument apparatus. Electric tokens were installed at Ponts Mill siding in October 1914, when they were also introduced at St Blazey and Luxulyan signal boxes.

Just beyond the ground frame a siding left the branch on the opposite, 'down' or west side to serve Prideaux Wood china clay dry prior to 1912. The only obvious remains of this today are the extended girders on the railway bridge over the River Par which clearly once carried an additional line.

The Prideaux works was built in the 1870s but all around the area was at one time heavily mined, mainly for tin. The planting of a substantial conifer forest by the Forestry Commission in 1960 has obscured many of the mining remains and the clay kiln was demolished by English China Clays immediately following closure in the early 1960s, although the settling tanks and base of the furnace room can still be traced. The origins of Prideaux Wood and South Prideaux Wood Mines are ancient. In 1881 the historian Robert Symons stated that "the open excavations in the coppice wood in which the sett is situated are enormous, if not unparalleled, partly done by the ancients – probably the Phoenicians – and partly by the moderns. The lodes are so numerous and the tinstone so thoroughly combined with the containing killas that the whole of it is fit for the stamps (crushers)."

As regards the Prideaux Wood china clay kiln, a narrow gauge line was opened, probably about the time the siding off the main CMR/GWR branch was closed, which ran from the linhay through a narrow and low bridge beneath the Newquay branch to a loading wharf, which adjoins the existing Ponts Mill sidings, although the standard gauge track serving the wharf has been lifted. The narrow gauge track and one of its turnouts on the wharf can still be traced (see photograph, page 77). In all probability the wagons were horse-drawn.

The single siding to the existing clay works branches away from the old tramway route on the 'down' side, and divides into two dead-end roads with the track set in concrete. Normally one train per day visits the works where once PGA wagons (now Tigers) are filled by front-loading tractors and

Plate 107. This surviving signal gantry indicates whether the train is bound for St Blazey yard or the spur to Par and the main line. There is no doubt that this ECC Rocks (Goonbarrow) to Carne Point (Fowey) train of CDA clay wagons will take to the main line. The locomotive, Class 37/5 No.37673 in new Raifreight livery, has the last three digits of its number on the front end. *JV*

VDA wagons have bagged clay on pallets loaded into them. Until recently the powdered china clay found its way to the Wiggins Teape mill near Fort William in the West Highlands of Scotland, for use in the manufacture of paper. Beside the works the main siding now ends with a simple stop block. There are no run-round facilities which is the reason for the train being propelled from St Blazey.

The line once passed the old canal basin at the foot of the Carmears Incline and the site of an old spur, which was once a china stone siding to the west of the location. Once across the access road to the works the track again divided, with the right-hand siding running to the Ponts Mill china stone works, which was open until the mid-1960s but which has now become heavily overgrown and partially flooded. The main siding then continued on the north-east side of Ponts Mill Viaduct on the Newquay branch, (by this point the structure carries the main branch high above the valley floor), to the foot of the old Treffry Tramway Carmears Incline. On the 'down' side is a solid-looking stone loading wharf where, after the railway to Trevanny Works (and much earlier Rock Mill and Orchard Quarries) was lifted, china clay was loaded from transfer lorry to railway wagon. On the 'up', or north-east side of the alignment, is an abandoned siding with mature trees grow ing between the sleepers, and immediately above this is the significant embankment which carried the original Treffry Tramway onto the incline. At the foot of the incline is a mystery bridge. Even the highly recommended 200-page report of the Cornish Archaeological Survey could not identify its precise purpose, other than to suggest that it may have been part of an 1835 scheme by Treffry to build a tramway up the floor of the valley, a project which proved to be abortive. "The bridge at the foot of the Carmears Incline is a very substantial structure whose purpose is to carry the incline over an obstacle of some importance. It has so far been impossible to establish if this was a road or trackway from Ponts Mill up the valley, or whether it was in fact the line of the early Tramway, preserved for some future use."

Thus at this point at the northern end of the Ponts Mill area, and at the south of the Luxulyan Valley, there is the present branch line standing high on Ponts Mill Viaduct, a loading wharf on the valley floor, the alignment of the valley floor tramway (described in the next section), an abandoned siding (with track overgrown but *in situ*), the Carmears Incline and the possible site of the original abortive tramway scheme. A visit to the location is highly recommended, preferably in the winter months for while the ground can be muddy the dense foliage of summer obscures many of the ruins.

It must be added that although the railways at Ponts Mill are broadly described, space does not permit detailed reference to the once-extensive crushing plant with its many stamps, the buildings of the New Consolidated Mines Company, the many mines such as Wheal Rashleigh, Wheal Treffry, etc., the fascinating array of machinery which pumped out mines, controlled the many leats and waterways or which powered the inclines, or the other buildings including early primitive cottages and tin miners' huts.

The latest and undoubtedly most significant development at Ponts Mill at the end of the 1980s has been the connection with royalty! The Prince of Wales owns, through his Duchy of Cornwall interests, vast tracts of land throughout the County of Cornwall. To visit his estates he regularly uses the Royal Train with its distinctive stock which includes sleeping accommodation. In past years the Royal Train used to be berthed overnight on the Bodmin General branch, just around the curve from Bodmin Road (now Parkway). Since the closure of that branch and its sale into private, preservationist hands, the Royal Train has, surprisingly, been berthed at Ponts Mill siding. On one recent occasion both Prince Charles and Princess Diana spent the night on the remote Ponts Mill siding, and bearing in mind that such workings are "topped and tailed" with a locomotive at each end, it may well be that the future King of England enjoys the last locomotive-hauled passenger train on the Newquay branch!

Plate 108. When long-distance locomotive-hauled trains to Newquay ceased at the end of the 1987 summer there was speculation that the through train phenomenon could end. However, this was not to be and InterCity 125 trains were utilised. Looking very incongruous on single-track bullhead rail and passing lower quadrant semaphore signals at 30 mph, on 10th June 1989, is the remarkable 06.55 Glasgow Queen Street via Edinburgh to Newquay – at this point 10½ hours away from Scotland's largest city! *JV*

Plate 109. On 22nd May 1959, Michael Mensing was capturing such gems as this on film. With a member of the footplate team leaning from the cab of 4500 class No. 5519, to collect the next single-line token, the 10.40 am Newquay to Par comprising two non-corridor coaches approaches St Blazey Bridge crossing and the A390 road. In the distance the now long-abandoned Prideaux Wood clay dry stack is belching smoke and steam. *M. Mensing*

Plate 110. In this charming scene, which is an epitome of the off-season Newquay branch service of the 1980s, Class 122 No. 55005 forming the 10.25 Par to Newquay, passes old lime kilns on the approach to St Blazey Bridge crossing. If the Newquay branch service is diverted via Burngullow–Parkandillack–St Dennis Junction this section of track will become a freight-only siding. *JV*

Plate 111. A magic moment on 30th August 1986 and a sight which is not now repeatable is Driver Percy Wherry winding Class 50 No. 50039 *Implacable* (since withdrawn) down from the Luxulyan Valley towards St Blazey Bridge with a rake of air-conditioned coaches forming the 17.10 Newquay to Wolverhampton. Note the Tywardreath Highway climbing the hill in the background, the approximate site of Fowey Consols. Percy retired in February 1991. *JV*

Plate 112. Based on a Collett design, the 5700 class pannier tanks, such as No. 9755 seen here, weighed 49 tons, fractionally less than a BR Class 08 shunter. On the china clay lines a great deal was expected of these tough little tanks such as hauling mixed freights (like that seen here) up the 1 in 37 climb through the Luxulyan Valley. The regulator is open as the train passes the laundry at St Blazey Bridge on 3rd August 1956. *Les Elsey*

Plate 113. At the foot of the Luxulyan Valley lies a small clay drying plant; ECC Ponts Mill. Trains run once a day, Monday to Friday, but there is always the "as required" factor. Clay wagons are propelled from St Blazey by a Class 08 shunter as there are no run-round facilities at the works. On 16th April 1985 No. 08945 propels six PRA wagons and an SR Lancing-built brake van past the junction with the Newquay branch (right). One of the two shunters is manning the ground frame. Note the two levers and the token instrument. *JV*

Plate 114. The whole of the Ponts Mill area abounds with industrial relics. Near Ponts Mill was Prideaux Wood Clay Kiln and a 2 ft gauge tramway ran from the linhay to a loading wharf located adjacent to the Ponts Mill siding. A low bridge took the track under the CMR/Newquay branch. Traffic was horse-drawn initially, but Industrial Railway Society literature suggests a steam locomotive was used. *JV*

Plate 115."No entry to BR without authorisation of the Shipping Captain" reads the sign outside of Ponts Mill works. With the Captain's permission no doubt, Class 08 No. 08955 removes two 80-tonne Tiger wagons with china clay bound for Mossend. After traffic to Fort William ceased at the end of 1989, and the withdrawal from clay duties of the PRA wagons, the track was strengthened to take these 80-tonne (gross) wagons. Photographed on 24th January 1991. *JV*

Plate 116. Ponts Mill was once a hive of activity with minerals coming down from Fowey Consols, ore being transferred from wagon to barge, granite arriving from the two main tramways and china clay being processed at the grinding mills and clay dries. The scene is now much more rural; witness this delightful sight of the Ponts Mill branch freight, powered by No. 08955, approaching the junction with the Newquay branch on 4th May 1989. *JV*

10 Luxulyan Valley to Goonbarrow Junction

Although there were clay driers and china stone crushing plants at Ponts Mill, and large volumes of china clay taken down the valley to the harbours at Par and Fowey, the granite within the Luxulyan Valley was not kaolinised and hence there is no china clay in the actual valley area. That is not to say that there was no mineral wealth, mining or quarrying activity. There was much activity in ancient times but in terms of railway lines it was Treffry's original plans for a tramway in 1835 which first brought rails to the valley.

Little is known about the original scheme but it is clear that, due to the difficult terrain, hard rock and incompetent contractors, work was abandoned. However, Treffry was determined to build the tramway to Mollinis, near Bugle, and eventually on to Newquay where he had just purchased the harbour. As detailed in the Treffry Tramway section, after detailed planning in 1837 work started on the tramway in earnest towards the end of that year. By 1841 the Carmears Incline up the eastern edge of the valley and the tramway along level ground, to what would become the eastern end of the Treffry Viaduct, and on to Colcerrow and Carbeans granite quarries, was ready for service. A combination of horse and water wheel power saw the first loads being transported down to Ponts

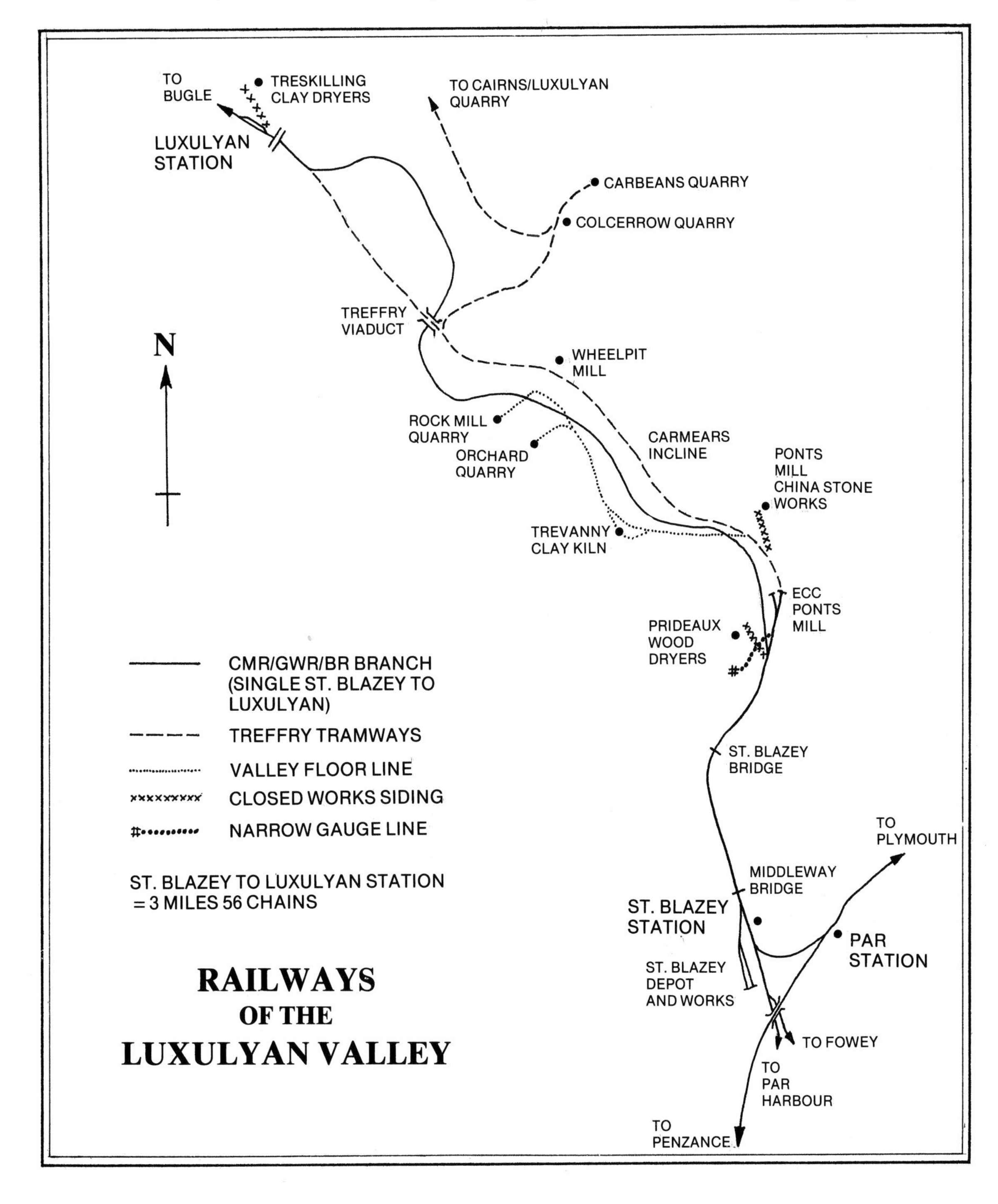

Plate 117. The standard gauge tramway along the floor of the Luxulyan Valley, as distinct from the CMR/present-day Newquay branch or the Treffry Tramway which ran up Carmears Incline, originally served Rock Mill and Orchard quarries, but in 1920 the Central Cornwall Clay Company opened Trevanny Dry, just visible on the left of this photograph. Latterly served by lorries, the dry closed in the early 1960s. The line was worked by a small Motor Rail "Simplex" petrol locomotive which was shedded in this corrugated structure. It is being surveyed by two gentlemen with long mackintoshes on 4th November 1956. *Maurice Dart*

Plate 120. *(Top near right)* Photographs such as this can be attempted only in the winter or spring, when the deciduous trees have lost their leaves. This view, north of Ponts Mill, is the only opportunity to give some appreciation of the Luxulyan Valley topography. Taken from Treffry's Carmears Incline on the east side of the valley, it is possible to see Ponts Mill Viaduct above, carrying the Newquay branch on the 1874 CMR route, while just beyond the tree-infested siding can be seen the trackbed of the valley floor line to Rock Mill and Trevanny Kiln. Photographed 14th April 1985. *JV*

Plate 121. *(Top far right)* In the 200-page report on the Luxulyan Valley, prepared by the Cornwall Archaeological Unit in 1988, it is stated that the remains of the Central Cornwall Company's Trevanny Kiln has become a sanctuary for wild life and plants – fauna and flora. This shows the remains of the building and its unusual all-brick stack in June 1989. *JV*

Plate 118. Wagons would often run down from Trevanny Dry under the control of a brakeman but this little ECLP-owned Motor Rail "Simplex" (2032 of 1920) was normally used for the interchange of wagons at the GWR and later BR Ponts Mill siding. By the time this photograph was taken, on 7th August 1956, the ageing machine was out of action. It was scrapped at Par by H. Orchard & Sons in 1965, after 45 years of service. *Maurice Dart*

Plate 122. *(Right)* Treffry's Tramway from Ponts Mill and up the Carmears Incline to quarries at Colcerrow and Carbeans was completed in 1841. There were many other quarries in the area, some going back hundreds of years. However, in 1868/70, a horse-drawn tramway extension had been constructed to serve Rock Mill and Orchard quarries (later acquired by the Penryn Company of John Freeman and therefore referred to as Freeman's Quarries). This tramway later served the aforementioned Trevanny Kiln. The view here shows the line running beneath Ponts Mill Viaduct on the Newquay branch in 1922. *L. T. George Collection*

Plate 119. Rambles along the old railways and tramways in the area can be very rewarding. Deep in the undergrowth near Trevanny Kiln a point lever has survived where the kiln siding left the valley floor tramway. Its pattern would appear to be almost identical to that visible on the old Gothers Tramway near St Dennis – see Plate 241. Photographed in 1989, with the aid of a flash gun due to the dark woods, one wonders if the track survives below the soil. *JV*

Plate 123. This area was surveyed by Mr Sherlock in May 1922 and through his camera he recorded the only known view of the valley floor tramway junction beneath Rock Mill Viaduct on the Newquay branch. This early line had been lifted in 1914 after the quarries closed but was relaid in 1922 only to be lifted again in 1938. Only the southern part was retained to serve the clay dry at Trevanny Kiln. The line to the right served Rock Mill and to the left Orchard Quarry. Research has revealed that many of the established dates concerning the opening and closing of such lines are unreliable. However, this photograph proves there were two lines and that some well-established maps are also unreliable. *L. T. George Collection*

Plate 124. A recent view on the decking of Rock Mill Viaduct in the heart of the Luxulyan Valley. Class 37/5 No. 37674 crosses the 1874 structure on 24th August 1987 with Goonbarrow to Carne Point clay hoods. Some of the granite from these quarries was used in the construction of Trevanny Kiln. *Brian Morrison*

Plate 125. The same view as Plate 123 but taken 67 years later! There are still traces of both wooden and granite sleepers and blocks but the old tramway is now a footpath and the area is very overgrown. Note the abutment of the Newquay branch Rock Mill Viaduct just visible on the right. *JV*

Mill, where they were transhipped to barge for the two-mile canal journey to the now-complete Par Harbour.

Historical reports refer to the Carmears Incline as double track with 'down' loads being balanced by 'up' loads, others show single track but with a passing section or loop half-way up, while the archaeological report is specific in stating that the incline was single track only. Further research shows that the incline was single track but judging by the width of the tramway in places it is easy to understand how some have made double-track assumptions. In the last week of February 1843 the magnificent Treffry Viaduct/Aqueduct was opened for traffic which later resulted in the first through loads to and from Bugle via Luxulyan Village. One historian commented that the Treffry Viaduct did *not* have the family crest sculptured on a shield on the stonework, another argued that it did. In a way they were both right, because curiously, the south side of the viaduct shows a blank stone shield whereas the northern face has the family crest proudly carved in a shield above the central arches. Water was carried across the structure beneath the huge granite slabs which supported the tramway. The water fed the leat which not only powered the Carmears Incline water wheel but also amplified the power of the Fowey Consuls leat.

Although there had been granite quarries around the Luxulyan Valley for many years, a form of pink and black coloured variety, known as Luxulyanite, was quarried in the area, and some of this is used in Westminster Abbey in London as part of the Duke of Wellington's tomb. In the early 1850s a branch from the tramway to Colcerrow and Carbeans Quarries was built. It formed a trailing connection with the branch in the 'down' direction and ran to the north-north-west past Gatty's Bridge to Cairns Quarry, a shallow working in the hillside behind Luxulyan. This quarry was disused by 1880 but the remains can still be traced (see Plate 12).

What was to become one of the most interesting tramways was a horse-drawn extension from Ponts Mill along the valley floor to further granite quarries at Rock Mill. This line was built between 1868 and 1870 with an inclined plane serving the southernmost quarry, called Orchard Quarry. When the Cornwall Minerals Railway built their well-engineered line up the valley in the 1872 to 1874 period, to enable locomotive-hauled trains to run from Fowey to Newquay via Bugle, effectively to replace the Treffry Tramway and making the Carmears Incline redundant, stone for the viaducts in the valley and the abutments was conveyed by horse on the valley floor tramway. The tramways at this time were an anachronism with only Pentewan surviving in horse-drawn mode in the County of Cornwall.

The quarry at the head of the valley floor tramway was Rock Mill and south of that was Orchard Quarry. These quarries had been in operation prior to 1840 and evidence of abandoned dwelling houses has been found. The tramway was built by the South Cornwall Granite Company. It diverged up the valley from the foot of Carmears Incline and the rails were anchored to granite block sleepers. The main tramway was to Rock Mill Quarry but just before what was to become the Newquay branch and Rock Mill Viaduct, a spur branched off to serve Orchard Quarry. About the turn of the century the Penryn company of John Freeman took over the quarries and on some early maps the name of the quarries are shown simply as "Freemans Quarry".

In the early part of the 20th century the demand for granite declined as cheaper imports from Scandinavia were readily available. While unlike other mining depressions, this did not finish quarrying overnight, the two quarries closed just before the First World War and the track from Ponts Mill to both Rock Mill and Orchard quarries was lifted. In the very early 1920s the Central Cornwall China Clay Company built their Central Cornwall Kiln, also known as Trevanny Dry. It was a conventional coal-fired pan-kiln with the linhay facing the valley floor tramway, which was relaid (and slightly diverted) through to the quarries further up the valley when Trevanny Dry was opened. The kiln was unusual in having an all brick stack, which still survives, although hidden in now dense overgrowth. The main buildings were built of granite and there is speculation that one of the primary reasons for relaying the tramway to the quarries was to bring down granite for the clay installation construction. There is some evidence that granite was sold from the quarry floor but little sign of post-First World War quarrying. The relaid standard gauge line was on wooden sleepers whereas the original valley floor tramway was, in common with the Treffry Tramways, laid on granite blocks, or setts.

The entire line from Rock Mill Quarry to Ponts Mill was lifted in 1938. It was reputed that no granite had come down from the Freeman-owned site since 1928. The track was relaid almost immediately with upgraded materials but only as far as Trevanny Kiln. From the date Trevanny Kiln had been opened small 4-wheeled Motor Rail "Simplex" petrol locomotives had been used to haul wagons to and from the clay dry. The machines used were No. 1943 of 1919 build and No. 2032 of 1920. One was called *Bessie* and the driver for many years was one Jack Arscott. The locomotives were not powerful and often loaded wagons were brought down from Trevanny under the control of a brakeman, without locomotive. The first of

Plate 126. Especially in the days of steam, there was always a man-against-nature competition in the climb to Luxulyan. The maximum load for an unassisted 'Grange' class 4-6-0 was a mere 180 tons or five loaded coaches. In this magnificent photograph, taken on 19th July 1958, 'Manor' 4-6-0 No. 7816 *Frilsham Manor* and 'Grange' No. 6832 *Brockton Grange* double-head the 3-coach 10.05 am Par to Newquay. The extra locomotive was required at Newquay for a returning full-length main liner. *Peter Gray*

Plate 127. Although published in past years, this classic picture of the 9.30 am Paddington to Newquay, blasting up the Luxulyan Valley, just had to be included in this volume. The 12-coach train would turn the scales at well over 400 tons but the maximum load for a 'Hall' and a GWR Mogul up the 1 in 37 would be 190 plus 180 = 370 tons. Therefore a tank engine banker had to be added to the formation. On 9th July 1955 No. 5972 *Olton Hall* and 4300 class 2-6-0 No. 6397 are assisted by 2-6-2T No. 5519. *R. C. Riley*

Plate 128. While the modern scene may not be quite so spectacular as the days of steam, the sight of immaculate Class 37 No. 37670 descending the valley is nevertheless impressive. Without having to worry about pinning down brakes the Railfreight machine heads a very mixed Goonbarrow to St Blazey ABS under the Treffry Viaduct on 14th March 1989. In recent years the farmers have removed the outcrops of rocks in the background to facilitate planting and grazing. *JV*

Plate 129. Forging its way towards Luxulyan Tunnel, with its clear chimney signifying warm temperatures, is 5700 class 0-6-0PT No. 9755, one of the St Blazey regulars. The train is the 2.15 pm Par to Newquay. Local trains of the period took about an hour for the $20\frac{3}{4}$-mile journey with five intermediate stops. *Peter Gray*

Plate 130. This most interesting view, immediately to the east of Luxulyan station, shows the siding which was the alignment of the original pre-1874 Treffry Tramway route. The track beyond the gate was out of use from 1933 when Colcerrow and Carbeans quarries closed. Horses would bring the wagons to the gate just visible behind the flat wagon in the siding where they were collected by GWR engines. Here, on 6th July 1955, No. 5526 leaves for Par with the 4.34 pm from Newquay. *R. C. Riley*

Plate 131. The same view as Plate 130 but taken 32 years later. On the Sunday following withdrawal of through locomotive-hauled trains to Newquay, BR showed some enterprise by organising an enthusiasts' special from Paddington. At 12.54 on 4th October 1987 an impeccable pair of Network SouthEast "Hoovers", Nos 50034 *Furious* and 50035 *Ark Royal*, looked and sounded superb as they livened up proceedings at Luxulyan. *JV*

Plate 132. A somewhat unusual view with a medium telephoto lens taken on 13th March 1989, from the end of Luxulyan station platform. A peep through the CMR-built overbridge finds 1,750 hp Class 37/5 No. 37673 hauling two VDA vans from St Blazey to Goonbarrow Junction. The other arch is for the river which feeds the leats down the Luxulyan Valley. *JV*

the small locomotives crashed about 1933 and the other was re-engined with a diesel in 1948. The track to Trevanny was lifted in the early 1950s and lorries then took the china clay down to a loading wharf near the foot of the Carmears Incline for transhipment to railway wagon as previously mentioned.

The Central Cornwall/Trevanny installation closed in the mid-1960s while in the ownership of ECLP and Trevanny siding was formally taken out of use on 31st December 1967. The slate roof on the kiln was removed in the early 1970s and, although largely still complete, the valley floor clay works is now little more than a nature reserve. In the undergrowth relics still survive including a point lever. Thus ended the valley floor railway story.

In the lower reaches of the valley there were a number of stone crushing plants but the last to be rail connected was Ponts Mill siding which was taken out of use on 31st December 1967. From this date there was thus no reason for the standard gauge line from Ponts Mill ground frame to cross the road beyond Ponts Mill driers.

Following closure of the Carmears Incline, shortly after the opening of the Cornwall Minerals Railway line in 1874, the Treffry Tramway was closed except for the section from Luxulyan (Bridges) to Treffry Viaduct, reversing to Colcerrow and Carbeans quarries. However, in 1890, the West of England China Clay Company opened their Wheelpit Mill at the head of Carmears Incline on the site of the incline wheel. A new waterwheel of 40 ft diameter was installed in the pit and this drove a pair of grinding pans. China stone was reputedly brought down to the mill along the old Treffry Tramway from Luxulyan station and loaded into the mill via wooden shutes. The crushed stone, in slurry form, ran down a 6-inch pipeline laid along the old Carmears Incline to Ponts Mill for drying. The Wheelpit Mill did not work beyond the First World War, closing as early as 1908. A major problem would have been bringing in the china stone in horse-drawn wagons from Luxulyan. Remains of some of the Wheelpit buildings can still be found.

Originally granite traffic coming off the Colcerrow and Carbeans line, and before 1880 the Cairns Quarry branch, joined the main Treffry Tramway from Mollinis and Luxulyan at a junction just at the south-east end of the Treffry Viaduct. From there it ran to the head of Carmears Incline for lowering by cable to the Ponts Mill area. However, once the CMR line (present Newquay branch) opened in 1874 traffic from the quarries reversed at the junction and was drawn by horses across the viaduct to a gate at a point on the tramway just before it joined the CMR, immediately east of Luxulyan station. From this point CMR, and later GWR, locomotives collected and delivered wagons. As aforementioned, the exception was between 1890 or so and *circa* 1908 when some clay wagons found their way to Wheelpit.

A delightful description of a walk recommended in an 1890 guidebook gives a remarkable insight to this area and is reproduced on page 191. Quotes include there being no risk in walking the tramway because "the trucks conveying the stone are drawn by horses" and on the Colcerrow branch "we may have to step aside to make way for trucks descending by gravitation". The branch up to Colcerrow and Carbeans was steep but well graded. There was a smithy at the quarry and a loading bank. Some of the track was relaid at the quarry end of the branch – on wooden sleepers rather than the original granite blocks. It seems the "new" track was ex-broad gauge and purchased from the GWR after 1892 (and, of course, relaid to standard gauge). The track to Wheelpit was lifted in 1915 having been disused for some years. The granite traffic dwindled although granite was quarried at Carbeans until the early 1930s when the tramway closed. The 1937 GWR Magazine refers to the line being open "until a few years ago". It seems traffic dwindled with the last load being taken down in 1933 by one of Mathew Hore's horses from Trethurgy. The Colcerrow track was mostly lifted shortly after closure but other track was removed in the summer of 1940. It was all removed to Par Beach and used in wartime defences against invasion. A short siding was retained at the Luxulyan end of the tramway, complete with protective gate (see Plate 130), but this was disconnected on 27th September 1964.

From Ponts Mill ground frame the branch climbs across the 52-yard Prideaux Viaduct, the 92-yard Ponts Mill Viaduct and the 52-yard Rock Mill Viaduct before curving under Treffry Viaduct. Still climbing, the single track enters a granite cutting and the 52-yard Luxulyan Tunnel before curving into Luxulyan station, once known as Bridges. The 1890 guide book states that "simple refreshments may be had at the Station Master's cottage". The train ride up the Luxulyan Valley is one of the most spectacular on British Rail and should be savoured while it is still possible. In the old days, if there was more than 20 wagons on a train, the Luxulyan porter had to assist the guard with pinning down brakes.

There was originally an 'up' and a 'down' platform at Bridges when opened by the CMR on 20th June 1876. A signal box controlled the passing loop and a siding. A simple station building was provided away from the platform and the GWR provided a pagoda hut shelter. In 1910 there were drastic changes to the station layout when a single island platform was provided. A new GWR signal box replaced the CMR example on 30th March 1911. The goods yard was extended on the north side of the line in 1916 when Treskilling Clay Works was opened. The passing loop was extended in May 1936 and a holiday "camping" coach appeared but, by and large, there was little change until 1964, when disaster struck.

On 27th September 1964 the goods yard was taken out of use. The signal box closed and the passing loop ('up' side line) was removed at the same time, as well as the Treffry refuge. Treskilling China Clay Works closed in 1975 and with it the narrow gauge line, which at first used horses and later a capstan, to move small clay wagons onto the standard gauge loading wharf. At this time the last siding serving the works also closed, leaving just a single track through the entire area. All the trappings of the days of steam disappeared such as water tower and water columns. Early in the 1980s the GWR shelter was replaced by a tasteless hut and by the late 1980s the station became a request halt. It had been unmanned since 12th July 1964.

West of Luxulyan the gradient eases slightly and relatively straight track takes the branch via Bowling Green and Goonbarrow Junction's fixed distant signal to Goonbarrow loop, adjacent to the vast English China Clay Rocks Works, on the fringe of Hensbarrow Down and clay country.

Plate 133. *(Above right)* Another before-and-after set of pictures. In this splendid July 1955 shot of Luxulyan the railway infrastructure includes branch train, water tower, signal box, token catcher, station building, clerestory camping coach, signals, pagoda hut, passing loop, sidings, goods wagons and water column. What a truly timeless scene! *R. C. Riley*

Plate 134. *(Below right)* Exactly 30 years later, at approximately the same time of day, all that remains is the basic platform, a train and a couple of the telegraph posts; a bleak and spartan scene. Heading a VIP Inspection Saloon towards Newquay on 17th April 1985 is No. 50037 *Illustrious*. In the Winter 1989/90 timetable five trains per day each way stopped here – on request. *JV*

Plate 135. The only known locomotives to have worked to Newquay since 3rd October 1987 have been the last day special, Class 47s "topping and tailing" a Royal train conveying HRH The Prince of Wales, the Class 20 hauled annual weedkilling train and Class 37s assisting failed High Speed Train units. The very last scheduled locomotive-hauled train was the 17.17 Newquay to Plymouth of 3rd October 1987 seen arriving at a wet and windswept Luxulyan behind No. 50026 *Indomitable*. *JV*

Plate 136. The winter months produce splendid lighting when the sun decides to shine, but the days are short and on the Newquay branch traffic is sparse. During the brief period when Railfreight liveried Class 37s could be photographed on the 30-year-old clay hoods, No. 37674 passes Bowling Green between Luxulyan and Goonbarrow with 'down' empties. *JV*

Plate 137. One of only two spoil trains which I have ever photographed in scores of visits to the line was No. 37142 on 11th June 1981. With half a dozen old 'Grampus' wagons and a 20-ton brake van the Type 3 locomotive is seen east of the massive ECC Rocks Works at Goonbarrow on its way from St Dennis Junction tip to Tavistock Junction. *JV*

Plate 138. Dumped in a field at Treskilling just beside the Luxulyan to Bugle road is this old 8-compartment coach used originally as a dwelling and latterly as a cow shed. At nearby Bowling Green there are still some railway coach dwellings including one rare ex-Metropolitan Railway rigid 8-wheeler. *JV*

Plate 139. Goonbarrow Junction is now the only passing loop between St Blazey and Newquay. Approaching the loop at the east end with empty CDAs from Carne Point on 16th June 1989 is No. 37670. It is clear from the semaphore survivors of a bygone age that trains can leave on the 'up' line from either sides of the loop, although those from the 'down' side must observe a 15 mph restriction. *JV*

Plate 140. The early bird catches the worm; in this case No. 37675 *William Cookworthy* arriving at Goonbarrow Junction at 07.20 on 4th May 1989, with two Tiger Railcar Leasing PAA wagons and the 'Carbis Wharf' Tiger No. TRL 11600. The train is seemingly passing the signal at danger but, in fact, trains for the freight sidings are controlled by a separate 'dummy' signal. *JV*

Plate 141. A real surprise for railway enthusiasts occurred on 26th January 1991 when Plymouth Laira depot repainted Class 50 No. 50015 *Valiant* in grey and yellow 'Dutch' livery before it hauled a Chartex over various Cornish branch lines. With newly painted all-blue No. 50008 *Thunderer* at the rear the special passes Goonbarrow Junction after a photographic stop (and reversal) at Bugle. Goonbarrow is open for two shifts, Monday to Saturday, with a single Sunday shift in the summer months. *JV*

Plate 142. One of Goonbarrow's resident signalmen is Peter Hamley, formerly of Bodmin Road and the Southern Region – when it ran to Wadebridge. He is seen here exchanging tokens with the driver of 'Skipper' Class 142 No. 142021 working from Par to Newquay on 11th June 1987. The 2-coach rigid 4-wheeled 'Skippers' were not a success in Cornwall as there was no sanding gear, they had transmission problems and the folding doors could fail. The designers lost much credibility with this technological disaster. *JV*

Plate 143. Until 15th December 1986 this would have been one of the tokens which the Goonbarrow signalman would have handed to the dmu driver, but from that date St Dennis Junction signal box closed and the tokens now show Goonbarrow/Newquay – see Plate 279. *JV*

Plate 144. With neither locomotive nor path available for the 'Carbis Wharf' Tiger, TRL 11600 languishes in Goonbarrow's 'down' sidings. Although the insignia on the wagon reads "ECC International", it is in fact being used by the Goonvean & Rostowrack China Clay Company. In the background, No. 37671 leaves for St Blazey, although the two Tullis Russell wagons are destined for Markinch in Scotland where the contents will be used for papermaking. *JV*

Plate 145. The Sulzer-engined 1,250 hp Class 25s replaced the diesel-hydraulic Class 22s by 1971. They were regular performers on china clay trains and hence the Newquay branch until 1980 when the Class 37s moved in. With the stack of Wheal Henry still standing in the left background, No. 25216 leaves a sunny Goonbarrow Junction with a train for Fowey. *Maurice Dart*

Plate 146. *(Top right)* The present vast ECC Rocks Works was built during 1960. Old clay dries of Hallivet, Rosevear and Wheal Anna were obliterated. In fact Rosevear once boasted a sidings signal box on the site of the present Goonbarrow box but that closed in September 1893! Gingerly reversing into the works with two wagons is immaculate No. 37175 on 23rd April 1987. This locomotive was fitted with special bogies designed to reduce track and wheel flange wear. Note Goonbarrow signal box on the left. *JV*

Plate 147. *(Bottom right)* The ECC Rocks Works is normally the patch of resident 4-wheeled diesel shunter No. P403D with Rolls-Royce engine (Sentinel 10029). With Wheal Henry's stack now cut short and with modern lighting equipment installed, the little machine stands beside No. 37671 *Tre Pol and Pen* on 4th May 1989. No. 37196 formerly carried this name, as did GWR steam locomotives in the past. *JV*

11 The Goonbarrow Branch

Although the GWR took over the operational side of the Cornwall Minerals Railway in 1877, the CMR was still very much in existence. With the china clay business in the ascent following a slump in the mid-1870s, the CMR proposed a branch line which was to penetrate the heart of clay country to serve numerous clay works including Higher and Lower Ninestones, Carbean, Bluebarrow, Caudledown, Cleaves, Old Beam, Imperial Goonbarrow, Rock Hill and many others. With a capital of £24,000 work started in 1890. Construction was slow due to the difficult terrain, which included embankments, bridges, a tunnel and severe gradients. An 1876-built Manning, Wardle tank locomotive called *Ringing Rock* was used on the construction of the line.

By 1893 the 3-mile 39-chain branch line was completed and it opened on 2nd October 1893. Leaving the Newquay branch at Goonbarrow Junction the line climbed at a steady 1 in 39 for nearly $2\frac{1}{2}$ miles. At the start of the branch, and adjacent to the sidings of ECC Rocks, which itself was built adjacent to the site of Hallivet, Wheal Anna and Rosevear driers, was Wheal Henry. This old pan dry was closed in the 1960s but the rails were set in concrete and in fact trains still use one of the sidings when shunting at Rocks. The stack survives, although it has now been "trimmed" in height.

The line then curved towards the village of Bugle, climbing hard to cross the main street on a high stone arch which has been demolished since the line closed. The main road to Roche was also crossed on a high bridge which in 1989 was still *in situ*. The first crossing was at Old Beam which was immediately followed by Old Beam siding at the 288-mile 35-chain point. This was taken out of use on 20th March 1969. After passing over Netley Crossing a siding diverged on the 'up' side at New Caudledown North and was crossed by a trailing connection from Imperial and Carnsmerry sidings. This "loop" line then served New Caudledown which rejoined the branch at New Caudledown South. Beyond was Rock Hill siding which closed back in July 1946. The ground frames at this point followed each other in quick succession, all on the 'up', or west, side; Imperial 288 miles 54 chains, New Caudledown North 288 miles 63 chains, Carnsmerry 288 miles 67 chains and New Caudledown South 288 miles 78 chains.

Some years after closure the preservationists moved in at Imperial Clay Driers and locomotives and stock belonging to the Cornish Steam Locomotive Preservation Society moved in. They accumulated a number of old goods wagons and other stock. Sadly, in 1987, the clay works environment was abandoned and the group moved their principal items to the Bodmin General preservation site. During their stay open days were held where visitors could travel the short distance from Imperial to New Caudledown clay dry.

The line continued to climb over the main St Austell to Bugle road and on the right was once located Caudledown (old) siding at 289 miles 18 chains. There was once a locomotive shed on the approach to Stenalees which housed the CMR locomotive *Goonbarrow* at the opening of the line. In later years the site of the long-demolished shed was located by a water tower. Next was the short Cleaves siding at milepost $289\frac{1}{2}$, which closed in 1933. After passing under a minor road the line entered the 345-yard long Stenalees Tunnel and again

Plate 149. The branch crossed the main St Austell to Bodmin A391 road on no less than three occasions. The steeply graded line included stretches at 1 in 39 and to Carbean even 1 in 35! There are now few conical clay tips but passing a splendid example on 22nd April 1961 is 1600 class pannier tank No. 1626, on the road overbridge at New Caudledown. *Terry Nicholls*

Plate 148. *(Left)* There are now but a few hundred yards of track left of the Goonbarrow branch which was opened by the Cornwall Minerals Railway in 1893. It ran through the town of Bugle and into the heart of china clay country at Stenalees and Gunheath, in total 3 miles 9 chains. From there the line reversed and ran down to Carbean, 3 miles 39 chains. On 12th June 1986 No. 37235 comes off the branch at Wheal Henry, Goonbarrow. *JV*

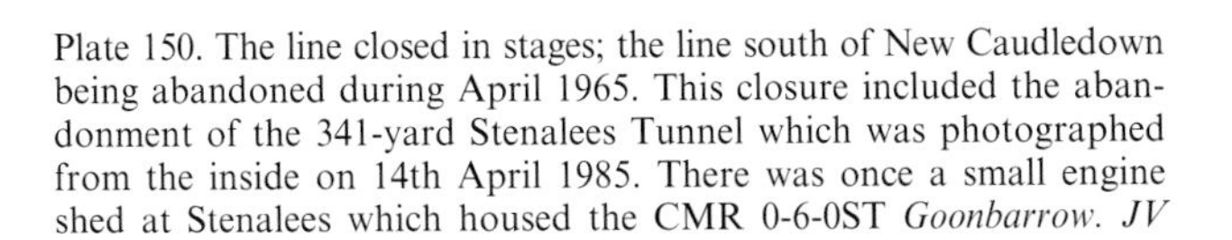

Plate 150. The line closed in stages; the line south of New Caudledown being abandoned during April 1965. This closure included the abandonment of the 341-yard Stenalees Tunnel which was photographed from the inside on 14th April 1985. There was once a small engine shed at Stenalees which housed the CMR 0-6-0ST *Goonbarrow*. *JV*

Plate 151. Another photograph of significant historical interest is this view of a train on the road overbridge at New Caudledown in the very last days of the CMR between 1893 and 1896. Double-heading this Gunheath-bound train is clearly one of the GWR converted CMR outside cylinder 0-6-0STs, with cab and bunker, and the CMR's own 0-6-0ST, purchased from Peckett & Sons at Bristol in 1893, which worked exclusively on the Goonbarrow branch. A total of six train crew pose for the camera on the 1 in 39 gradient. *Maurice Dart Collection*

Plate 154. *(Below right)* Carbean siding is now completely overgrown, although it can be glimpsed by climbing through a hole in the wall adjoining the A391. The line terminated in the immediate proximity of several high-volume china clay works such as Single Rose, Higher and Lower Ninestones and Carbean. With typical china clay country scenery all around, No. 1626 simmers by the loading dock at Carbean during the 1961 tour. *Terry Nicholls*

Plate 152. On 22nd April 1961 the Plymouth Railway Circle took a brake van special onto the Goonbarrow branch. Having just dropped down the 1 in 40 gradient to Gunheath, participants bail out for rambling and photographic opportunities. The motive power provided was again the well-travelled No. 1626. The line switches back to drop down to the terminus of Carbean, which then ran in front of the cottage on the right. *Maurice Dart*

Plate 153. In book research this is the only photogaph discovered of Gunheath. The photographer admits the scene was recorded with a box camera on 25th November 1956. The line on the right descends from the Goonbarrow direction at 1 in 40 while the photographer is standing on the Carbean extension which falls away initially at a similar gradient. Note the siding gates and the wagon on the right. *Maurice Dart*

crossed the St Austell to Bugle road, which marked the summit of the line. Immediately across the road on the 'down' side was Oil Siding, 290 miles 9 chains, opened in 1926 and which was situated on an earlier alignment of the branch. The deviation took place early in the present century following the extension of Carbean Clay Pit. The line then descended at 1 in 39 past Gunheath New Siding to reach Gunheath, where there were sidings and loading wharfs, 290 miles and 48 chains from Paddington, via Bristol!

To continue to Carbean trains had to reverse at Gunheath. A loop was provided and locomotives could run round their trains. The line dropped away at 1 in 40 and then at a staggering 1 in 35 towards Carbean and at 290 miles 51 chains Carthew Crossing was reached. After passing the crossing gates Carbean was reached a mere 24 chains further on. The track layout at Carbean was very cramped with a loading wharf, a short run-round loop and a headshunt.

Restrictions have always been so severe that only short wheelbase tank locomotives have been passed to work the branch. Following the early workings by the converted CMR 0-6-0 saddle tanks, locomotives of the 2021 and 2181 classes worked the line. The latter were modified versions of the former, having increased brake power for heavy gradients – such as the Goonbarrow branch. The final class of steam locomotive to work the line was the 41-ton 1600 class 0-6-0PTs. On rare occasions 4500 class Prairies worked over part of the branch, but special permission had to be given in such circumstances. In later years 350 hp diesel shunters and Class 22 diesel-hydraulics appeared on the branch, and once a Class 25 diesel-electric appeared. However, in the case of the latter the train worked only to New Caudledown, the line beyond having been closed on 29th April 1965.

Normally one train per day traversed the branch. In the late 1950s the branch freight left St Blazey at 8.10 am returning from Carbean at 1 pm. As sidings made both facing and trailing connections with the branch, a single locomotive would call at certain sidings on the way down and the remainder on the return journey. However, some days saw a locomotive at both ends of the branch freight, with each of the locomotives returning with its own train, normally one from the New Caudledown area and the other from Gunheath and Carbean.

Traffic on the branch gradually declined due both to the closure of the old coal-fired pan driers and an improvement in pipeline technology. The last two miles of the branch closed in 1965, as mentioned above, and the section from New Caudledown to a point near Wheal Henry closed on 3rd December 1978.

The last train over part of the branch was on 1st December 1978 when No. 25206 delivered stock to the Imperial Clay Driers preservation site. Today many remains of the Goonbarrow branch can be found, albeit with a bit of "bramble bashing" in some locations. Much of the land remains in ECC hands and the Stenalees Tunnel is still clear. Only one of the four main road overbridges remains, although the sites of those demolished are readily identified with the aid of an Ordnance Survey map. The line was greatly under-photographed and illustrations of trains in action have been hard to locate.

The line never had a passenger service and there were no signals beyond Goonbarrow Junction. A couple of enthusiasts' specials travelled over the line before closure, with the participants enjoying a journey in the much-lamented brake van. Now only a few hunded yards of the branch remains as testimony to the CMR's last significant development.

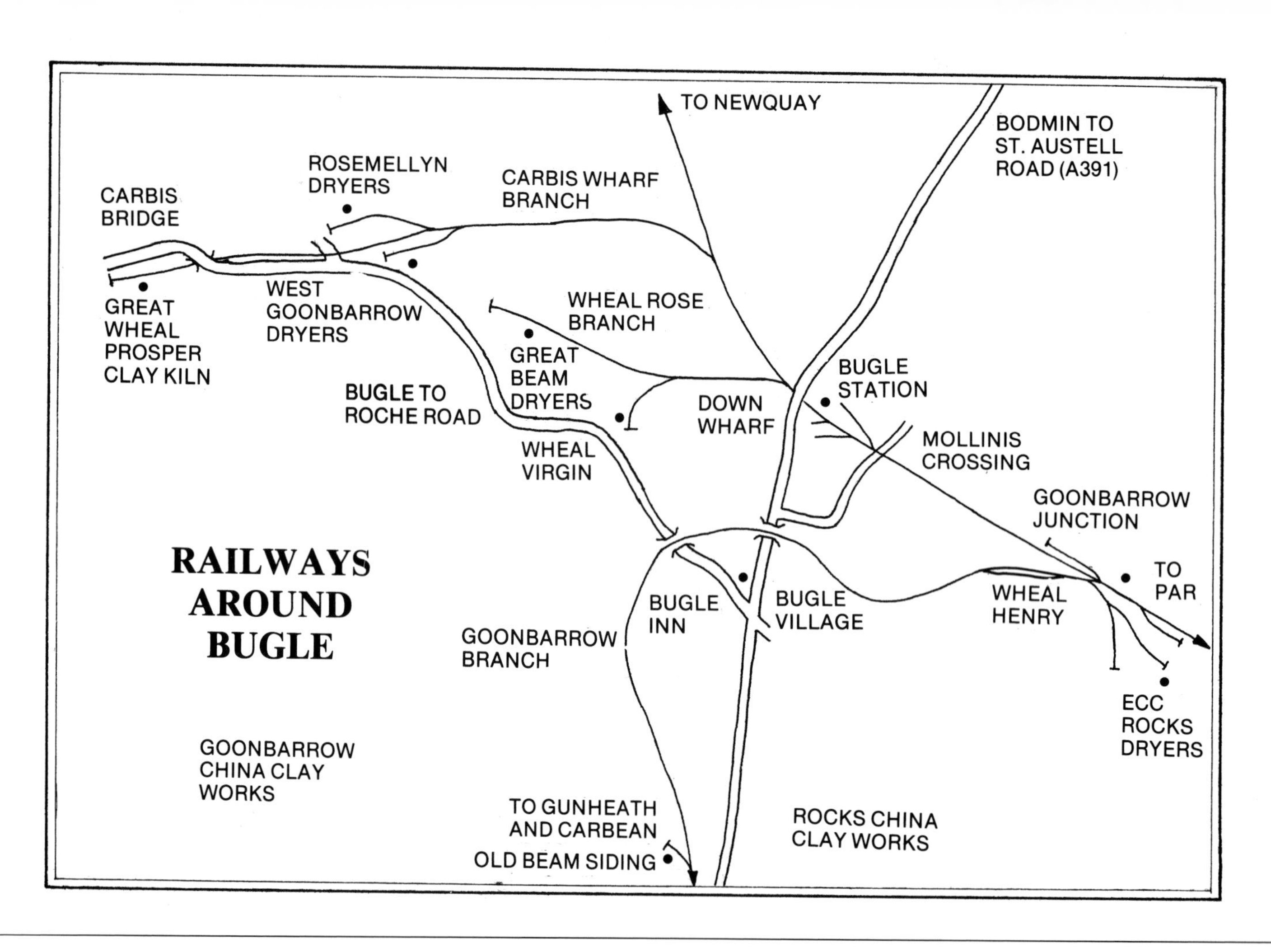
TO NEWQUAY
BODMIN TO ST. AUSTELL ROAD (A391)
ROSEMELLYN DRYERS
CARBIS WHARF BRANCH
CARBIS BRIDGE
GREAT WHEAL PROSPER CLAY KILN
WEST GOONBARROW DRYERS
WHEAL ROSE BRANCH
GREAT BEAM DRYERS
BUGLE STATION
BUGLE TO ROCHE ROAD
DOWN WHARF
MOLLINIS CROSSING
WHEAL VIRGIN
GOONBARROW JUNCTION
RAILWAYS AROUND BUGLE
TO PAR
BUGLE INN
BUGLE VILLAGE
WHEAL HENRY
GOONBARROW BRANCH
ECC ROCKS DRYERS
GOONBARROW CHINA CLAY WORKS
TO GUNHEATH AND CARBEAN
ROCKS CHINA CLAY WORKS
OLD BEAM SIDING

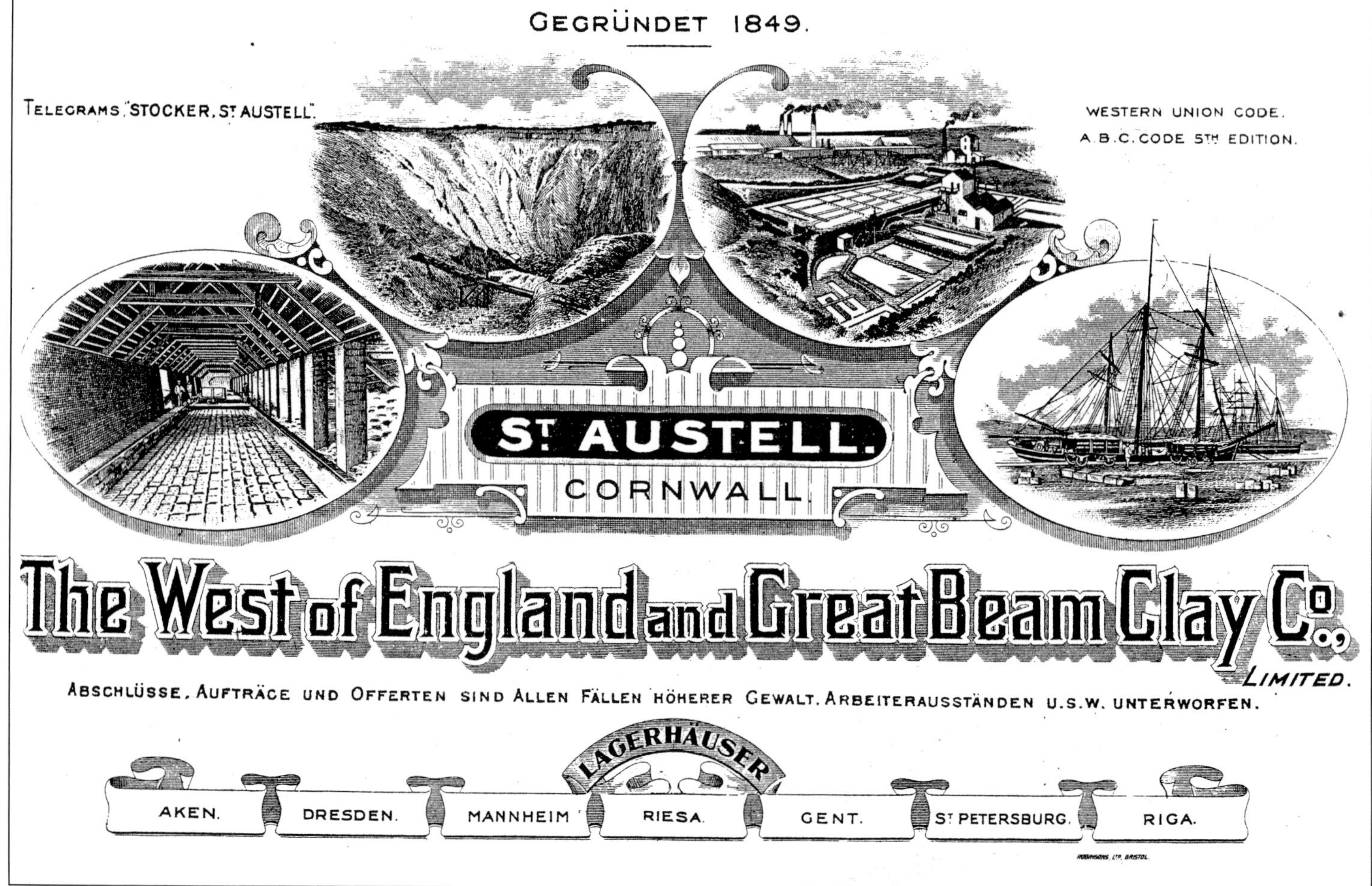
GEGRÜNDET 1849.
TELEGRAMS "STOCKER, ST AUSTELL".
WESTERN UNION CODE.
A.B.C. CODE 5TH EDITION.
ST AUSTELL.
CORNWALL.
The West of England and Great Beam Clay Co.,
LIMITED.
ABSCHLÜSSE, AUFTRÄGE UND OFFERTEN SIND ALLEN FÄLLEN HÖHERER GEWALT, ARBEITERAUSSTÄNDEN U.S.W. UNTERWORFEN.
LAGERHÄUSER
AKEN.
DRESDEN.
MANNHEIM.
RIESA.
GENT.
ST PETERSBURG.
RIGA.

12 Goonbarrow Junction to Bugle

For a stretch of railway line with a length of only half a mile the Goonbarrow Junction to Bugle part of the branch has had a history of mixed fortunes. The alignment was part of the original Treffry Tramway, dating back to 1844 when horses used to haul a wagon or two from the top of Carmears Incline near Luxulyan to Mollinis, near Bugle. With the coming of the Cornwall Minerals Railway in 1874 the line was upgraded to take locomotives and heavier loads. At the location of Goonbarrow Junction signal box was once located Rosevear siding signal box which controlled a junction with the siding that served a clay loading point.

Rosevear signal box was closed in 1893 and Goonbarrow Junction box was opened. This was to coincide with the opening of the CMR Goonbarrow branch to Stenalees and Carbean. Also, Wheal Henry siding opened in the area adjacent to Rosevear siding. This was followed in later years by a series of sidings serving clay driers at Rocks, Wheal Anna and Hallivet as well as the aforementioned installations. A new signal box replaced the 1893 product in 1909 which, at the time of writing, remains in use. The sidings on the south side of the signal box were added at the same time. An 'up' siding was added in 1924. Not only does it survive but it still has some of the original chairs holding the track *in place*.

By 1930 traffic was heavy, with more china clay trains, combining to cause pathing problems with the branch trains. Also, in the summer months, the branch was carrying an increasing number of holidaymakers to the resort of Newquay. Accordingly, the GWR set about doubling the track between Goonbarrow and Bugle. Work was completed on 20th July 1930. The track between the two points was straight with a slight curve to the north approaching Bugle station. Just before Bugle at Mollinis level crossing a signal box was installed. Bugle was an important railway centre which was also subject to a number of changes over the years.

The original Treffry Tramway from Ponts Mill terminated at a point near the old Bugle Inn, at Mollinis. The name Bugle is in fact derived from the bugle in the badge of the Cornish Regiment whose soldiers frequented the inn regularly as they traversed the main Bodmin to St Austell road. At the site of the two 'down' sidings at Bugle there was once a substantial clay loading wharf where horse-drawn wagons from near-by pits, such as Single Rose, would unload. Although long abandoned the wharf can still be seen. There was an 'up' side goods yard which handled general produce, ranging from coal to cattle, and in 1874 and 1893 respectively the CMR opened branch lines to Carbis Wharf and Wheal Rose. In 1874 they also extended the railway to Roche and across Goss Moor to link up with the Hendra to Newquay tramway, at Bodmin Road Junction, later St Dennis Junction.

When the passenger service between Fowey and Newquay commenced in 1876 Bugle had a single platform with a CMR signal box at the east end. This was the last CMR box to survive – until 1916. The original wooden station buildings were allegedly once lived in by the navvies building the line. There were minor track changes in 1910 at the west end of the station and an additional siding was laid in the 'up' goods yard. In preparation for doubling the track from Goonbarrow a single island platform was built. Access for passengers was by steps from the main road overbridge, which was modified to take the extra track. Bugle was at its peak in the late 1930s.

After the Second World War some of the clay dries never recovered; more buses and lorries came onto the roads, traffic dwindled and by 1964 rationalisation was in prospect. The Wheal Rose branch closed on 29th November 1964; at the same time the 'up' goods yard was closed and effectively the line to Goonbarrow was singled for branch line working. The east end crossover was also removed. The "other" track was used only for freight to Bugle 'down' wharf or Carbis. The signal box located at Mollinis Crossing, at the 'up' end of the station, was reduced to groundframe status and only a single platform face was used. In later years the 'down' wharf sidings were removed and from 1973 Mollinis Crossing was "open" as the gates were removed and the ground frame abolished.

It was difficult to imagine that the scene could become much bleaker with just the two single lines from Goonbarrow taking trains to Newquay and very rarely to Carbis Wharf, without a siding or crossover in sight. However, from the end of August 1989 the Carbis Wharf line closed to traffic, leaving only a rotting hut on the single platform at Bugle station. If the Newquay branch trains are eventually diverted via Burngullow and St Dennis Junction, then the line through Bugle station will be closed leaving Bugle rail-less for the first time since 1844.

Plate 155. The track from Goonbarrow Junction to Bugle was double track throughout but following rationalisation in 1973 the second track (seen here in the left foreground) became the long Carbis siding and passing facilities were confined to the loop immediately in front of the signal box. Leaving the loop on 13th June 1989 and forming the 10.52 Par to Newquay is one of the Class 142 'Skippers', No. 142027. The units had a short life on West Country metals. *JV*

Plate 156. I confess to being fascinated by the area around Bugle station and these past and present photographs simply whet the appetite for a return visit. In June 1958 4575 class No. 5521 crosses Mollinis Crossing, just east of Bugle station, on its way from Newquay to Par. The GWR signal box can be seen on the left (see Plate 35). *C. H. A. Townley*

Plate 157. The same scene 31 years later, on 10th June 1989, finds the most amazing sight of the "Atlantic Coast Express", comprised of a 125 mph HST set travelling through the grass at a regulation 10 mph! The "ACE" started life in 1927 on the Southern Railway and died towards the end of steam in the early 1960s. Although the SR directors would turn in their graves at the WR (GWR) "stealing" the title, they could not argue that the train does not travel from the Atlantic Coast to London, this being the 11.25 Newquay to Paddington (SO). The line on the left now goes only to Carbis siding but following closure in August 1989 will no doubt be lifted soon. *JV*

Plate 158. Even in its heyday the Carbis branch saw only one train a day, Mondays to Fridays. It was always a "freight-only" line, with trains being propelled from Bugle because of the absence of run-round facilities. In this 1957 view the Carbis service was double-headed by a pair of 1600 class pannier tanks with No. 1626 leading. The clay will have come from both West Goonbarrow and Great Wheal Prosper clay dries. The track on the right is the 'down' branch loop and two wagons are being loaded at Bugle Wharf. *C. H. A. Townley*

Plate 159. In a brutally stark comparison, Class 37 No. 37669 propels through the weeds at 06.50 on the morning of 5th May 1989 with what by then was an approximately monthly train. The scene is one of dereliction, but one which could be even worse if the Carbis branch is lifted following closure and if the Newquay branch trains are diverted via Drinnick Mill, rendering Bugle completely rail-less. *JV*

Plate 160. Another fine view of Bugle station, probably taken in the late 1940s or early 1950s, sees no less than five passengers alighting from an 'up' train at about lunchtime. In the background the 'up' side goods yard seems to be doing good business with a range of cattle wagons and box vans visible. The raised letter sign survived until the late 1970s. *JV Collection*

Plate 161. My first photograph at Bugle was, I am ashamed to admit, not taken until 20th June 1970, a mere twenty years ago. This was it! Pausing beside a fixed distant signal is a summer Saturday strengthened Newquay to Par working with two 3-car suburban dmus forming 2C74. Of note is the white crossing gate under the bridge which was the "entrance" to the then closed Wheal Rose branch. *JV*

Plate 162. Just a simple hut and a single lamp adorn the platform at Bugle on 21st October 1989. The 'up' side goods yard has been ripped out and the 'down' loop and the loading dock are trackless. The now defunct line to Carbis Wharf is on the right. As trains now stop only by request and on this day at this time there were no passengers to either board or alight, Class 122 No. M55012, working the 10.25 Par to Newquay, ran through the station non-stop. *JV*

Plate 163. With 14$\frac{1}{2}$ miles of its 281$\frac{1}{4}$-mile journey completed, NSE Class 50 No. 50002 *Superb* rounds the curve west of Bugle with its rake of NSE liveried Mark 1 coaches forming the 10.40 Newquay to Paddington of 15th August 1987. Other Saturday departures took through trains to Newcastle and Manchester. Note the fixed distant signal. *Brian Morrison*

13 The Wheal Rose Branch

In common with the Goonbarrow branch the Wheal Rose branch was a late arrival. The name is capable of being confused with the East Wheal Rose branch, the original Treffry Tramway line from Tolcarn Junction, near Newquay. The branch was little more than a half-mile long siding which left the Newquay branch just beyond Bugle station. The branch opened in October 1893, although part of the line to the old Wheal Virgin Air Dry may have been opened some years before.

A single crossing gate protected the branch and this had to be opened by the train crew before proceeding. The main reason for the gate was a dirt road which crossed the line just beyond the St Austell to Bodmin road bridge. On the 'down' side of the branch, just beyond the junction, was Wheal Hope Clay Driers (also known as Treleavens Kiln), followed by East Goonbarrow Kiln on the 'up' side. Both had rail loading facilities facing the branch without individual sidings. There followed a shallow cutting and the junction shown in Plate 165. The old line curving to the south served Wheal Virgin Air Dry and Boss Allen's Timber Wharf.

The primary branch then looped, with the 'down' track serving Martins Goonbarrow and Great Beam No. 1 and No. 2 kilns. All of these were of the coal-fired pan dry kiln type, most of which passed into oblivion during the 1960s. The Old Beam sidings were set in concrete and beyond the loop a single track continued to a stop block which was located but a few hundred yards from the Carbis Wharf branch.

The line formally closed from 29th November 1964. The track was left *in situ*, pending the outcome of evaluation of the transportation of acid by rail tanker to Wheal Rose but this came to nothing. The line gradually decayed and it became buried under a mixture of mica, stent and overgrowth. It is still possible to detect a little track just beyond the junction at Bugle and the track set in concrete at Old Beam. Curiously, despite years of research, no photograph of a train on the line could be found. In 1988/89 the last two stacks at the junction were felled leaving only the Great Beam stacks as testimony to the once great industrial activity in the area. Wheal Rose china clay was still (unusually) laid out in blocks to dry in sheds at the turn of the century but after replacing Crown Filley in 1912, Wheal Rose and Great Beam both became part of the vast West of England and Great Beam China Clay & Stone Company who introduced more modern techniques. The company was later absorbed by English China Clays.

Plate 164. On 2nd October 1985, when the aftermath of Hurricane Gloria hit the West Country bringing with it gales and rain, a train ran to Carbis Wharf. No. 37207 *William Cookworthy* approaches the junction with the abandoned Wheal Rose branch at Bugle. The ivy-covered stack which once belonged to the demolished Wheal Hope Kiln was felled in 1989. *JV*

Plate 165. The Wheal Rose branch was less than half a mile in length and it was always regarded as a siding from Bugle, it being opened in 1893, at the same time as the Goonbarrow branch. Access to the single line was gated. The line served Wheal Hope, East Goonbarrow, Martins Goonbarrow, Great Beam and Wheal Rose dries. A siding off the branch served Wheal Virgin Air Dry and Boss Allen's Timber Wharf. This May 1968 view, taken after closure, shows the Wheal Virgin siding left and the main track to Martins and Great Beam right. *Maurice Dart*

Plate 166. Although parts of the Wheal Rose branch are impenetrable due to heavy overgrowth, the loop set in concrete at Great Beam No. 1 and No. 2 kilns is easily surveyed (with ECC permission). In this October 1988 shot the stacks and clay dries are deteriorating and have partially collapsed. In the distance are the West Goonbarrow and Rosemellyn stacks on the Carbis branch. The line closed on 29th November 1964. Research did not produce a photograph of a train on the line. *JV*

14 Carbis Wharf

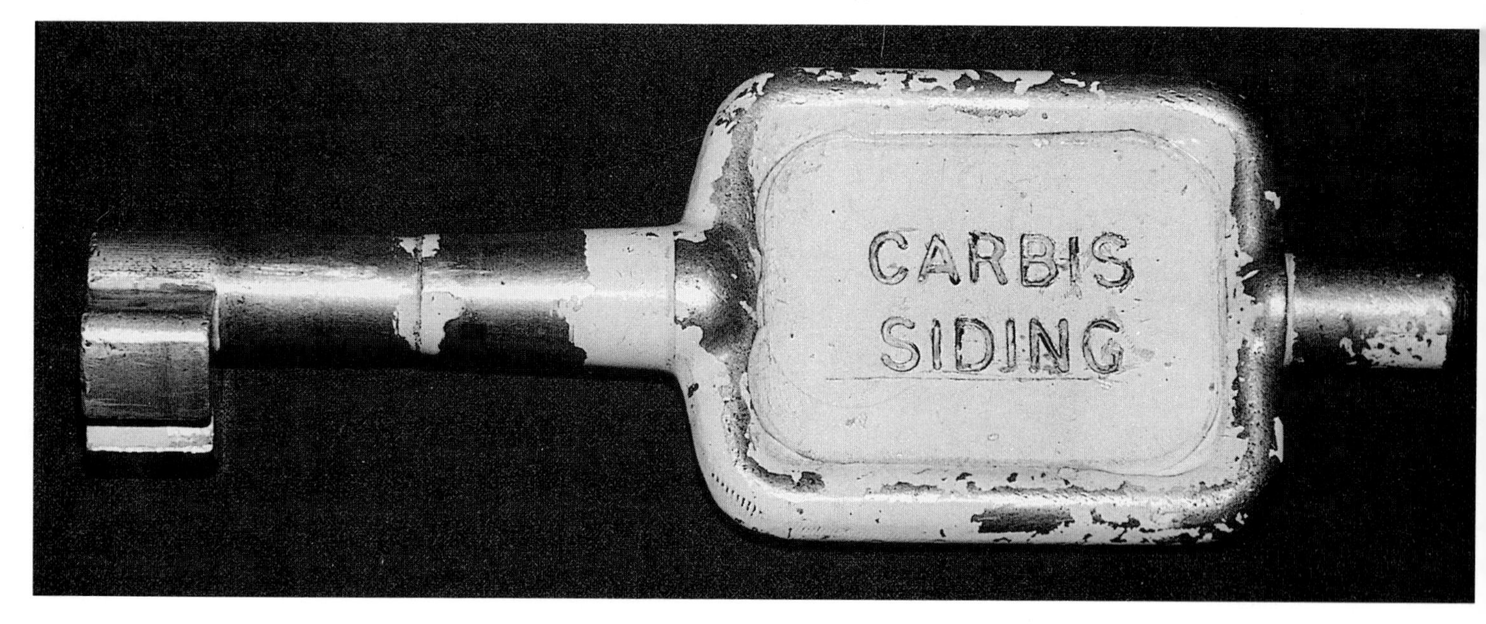

Plate 167. Since December 1986 only one train could be west of Goonbarrow signal box at any one time, which meant that the Carbis freight had to find a gap in the branch public timetable to be able to undertake its three-mile round trip. On the rare occasions that it did run the driver would be handed this token by the signalman. It is interesting to note that the word "siding" seems to be sufficient to describe the line. *JV*

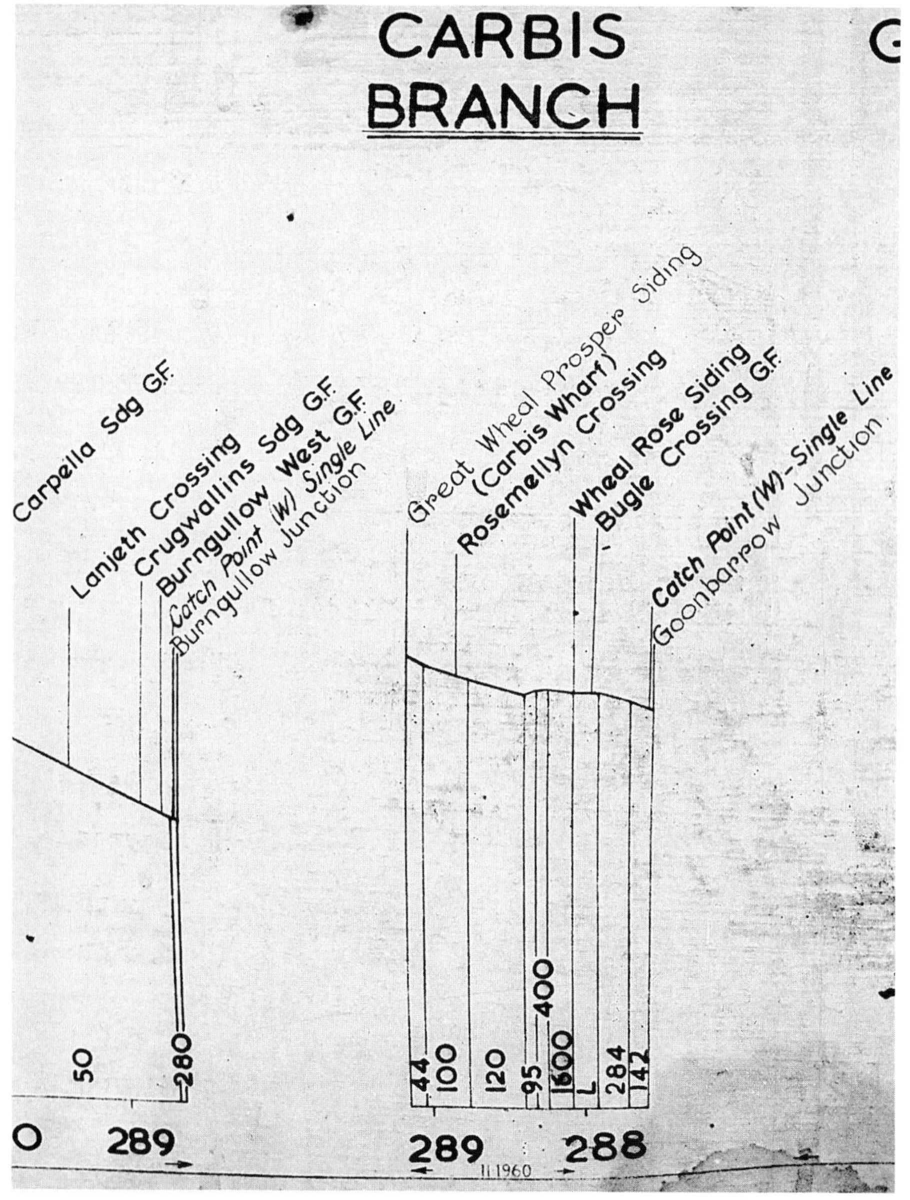

Plate 168. The section of the gradient chart which includes the whole of the Carbis branch. Only the last half-mile would seem to present any problems. In this 1970 diagram neither West Goonbarrow nor the long-closed Rosemellyn clay dries are mentioned but Carbis gets the full Great Wheal Prosper Siding treatment. *JV*

Plate 169. A surprising discovery on this farm crossing gate in 1984 was the survival of a Victorian warning sign threatening a penalty of forty shillings (£2) for not fastening the gate. Predictably, on the next visit to the site, the junction of the Carbis branch with the Newquay branch, the sign had "disappeared". In recent years the gate was permanently open! *JV*

Plate 170. Let nobody be mistaken, when in 1989 BR stated that one of the reasons for closure was the condition of the track, they were not exaggerating. This completely rotten sleeper was photographed near the junction on 21st October 1988. Note the GWR chair, the wooden key and the bullhead track. Safety must become a factor when a 107-tonne Class 37 passes over such track, which would have cost a fortune to replace. *JV*

The Bugle area was rich in china clay works and by the mid-1850s the transportation of an increasing yield was becoming a problem. As recorded elsewhere, the dependence upon horses drawing 3-ton wagons over very poor-quality roads was slow and costly. The line of just over a mile from Bugle to Carbis was incorporated in the 1873 Cornwall Minerals Railway Act. Treffry had already reached Mollinis at a point near the Bugle Inn in 1843 and substantial amounts of clay were loaded from the wharf at the terminus. However, an extension of the railhead to the growing Rosemellyn Works and Great Wheal Prosper Clay Kiln was attractive for the clay producers, who in many cases were also the landowners of the envisaged trackbed.

By February 1874 work had still not been commenced on the line to Carbis (then Carbus) but it was, nevertheless, ready for service together with the rest of the CMR on 1st June 1874. William West's foundry at St Blazey produced the ironwork and a suitable inscription can still be seen in the main iron support span beneath the weight-restricted Carbis Bridge (see Plate 26). Although towards the end of the short branch there was a 1 in 44 gradient, construction was relatively straightforward.

In the words of the original Act the line was to terminate at a point near Great St George Clay Works. At the end of the line accommodation was tight with the single-track line dividing into two for the last few yards to the end of the loading dock. One of the two lines served Great Wheal Prosper Clay Kiln, where the clay from the works of that name was dried, and the other was a general wharf where clay and other merchandise was loaded onto railway wagons. The two tracks at the terminus were so short that a run-round loop could not be provided, with the result that for the 115 years of the line's existence trains were always propelled on the outward ('down') run. In 1901 the length of the sidings was doubled and the

Plate 172. *(Top right)* Rosemellyn Clay Works was rail-connected to the CMR Carbis branch shortly after opening in 1874. In the 1880s a single-track siding served the clay dry but by the turn of the century the siding branched into two roads near the works. In this *circa* 1908 view china clay in casks can be seen in the left background, while on the right is the coal brought in by the railway to fire the kiln for drying the clay. The gentleman with the whiskers is Captain John Pinch. *Maurice Dart Collection*

Plate 173. *(Bottom right)* Despite closure many decades ago Rosemellyn stack survives and this view is the nearest comparison now possible with the above photograph. In its heyday the works was renowned for producing top-quality china clay; so good that in 1877 the clay was selling at £1 4s (£1.20) per ton, some 50 per cent above its rivals. A few yards of the original loading dock can still be found in the shrubbery. *JV*

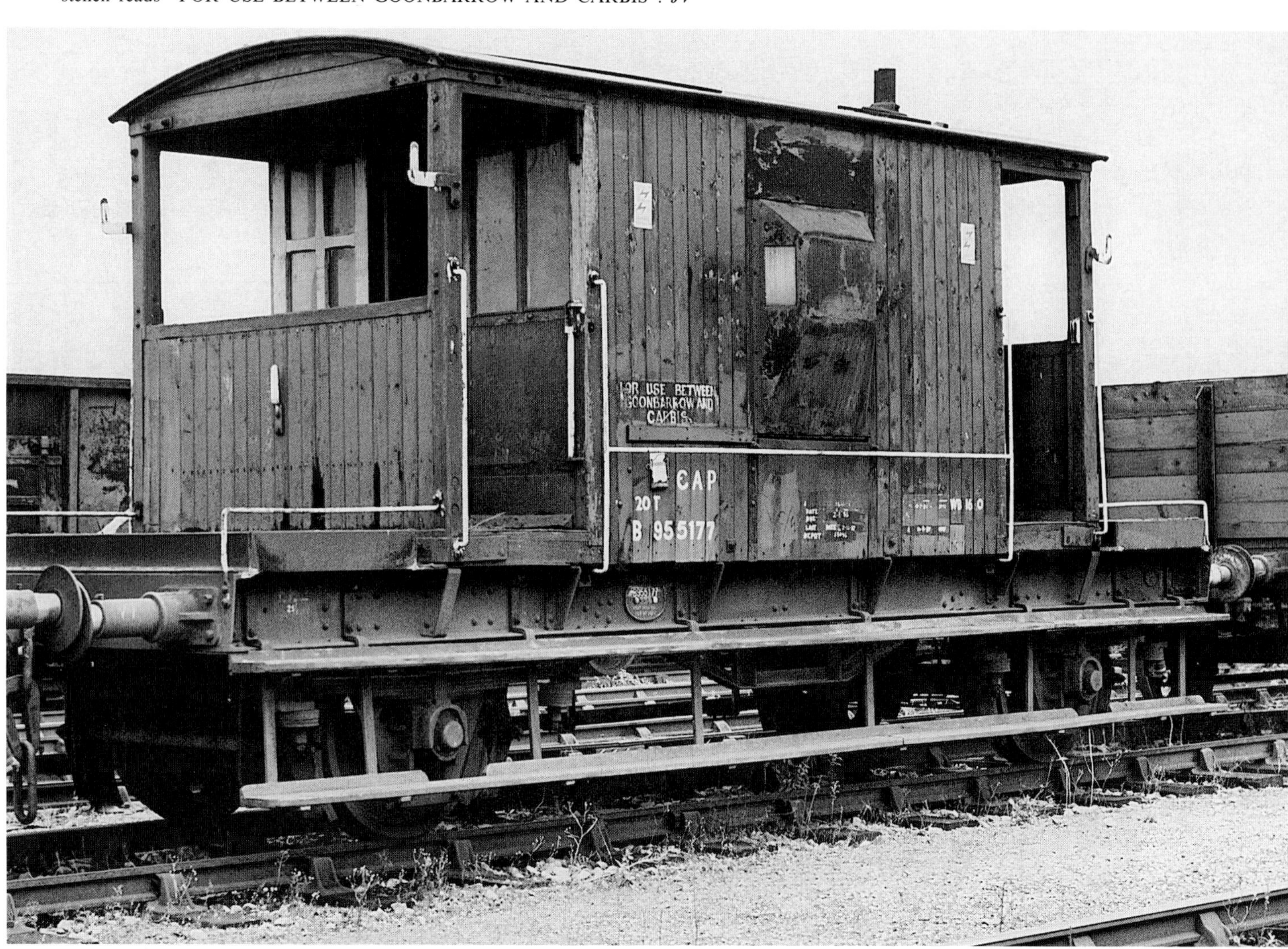

Plate 171. For many years the Carbis branch had dedicated brake vans. This 1962 Ashford-built 20-tonner replaced two GWR examples. It probably ceased its dedicated use when brake-fitted wagons were introduced. By the time I caught up with No. B955177 it was in the scrap line at Radyr Yard near Cardiff where, on 19th November 1988, it was waiting for its last run to Woodhams at Barry for breaking up. The stencil reads "FOR USE BETWEEN GOONBARROW AND CARBIS". *JV*

agreement between the Great Western Railway Company and the Great Wheal Prosper China Stone & Clay Company shows the work cost £331 16s 7d (how's that for preciseness). The single point was moved nearer to Carbis Bridge but there was still no run-round provision. Originally a catch point was located on the west side of Carbis Bridge but in later years it was between the wharf and Rosemellyn Gates.

Shortly after opening, a siding at 288 miles 56 chains was provided to serve Rosemellyn Clay Works. The works produced fine-quality clay, reputed to be the best available, and which, in 1877, commanded a price 50 per cent higher than its rivals. By the turn of the century the single-track siding had also been enlarged to two "roads" at the works end (see Plate 172). By 1912 a further substantial pan dry had been opened, this time on the south side of the line, called West Goonbarrow. The junction for the West Goonbarrow siding was at 288 miles 54 chains; just 40 yards east of the Rosemellyn line. ECLP acquired the Rosemellyn Works in 1936 and it was subsequently to be the first of the sidings to close in 1948. West Goonbarrow closed in the early 1960s, although unlike Rosemellyn the track was still *in situ* in 1968. Also in the 1950s and 1960s it was observed that there were some vintage South Devon Railway chairs in the trackwork at Carbis Wharf – a leftover from the Victorian era!

The line has always been worked as a siding; from Bugle between 1874 and 1973 and from Goonbarrow Junction from 1973 until the line closed in 1989. For many years the Carbis branch had a daily train which would propel empty clay wagons and loaded coal wagons to the various works and reverse the situation on the return journey. The line was worked by small 0-6-0 pannier tanks and on occasions two locomotives were used. The line had dedicated brake vans which were stabled at Goonbarrow Junction. In recent years the token for the line had simply "Carbis Siding" engraved in the alloy.

Since the closure of West Goonbarrow the only works served has been the Great Wheal Prosper Clay Kiln which was acquired by the Goonvean & Rostowrack Company in 1937. Gradually the output from this drier was diverted from rail to road by the company. This private company is one of the few not to have been subjected to the progressive ECC takeovers and is the only company other than ECC to have its own railheads. The principal shareholder and an extensive landowner in the area is Lord Falmouth. The service gradually dwindled from daily to weekly, as and when required. In the early 1980s there were reports that the line had closed and this seemed to coincide with the changeover on the long-distance trains from the wooden-bodied, short wheelbase, vacuum-braked PBA wagons to the new French-built, long wheelbase, bogie, air-braked wagons, in 1982.

To support the use (and no doubt the weight) of the new 80-tonne gross wagons a new concrete loading "base" was constructed at Carbis Wharf. A Tiger wagon from the Tiger Railcar Leasing "ECC International" fleet was used to convey clay to a Scottish customer. Between 1982 and June 1989 this dedicated Tiger wagon, No. TRL 11600 was used on the Goonvean circuit which normally saw the wagon traversing the branch every three to four weeks. On rare occasions, and between June and August 1989, smaller 32-tonne PGA wagons were used. On occasions, the single wagon would be taken to Carbis where it would be loaded the same day, although sometimes it would be a next-day collection and it was, albeit unusually, occasionally left for a few days or over a weekend. While at Carbis, wooden chocks were placed under the wheels of the wagon to prevent a runaway down the 1 in 44 gradient towards Rosemellyn Crossing. The railway wagon was loaded by a front-loading tractor or a small conveyor-belt system. During 1988 a new conveyor system was built for loading Goonvean lorries and the base was on that provided for the Tiger rail wagons which subsequently rested on the crumbling track. For a very brief period during the 1988/89 winter, PGA wagons used the line on a weekly basis.

Operationally the Carbis branch was a nuisance to BR. Especially after St Dennis Junction signal box closed it was difficult to find a suitable path for the branch freight. Due to the crossing mechanism at Mollinis, near Bugle, it was not possible for more than one train to be west of Goonbarrow Junction at the same time, even though the Carbis line was all but separate from the "main" Newquay branch by using the old 'down' line of the former double-track section as far as Bugle. Accordingly, the Carbis normally ran between 06.30 and 07.15, before the first branch passenger train from Par reached Goonbarrow. With slick working there was also a lunchtime path at 13.25. With the slow speed restriction, gate opening, catch point changing and wagon coupling, a run to Carbis was time consuming, taking about half an hour for the two-mile out and back journey.

A number of circumstances contributed to closure. The condition of the track in places gave cause for concern and it was clear that substantial sums would soon need to be spent on renewal. For the volume of traffic the return on capital would have taken decades to achieve. As already mentioned, the workings were operationally inconvenient and BR had deliberately not included the branch in the weedkilling itinerary for a couple of years. The Goonvean Company had installed a pipeline from Great Wheal Prosper to their other railhead at Trelavour, near Parkandillack, and the autumn of 1989 saw the interface equipment ready for service. There were also health and safety considerations because, latterly, train crews had had to contend with waterlogged track, clay slime and brambles. Although these problems could have all been remedied they would have exceeded the small fixed maintenance charge paid by Goonvean. Eventually, even the 107-tonne Class 37s slipped badly on the grass over the track and it was clear the end was in sight. Closure was obviously on the cards because in the early months of 1989, following a gate-crushing contretemps, brand-new wooden crossing gates were fitted at Rosemellyn Crossing!

It is amusing to relate the story of the Carbis gateway. Effectively this gateway was an aperture in a hedgerow which was used by the Goonvean & Rostowrack China Clay Company for coal deliveries to the Great Wheal Prosper Clay Kiln. Lorries would use the unpaved track to provide coal for what is the last coal-fired pan clay dry in Cornwall. Under an old 1943 agreement the clay company paid the GWR and later BR an annual rent of 10s 6d (52½p) for use of the "road". No less than 45 years later BR woke up to this peppercorn rent and demanded £15 from the clay company – a 28+-fold increase – or an annual inflation factor of over 60 per cent simple!

The very last wagon arrived for loading at Carbis on the morning of Friday, 25th August 1989 and it was collected the same day at 17.25. There followed a three-month trial where, pending the completion of the aforementioned pipeline, Great Wheal Prosper's clay was delivered by road to Trelavour for loading into railway wagons. The trial was successful. Thus ended 115 years of railway history. The Carbis line was the last of its kind. It not only oozed with atmosphere and had eccentric workings but it served an old dry with a typical Cornish stack which still carries its smoke and steam into the sky. The line never had a passenger service, although an enthusiasts' special or two traversed the line. The little line will be held in the memory with considerable affection.

Plate 174. The mood of early morning is captured in this image of the Carbis branch. Having deposited a single wagon at Great Wheal Prosper a Class 37 locomotive heads for Bugle and Goonbarrow. In recent years photography on this line would be impossible without inside information unless, of course, one could spend three weeks to a month camping beside the line! *JV*

Plate 175. Looking in the opposite direction to the above plate but on a day in 1968 rather than 1989 shows the point where the siding to West Goonbarrow branched off. Note the catch point on the abandoned line. On the right, just across the fragile bridge over a stream, the siding to Rosemellyn diverged; two chains beyond the West Goonbarrow point. *Maurice Dart*

Plate 176. It should have been entirely predictable that the Carbis line would see its last train in August 1989 because earlier in the year the infrequently used crossing gates at Rosemellyn Crossing, seen here, were replaced! The Goonbarrow shunter has opened the gates for Railfreight Class 37 No. 37669 which is returning to the junction light at 07.10 on 5th May 1989. *JV*

Plate 177. The gradient from Carbis Wharf to Rosemellyn Crossing was 1 in 44/100 and to ensure that any runaway wagons never reached even Rosemellyn Crossing a catch point was provided at milepost 289 – seen here. The shunter prepares to move the point lever as a special working comprising three clay hoods leaves the works. West Goonbarrow can be seen, right background, and Rosemellyn stack on the left. The locomotive is No. 37207 *William Cookworthy. JV*

Plate 178. Great Wheal Prosper Kiln at Carbis was the last coal-fired china clay pan dry to be served by rail. It was owned and run by the Goonvean & Rostowrack China Clay Company, a private company. Carbis was also once well known for its brick making and the brick works stack can be seen behind and to the right of the clay dry stack. In the distant right background is the famous Roche Rock landmark. Finding a path through the weeds with an 80-tonne Tiger wagon with china clay, for a customer in Scotland for use in ceramic products, is No. 37669 on 5th May 1989. The line closed 16 weeks later. *JV*

Plate 179. Whenever a Tiger wagon was not available and after TRL 11600 was returned to ECC traffic, the smaller 32-tonne PGA wagons were used. Already loaded and awaiting collection on 1st September 1988 was this example. Carbis Bridge can just be glimpsed and the conveyor-belt loader in the foreground is used to load lorries. The dry may not last far into the 1990s because a new pipeline now takes Great Wheal Prosper's clay to the company's main plant at Trelavour, near Parkandillack. *JV*

Plate 180. In times gone by the catch point at Carbis was on the works (west) side of Carbis Bridge. Also there were two roads at the terminal point; Great Wheal Prosper Dry on the left, with empty wagons waiting to be loaded, and Carbis Wharf itself on the right. The road on the left was used for coal deliveries. Photographed on 6th April 1956. *Maurice Dart*

Plate 181. Over the years the large international company of English China Clays has absorbed well over a hundred smaller clay companies. One of the few remaining private companies is the Goonvean concern of which Lord Falmouth is the principal shareholder. The photograph shows a truly Cornish sign at the clay dry. *JV*

15 Bugle to St Dennis Junction

Prior to 1910 the junction for the Carbis Wharf branch was to the west of the station but, after that year, access was possible from the 'down' branch line loop or the second 'down' line which served the loading wharf by the station and the Wheal Rose branch.

The other 'down' line from Bugle, once clear of the junction with the Carbis branch, headed in a north-westerly direction towards Roche. This section of track was always single as far as the loop at Roche station. The track is level for the first mile or so beyond Bugle but then it climbs steeply to the summit of the line just beyond Roche station. The line leaves china clay country and runs through pleasant rolling farmland. Although this section of track was not opened by the CMR until 1874 it was 1876 before passenger trains served the community.

Roche station was originally known as Holywell but was changed to Victoria, reflecting the name of the near-by hamlet, in 1879. A third name was used from November 1904 when the station became Roche, the name of the village some three-quarters of a mile to the south. Roche is derived from the French name for rock and in fact it is Roche Rock which is the most famous of near-by landmarks. The 100 ft high rock has a hermit's castle built towards the top of it and the area is strewn with huge boulders.

The station was served by a single platform in CMR days but eventually a second platform was provided and on the 'up' side a signal box controlled the passing loop and the sidings, which comprised the 'up' side goods yard. Additional freight sidings were provided by 1920 and on 3rd July 1936 the passing loop was extended to take full-length trains. On summer

Plate 182. Oh for the chance to travel on this Plymouth Railway Circle brake van special today! In this busy scene at Bugle, North British Class 22 No. D6323, working a Par to Newquay local, passes the mineral line tour which comprises 4500 class Nos 4564 (1906 series) and 5531 (1927 series) and no less than eleven brake vans. Participants are obviously enjoying their pause on 28th April 1962, the last day of steam at Bugle. *Terry Nicholls*

Saturdays, when many of the trains to and from Newquay had banking locomotives, many engines were detached at Roche. Roche is one of the quieter stations on the branch; it never possessed any grandiose buildings and its decline occurred at the same time as other stations on the line. Goods facilities ceased at the end of 1964 and the passing loop was removed and the signal box taken out of use in 1965. From 3rd January 1965 the 'down' line was taken out of use, but in July 1965 BR decided it would be the 'down' line which would be retained and the 'up' line and sidings were removed in October that year.

The line continues through a cutting and under the A30 road to reach Goss Moor. This gorse-covered expanse is a wild and windswept area at an elevation of over 400 ft above sea level. The railway crosses the A30 on a narrow, low, girder bridge which could become the downfall of the existing line, and runs across the moor for three miles to reach St Dennis Junction. After crossing the A30 the line descends from its "skew" on an embankment which, during construction, required thousands of cubic yards of spoil from other excavation sites on the CMR.

At the 292-mile 31-chain mark there is a level crossing called Tregoss Moor. The gates were controlled from a small signal box opened in 1914, which was replaced on 10th September 1921, when the two miles from Tregoss to St Dennis Junction were doubled. Trains passing this crossing once included not only the Par to Newquay branch trains but clay wagons to and from St Dennis Junction, for both the Retew branch and the Newquay & Cornwall Junction line to Drinnick Mill and Burngullow. The signal box was reduced to ground-frame status on 3rd January 1965 and was closed altogether on 25th May 1973 when the crossing became open with flashing-light warning signals and a railway speed restriction.

St Dennis Junction was once an important focal point for the Newquay branch and branches. Originally known as Bodmin Road Junction, because the Truro to Bodmin road passed nearby (and nothing to do with the distant main line Bodmin Road station), lines from Newquay, Par, Retew and Burngullow all met at St Dennis. The village of St Dennis was nearly two miles away to the south-east. The site saw its first tramway in 1849 when Treffry opened his rail link between Hendra and Newquay as a means for shipping china clay from

Plate 183. The summit of the line from Par (and formerly Fowey) to Newquay is at Roche where an altitude of about 600 ft is attained. Roche station started life with the name of Holywell which was later changed to Victoria and finally, in November 1904, to Roche. Approaching Roche with the 2.40 pm Par to Newquay on 19th July 1958 is 5700 class 0-6-0PT No. 3635. Which locomotive helped it to climb Luxulyan with six bogies? *Peter Gray*

the pits he owned south and east of St Dennis. But it was the CMR which opened up the area with the completion of the line from Bugle, the N&CJR line to Drinnick Mill and the new Retew branch to Melangoose Mill.

The track layout on the south-west side of the junction was quite complex with not only the signal box but also five ground frames to control movements. However, St Dennis was not a marshalling yard as such and most of the trackwork comprised various loops for locomotives to run round their trains. All clay trains from St Blazey to Retew or Drinnick Mill had to reverse at St Dennis Junction and on the Retew branch, banking locomotives were removed there from 'up' trains. A pair of sidings curving away to the east served as a tip for many years and spoil trains containing old ballast, etc., in "Grampus"-type wagons, and later "Turbots" once discharged their loads at St Dennis.

From 1965, when the double-track section to Tregoss was singled, St Dennis was regularly used as a passing loop by 'up' and 'down' branch trains, and the signalman was kept busy exchanging single-line tokens with train drivers. However, with the closure of the St Dennis Junction to Parkandillack section of the N&CJR line, and the gradual but relentless closure of the Retew branch clay driers from 1965 to the late 1970s, freight traffic all but disappeared. The Newquay branch lost its pick-up freight in 1964 and by the early 1980s St Dennis was used as a passing place only on summer Saturdays. Predictably, the signal box closed in December 1986 leaving Goonbarrow Junction as the only passing place on the Newquay branch between St Blazey and Newquay. Newquay signal box also closed in October 1987 and, except for the St Dennis ground frame and a couple of rarely used sidings, rationalisation is virtually complete.

Plate 184. This is one of those occasions where, with the forbearance of the train crew, a gricer leaps from a train, takes a photograph and reboards. Normally the results are not successful! What helps in this instance is the mixed unit No. 862 of Laira depot which comprises Class 108 No. 51570 leading and Class 101 No. 51179 trailing, the tiny shelter, semi-ornate lamp-post and weed-covered platform – plus a glimpse of the sun. The location is Roche and the train the 17.40 from Par in June 1989. *JV*

Plate 185. This is the only occasion the author saw a pair of Class 142 'Skippers' working the Newquay branch. With a pair of alighting cyclists providing some welcome animation (a rare sight at Roche!), Nos 142017 and 142025 leave for Newquay with the 11.23 from Par on 23rd August 1986. The units were attractive to look at but ill-designed. There is little trace of the former 'up' platform or the once-thriving goods yard. *JV*

Plate 186. The major problem which is likely to lead to the rerouteing of the passenger service to Newquay in the early 1990s is the narrow, 14 ft 3 in clearance bridge over the main A30 road on Goss Moor. The road is heavily congested with holiday traffic in the summer months and a dual carriageway is called for. If the line from Goonbarrow to St Dennis Junction is closed and lifted the new road would run down its alignment. On 10th June 1989 the 09.50 Newquay to Glasgow IC125 crosses the busy road. *JV*

Plate 187. There was less traffic on the A30 on 8th July 1955! With only one caravan visible, 'Grange' class 4-6-0 No. 6809 *Burghclere Grange* catches some late afternoon sunshine as it leaves the barren Goss Moor with the 4.34 pm Newquay to Par local. The spoil for these embankments was that removed from cuttings when other parts of the CMR were built. *R. C. Riley*

Plate 188. Tregoss signal box in the middle of Goss Moor closed from the 25th May 1973, having had only ground-frame status since 1965. West of the box a double-track stretch of line was laid in the 1930s as far as St Dennis Junction, but this was lifted when the box was closed. This view from the west shows the single-track gates, the crossing keeper's cottage on the left and the short box on the right. *Royal Institution of Cornwall/ D. C. Vosper*

Plate 189. The crossing keeper's cottage and some wooden fencing are all that remains at Tregoss and the ungated crossing is "guarded" by visual and audio warnings of approaching trains. Contrary to the warning sign there are no steam trains now, only 'bubble' car dmu No.55003 heading east with the 16.35 Newquay to Par on 8th June 1990. *JV*

Plate 190. In this view from the footplate of 'County' class 4-6-0 No. 1002 *County of Berks*, its train, the 12.41 pm from Par, has been brought to a stand by adverse signals at St Dennis Junction. The reason is probably visible here; the passing of the 12.50 pm Newquay to Par headed by an all-green 1,100 hp Class 22 diesel-hydraulic on 23rd September 1960. *R. C. Riley*

Plate 191. The energies of the shunter at St Dennis Junction 'tip' knows no bounds as he takes the word perhaps too literally! 'Grampus' spoil wagon No. 984695 adopts the 45-degree posture at St Dennis in 1963. The tip is now very rarely used with the Bristol Parkway disposal point, being preferred. *Carey Batchelor*

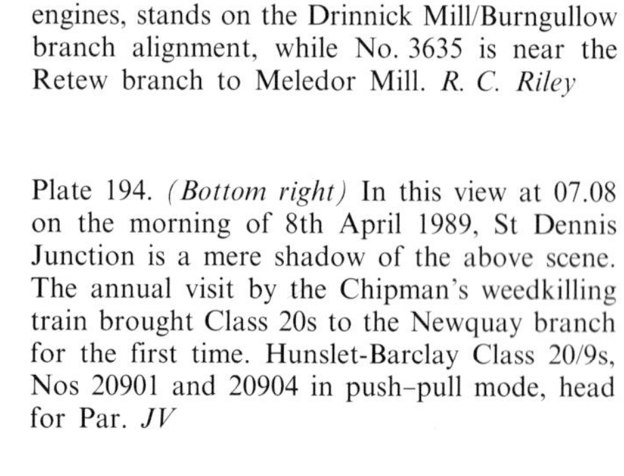

Plate 193. *(Top right)* Another of the few previously published photographs in this volume is this ultimate study of steam action at St Dennis Junction, looking east from the A30 road bridge. On 11th July 1955 'Hall' class No. 5969 *Honington Hall* leaves the junction with the 4.05 pm from Par, which includes three through coaches from Paddington detached from the 'Cornish Riviera Express'. No. 4526, the left of the two tank engines, stands on the Drinnick Mill/Burngullow branch alignment, while No. 3635 is near the Retew branch to Meledor Mill. *R. C. Riley*

Plate 194. *(Bottom right)* In this view at 07.08 on the morning of 8th April 1989, St Dennis Junction is a mere shadow of the above scene. The annual visit by the Chipman's weedkilling train brought Class 20s to the Newquay branch for the first time. Hunslet-Barclay Class 20/9s, Nos 20901 and 20904 in push-pull mode, head for Par. *JV*

Plate 192. A 1922 view of the west end of St Dennis Junction finds some ancient wooden signals, water tower on a brick and stone support and a typical GWR building on a curious short platform. *L. T. George Collection*

5969
295

16 Newquay & Cornwall Junction Railway

Plate 197. Looking east from the overbridge at Burngullow, the massive ECC Blackpool plant dominates the scene. The tall concrete clay silos were something of a white elephant and are now disused. Shunting clay hoods, on 19th May 1976 in pouring rain, is one of the much-loved 'Western' class diesel-hydraulics, No. D1023 *Western Fusilier.* The Drinnick Mill branch, or the N&CJR line, is on the left. *JV*

Plate 195. *(Top left)* The Cornwall Railway main line from Saltash to Truro was opened in May 1859. About this time there were proposals to build a branch line into clay country to the north-west of St Austell. After several abortive efforts a scheme to link the CR with Treffry's Tramway at Hendra, near St Dennis, was approved and the first sod was cut near Burngullow in 1864. It was to be a further five years before the broad gauge line opened and then only to Drinnick Mill. In this splendid June 1922 scene, Burngullow main line station was still open. The Drinnick Mill line diverges on the right beside the small, former broad gauge engine shed. The station closed on 14th September 1931. *L. T. George Collection*

Plate 198. The scene at Blackpool Driers, Burngullow on 27th February 1990. The main line changes from double to single track and the old loading dock visible in Plate 197 has been removed. No.37412 formerly *Loch Lomond* has just arrived from St Blazey with slurry and Tiger wagons, and is seen propelling back into the yard. In the background is an old abandoned siding to Wheal Louisa, and the site of Parkyn and Peters siding. The former BR class 08, No. P400D carries the name *Susan. JV*

Plate 196. *(Bottom left)* Recorded from the same spot 68 years later the comparison can only be described as dramatic. The main line has been singled and the freight-only branch survives, but only a brick wall, the disused signal box and a former 'up' side station building survive. Arriving light locomotive from Penzance is Coal subsector Railfreight Class 56 No.56013. This rare visitor was spending the day in Cornwall with a view to replacing pairs of Class 37s on some long distance trains. It later traversed the Drinnick Mill branch for clearance tests. *JV*

Plate 199. ECC spent over a million pounds on modifying the track layout and loading facilities at their Blackpool plant at the beginning of 1989. In part this was to cater for an increase in the clay slurry business and a change in rolling stock. One of the new workings was from here to Irvine in Scotland with clay slurry for the Caledonian Paper Co. In grim June weather, in an otherwise fine 1989 summer, No. 37674 leaves Burngullow with a half-load of six 90-tonne wagons. *JV*

Plate 200. At the start of the Drinnick Mill line names can get confusing. On the south-west to north-west curve the site of Burngullow West sidings and clay dry is passed, followed by the still open Crugwallins sidings seen here. However, the ECC sign outside the works clearly states ECC Burngullow! Paying a (very) spasmodic visit to Crugwallins on 16th June 1989 is Railfreight Class 37/5 No. 37674 with air-braked CDA wagons. *JV*

By the fourth decade of the 19th century the owners of the many clay pits which were expanding on the high ground north of St Austell, and across the greater Hensbarrow area, had still not tackled their chronic transportation problems. Horses were still hauling 3-ton wagons over difficult terrain and appalling roads. The tramway from Pentewan Harbour to St Austell, with its primitive horse-drawn wagons, had opened in 1829, but with Pentewan Harbour continually silting up and the terminus at St Austell being some way away from the clay driers, transhipment to the railhead was still necessary.

There were a number of plans produced which included not only an extension of the Pentewan Railway but new ventures which would build a railway towards the St Stephens area and north-west towards the village of St Dennis. One of the most important proposals was publicised in November 1843 for a St Austle (*sic*) & St Stephens Railway. It would have been necessary to purchase 257 parcels of land and the railway would have linked Pentewan with Gover Mill and then run via Trewoon, north of Methroes, High Street, Carpella, Foxhole, Drinnick, Nanpean and ending at Little Treviscoe. The line would climb a total of 428 ft in 5¼ miles. The ruling gradient would have been about 1 in 60 but there would need to be one incline on a 1 in 12 section. This and further schemes in 1858 and 1862 came to nothing. In the meantime, as detailed in Section 1, Treffry had opened his standard gauge tramway from Newquay to Hendra Village in 1849 with an extension on an incline to Hendra Downs, which included two inclines at 1 in 9 and 1 in 20, in 1852.

In 1864 there was a proposal to build a 5-mile 13-chain single line from Burngullow, on the Cornwall Railway main line, through clay country and thereby serving several pits, to link up with the original Treffry Tramway near St Dennis. The line was to be known as the Newquay & Cornwall Junction Railway and it would, in common with the main line, be broad gauge throughout. The railway was authorised on 14th July 1864 with capital of £27,000 in 1,350 shares of £20 each. Easy payments were advertised for those wanting to invest and deposits of £2 per share were invited. The chairman of the N&CJR was to be Brydges Willyams of St Columb. The prospectus made fascinating reading: "The proposed line of railway is intended to be constructed from Burngullow station of the Cornwall Railway through the heart of the important china clay and china stone district of St Stephens and St Dennis to a junction with the St Dennis branch of the Par and Newquay Railway near the village of Hendra." The announcement optimistically continued: "It is also intended to apply for powers to improve the Par and Newquay Railway so as to adapt it for locomotives as far as Ruthvoes within a little more than two miles of St Columb (to which it is intended to continue the railway if sufficient funds shall be prescribed for the purpose). The line to Hendra will be about five miles in length affording direct communication with Newquay, Par, Fowey and Falmouth."

There was also some quantitative information in the announcement: "The curves and gradients will be easy and there will be no tunnels, viaducts or other heavy works. It is estimated that 80,000 tons of merchandise would annually pass over the line besides passengers. Needless to say, this would afford a very handsome return of the limited capital required." Needless to say, the N&CJR were being economical with the truth.

The diaries of William Pease deposited in the County Records Office, Truro, make interesting reading. Pease had been the steward of J. A. Treffry but he was also a landowner in his own right. On 22nd February 1865 Pease, by then the steward of the Fortescue family, walked the route of the proposed railway over his land and two weeks later one Mr Geech was valuing the land on behalf of the N&CJR. Finally, in May 1865, the railway purchased parcels of land from Pease at £100 per acre. There seems to have been something of a "gentleman's club" with plenty of communication between the land and clay works owners. For example, William Pease makes note of a visit to Mr Lukes' clay works (there were later sidings on the branch named after the owner). The N&CJR tried to tempt the important West of England China Clay Company to invest in the railway but at the time of the approach they were carrying a £5,000 overdraft and the proposition was unsuccessful.

The first sod was cut in a field near Burngullow on 15th November 1864 and an inscribed wine cooler was presented to the wife of the chairman, who performed the ceremony, by William West & Sons of St Blazey who had been nominated contractors. The company was soon in difficulty with construction and financial problems. It was another well-known landowner of the period, George Fortescue, who although irritated by the N&CJR selecting broad gauge for the line, loaned the railway a further £1,000 in 1867 and allowed the monies from the sale of his lands to be appropriated to the construction of the line. In 1868 it appeared that a deviation line from the original 1864 plans would be necessary, and a further Act was secured to allow the 1-mile 2-chain deviation to be built, and for an extra £3,000 in funds to be raised. After two further years of activity the railway reached Drinnick Mill in 1869 and the railway was opened on 1st July that year, but completely devoid of funds for the further work required to reach St Dennis.

Plate 201. A view inside Crugwallins driers finds the common practice of setting the track in concrete. The linhay is on the right with settling tanks and clay waste behind. This is now a rotary clay dry and the old stack, which was used when this was a pan dry, has been cut short. *JV*

Plate 202. A half-mile further up the branch, which climbs at a consistent 1 in 50, is Lanjeth Crossing. This has always been protected by stop boards but in past years there were also crossing gates which were operated by the train crew. With a staggering 1,010-tonne load behind it No. 37673 leaves the crossing with a St Blazey air-braked freight on 5th May 1989. *JV*

Plate 203. A further three-quarters of a mile up the branch, $1\frac{1}{4}$ miles from Burngullow, is the site of High Street sidings. This was the site of a public wharf and the Beacon Clay Company's Beacon Kiln. Still to be found on the abandoned linhays are the remains of a narrow gauge railway used to transfer the clay from the kiln to the standard gauge railway wagons. The Drinnick Mill line is behind the bushes, far right. A 1989 view. *JV*

Plate 204. Descending on the post-1922 alignment between Old and New Carpella sidings on 13th July 1961 are a pair of pannier tanks of the 5700 and 1600 classes, Nos 9755 and 1624. The pair will be bringing down china clay from the variety of pits in the Drinnick Mill area but the three leading wagons are empty and will be shunted into New Carpella. *Peter Gray*

Plate 205. Attacking the short section at 1 in 45 near Drinnick Mill South with clay empties for Drinnick and beyond, on 30th July 1954, is 1906-built 2-6-2T No. 4508. Near to this point is the village of Foxhole and if, or perhaps when, the Newquay trains are diverted this way, there could be a halt here. *Maurice Dart Collection*

William West & Sons used two broad gauge steam locomotives in the construction of the line, although historians argue about the detail. One of two engines was a Manning, Wardle 0-4-2T – No. 136 of 2/1866 – purchased by West & Sons from the South Wales Mineral Railway in 1869. The other was said to be built by (but more likely last overhauled by) the Brotherhood firm of Gloucester in 1863. It was a 6-wheeled, 4-coupled locomotive with 16 by 22-inch cylinders. They were named *Newquay* and *Phoenix* respectively. There are stories of a third locomotive called *Cornwall* working the line but there is no proof of this. The contractor's locomotives worked the line for some time, but when the GWR took over the running of the line, they refused to have them in their stock and both were sold to N. J. Barton, an iron dealer at Par, for scrapping – probably in 1879.

The first two miles of the N&CJR to Higher Carpella had cost some £22,000 and the long cutting to Nanpean was through granite and very costly. Although the railway was operating it was not maximising its potential and it was not until the Cornwall Minerals Railway Act of 1873 that this situation was addressed. The 1873 Act recognised the N&CJR efforts but stated that ". . . powers for the construction of the remainder of their railway . . . have expired and they have not taken any land for the purposes of the said portions of their undertaking, but they have entered into contracts for the purchase of certain lands". Details of the N&CJR's indebtedness were included in the Act, as was the CMR proposal to build a railway "2 miles 4 furlongs and 5 chains in length wholly situate in the County of Cornwall and commencing by a junction with the N&CJR near the termination thereof at Drinnick Mill in the Parish of St Stephen in Brannell, and terminating by a junction with the New Quay Railway about 300 yards northward of a place called Hendra Crazey in the Parish of St Dennis".

Thus it was the Cornwall Minerals Railway, headed by the entrepreneur Roebuck, which completed the link between the broad gauge N&CJR and the standard gauge CMR. The line opened throughout on 1st June 1874, the date when the entire CMR network, as defined in the 1873 Act, also opened. The work was carried out with the full co-operation of the clay companies and many sidings serving various clay driers were paid for by the clay works owners. There was a break of gauge at Drinnick Mill, a situation which persisted until the abolition of the broad gauge in 1892. In fact the 1873 Act stipulated that a third rail should be provided from the end of the Newquay Railway to Burngullow to allow mixed gauge running, but the CMR did not comply.

This was to lead to the Cornwall Railway insisting that the CMR provided a third rail to St Dennis and as a result of inactivity, the CR commenced legal proceedings against the CMR in 1875. The CMR consequently laid a third rail but in such a way that it was quite unusable and broad gauge wagons never worked beyond Drinnick Mill. The matter was never subsequently pursued by the CR.

Although provision in the original N&CJR prospectus and the CMR Act was made for passengers in terms of publicity and rates per mile, the line from Burngullow to St Dennis Junction has never had a passenger service, and the only passenger trains to traverse the line have been occasional railway enthusiasts' specials. There was an unconfirmed report of a one-off diversion during the Second World War which used the route. Curiously, there was at one time a sign at the entrance to Drinnick Mill Goods Yard which read "To the Station".

Just to the east of Burngullow station are the sidings of the massive Blackpool Driers loading point. The sidings are where English China Clay International load china clay slurry into railway tank wagons for customers who prefer their white gold in liquid form. In the 1960s some huge concrete clay silos were constructed which can be seen for miles around, but these turned out to be "white elephants" and they are no longer used. In the past there were other clay driers in the immediate vicinity as well as Blackpool, including Wheal Louisa, Cornish Kaolin, Parkyn and Peters and Methrose.

Burngullow station was opened by the Cornwall Railway in 1863. The station was re-sited a little further to the west in 1901 but there was no significant centre of population and the GWR closed it as long ago as 14th September 1931. Although the station was located at the junction with the N&CJR, a branch platform, in the absence of a passenger service, was never built. There was a broad gauge engine shed located to the north of the station which once accommodated a broad gauge locomotive. The signal box was closed in October 1986 but the 1901 structure still stands for use by permanent way staff. After being used as a standard gauge shed until April 1922 (see photograph), the shed was demolished in the late 1920s. Burngullow East signal box, opened in 1899, was closed from 24th March 1935.

The N&CJR, also known as the St Dennis branch and sometimes the Drinnick Mill branch, curves sharply away from the main line at Burngullow at the 288-mile 50-chain mark. Within a few yards, the first of many clay company sidings was encountered; that to Burngullow West. Now an abandoned shell, the dry closed in 1974 after three-quarters of a century of clay production. The line curves to the north-west climbing at 1 in 38 and then 1 in 50. Although in days of old the direction from Burngullow to St Dennis was 'up', on the basis of the presently truncated branch, the "up to London" approach has been adopted in describing the position of sidings. Only 200 yards beyond West Burngullow is the surviving Crugwallins siding where the adjacent driers have been producing china clay for loading onto railway wagons since 1907. Traffic is erratic and a photograph of a train calling at the driers is well worth having.

The branch continues to climb at 1 in 50 to Lanjeth Crossing. Until the crossing gates were removed on 14th November 1966, trains stopped at the stop board and the train crew opened the gates. Except for a give way road sign and a stop, and blast of the warning horn by the train driver, the crossing is now unprotected. At 289 miles 71 chains was Beacon siding, where in August 1928, the Beacon Clay Company brought the siding into use. The old wharf can still be seen but the siding closed in 1963. Immediately beyond Beacon and also on the 'up' side was High Street siding. Here narrow gauge lines carried dried china clay from the linhay to the loading dock before closure in 1967.

In 1907 there was potential disruption for the branch line when the Carpella United Clay Company gave notice of their right to extract china clay from ground beneath the railway line. The GWR took the matter to court on the grounds that the activities of the company were not tantamount to the extraction of minerals, which was permitted under their preserved mineral rights retained when the N&CJR first used the land. The House of Lords adjudicated that china clay was a mineral and the company had the right to require removal of the track while excavating. Accordingly, the line was severed between 290 miles 20 chains and 290 miles 40 chains as and from 16th December 1909. From that date through running was not possible due to the "Carpella Gap".

On Tuesday, 18th April 1922 the GWR announced the opening of a deviation line to avoid the break and re-established through working between Burngullow and St Dennis Junction.

South of the break, New Carpella siding had opened on 19th September 1921 on the 'down' side of the line and the truncated 'stubs' of the original route were retained as sidings for some years. The deviation was from the 290-mile mark to 290 miles and 62 chains. Old Carpella siding (which was part of the old pre-deviation line) closed in 1949 and at 290 miles 64 chains was Carpella siding on the 'down' side, which lasted until 1968. The latter was served by the Mid Cornwall Tramway and its two distinct sections delivered the clay to the wharf at Carpella. Drinnick Mill's ringed fixed distant signal was located near to this point and 33 chains further on was Drinnick Mill South ground frame which, until May 1966, was the start of a 170-yard loop on the 'down' side. Part of the loop is still used as a siding for china clay wagons.

On the 'up' side, at 291 miles 31 chains, was a very old clay dry dating back to the original line opening date. Known as Dubbers No. 2 siding the installation closed in 1973. Just beyond is the junction where a spur leaves the "main" branch on the 'up' side and runs down to Drinnick Mill Goods, – known as Nanpean Wharf – 291 miles 60 chains. On the 'up' side of the spur, at 291 miles 40 chains, was Dubbers No. 1 siding which opened and closed at about the same time as No. 2. At 291 miles 46 chains is a trailing connection which runs down under the "main" branch to Drinnick Mill itself, where there were numerous clay dries, as well as coal staithes. It was here in 1936 that a power station was opened which, with the aid of eleven substations, provided the power for much of the surrounding area. Also served were Carloggas, Barne and Rottery sidings. In 1989 clay was again loaded at Drinnick Mill, although a brief resurgence of coal traffic, this time for local distribution, which had recommenced in 1985, ended in 1987. Cornwall's coal is now distributed by road from Exeter!

Nanpean Wharf dates back to the original days of the line and the photographs herein show the changing scene. Other than a head shunt with two tracks and one loading dock, only calcified seaweed is now loaded at Nanpean, a long way from those far off days when teams of horses with their 3-ton wagons of china clay queued for unloading and transhipment. The line, which drops down to Drinnick and Carloggas, passes under the N&CJR via a limited clearance stone bridge.

At Drinnick Mill Junction there once was a signal box but

Plate 206. Surrounded by the unique china clay country, comprising old waste tips, pipelines and in the foreground a huge mica dam, Railfreight Class 50/1 No. 50149 *Defiance* (now No. 50049) clings to the ledge below the village of Foxhole with two 80-tonne Tiger wagons on 3rd February 1988. The clay had originated at ECC Parkandillack and was bound for Stoke-on-Trent. *JV*

Plate 207. On 22nd July 1986, when Cornish Railways enjoyed a degree of autonomy, No. 37207, the original *William Cookworthy*, works 20 clay hoods from Treviscoe to Carne Point away from Drinnick Mill. Sadly, the magnificent artwork of crest and legend were scrubbed out before the locomotive was transferred to South Wales. Note the tips in the background. *JV*

Plate 209. *(Top right)* A June 1986 photograph of Drinnick Mill Junction and Goods Office from the site of Dubbers No. 2 siding. Class 37 No. 37204 had arrived from Parkandillack on the left-hand line, uncoupled, reversed down to Nanpean Wharf and reversed again to recover the coal wagon, brought it up to Drinnick, wagon leading, reversed to pick up the Tigers, moved forward uncoupling the coal wagon, reversed onto the Nanpean line, with the coal wagon being run back on gravity for the Class 37 to collect and continue to St Blazey! *JV*

Plate 210. *(Bottom right)* Drinnick Mill once boasted a signal box and a Station Master, even though there was never a passenger service. Until 1892 there was also a change of gauge there. Arriving at Drinnick Mill from Nanpean Wharf and passing one of the old gates, which were once shut across the majority of sidings, is newly refurbished Class 37/5 No. 37696 on 22nd July 1986. *JV*

Plate 208. Just beyond the junction at the Drinnick Mill offices, seen in Plate 209, the right-hand line drops down to Nanpean Wharf. Many years before there was a further line to Dubbers No. 1 clay dry before the 'switch back' to Drinnick Mill works and Carloggas. On 1st October 1955 there are clearly wagons on the Dubbers line, right, and the Carloggas line, left – probably coal wagons to "feed" the kilns. The clay tip is at the Hendra pit. *Maurice Dart*

G. W
31241
PAR HARBOUR

Plate 211. *(Top left)* This double page is, pictorially, a Nanpean Wharf spread. When this interesting picture was reproduced in *An Illustrated History of West Country China Clay Trains* the location was described as not known. In fact the frantic loading activity from horse-drawn wagon to railway wagon is taking place at Nanpean Wharf. In this very old view the two wagons, foreground left, are for china clay, the dark wagon is for terracotta and bricks while the other wagons are all full of coal for the kilns and boilers of the clay dries. *ECC*

Plate 212. *(Bottom left)* The common features of all these views are the two track sidings, the houses beyond the stop blocks and the hill behind. In terms of time scale this "intermediate" view shows an "all in a day's work" scene with the little pannier tank already having seen plenty of clay country in its travels, with the 5.35 am from Par. On 16th June 1958 a 5700 class 0-6-0PT shunts Nanpean Wharf with a variety of wagons visible, which have long since disappeared. *C. H. A. Townley*

Plate 213. By 1986 the roads were covered with concrete and tar, the stream seems to have disappeared beneath concrete, some trees have sprouted and the clay tip has been graded. With some crippled wagons stabled on the right, No. 37696 shunts coal and calcified seaweed wagons. The pelletised seaweed is now the only commodity loaded here. *JV*

this was closed in May 1966 and subsequently demolished. Now the only sign of life is the Drinnick Goods Office normally inhabited by shunter and despatcher Ivor Trudgeon. He is in telephone and telex contact with the main BR network, especially St Blazey from where all movements are controlled, although once a train is on the branch Ivor is in charge! Drinnick was once a block post but, at least until the line is resignalled for Newquay branch trains, there is no signalling on the branch.

On leaving Drinnick Mill the West of England China Clay Company's siding branched off on the 'up' side at 291 miles 47 chains. Snells stone wharf was also served. This once-important siding was served by the Hendra Tramway and china clay and stone from both the West of England China Stone Quarries and the Hendra China Clay Works was loaded there. After over a hundred years of service the siding was abandoned in 1973 and lifted in 1975. Climbing at 1 in 40 again, the branch curves around the clay tips. Luke's Old siding, which faced on the 'down' side at 291 miles 63 chains, was closed early in 1960 and Luke's New siding at 291 miles 77 chains, 'down' side facing, closed in 1963. The next two short (and long removed) sidings, known as Slip sidings, belonged to the Goonvean & Rostowrack China Clay Company. Wagons were loaded with china stone until the early 1960s. Another Goonvean siding left the branch by a trailing connection on the 'up' side just seven chains further on. Known

Plate 214. From Nanpean Wharf there is a trailing connection to Drinnick Mill and Carloggas which passes under the "main" branch to Treviscoe and Parkandillack. How the driver can see to avoid "lorries loading" in accordance with the sign is a mystery. On 15th April 1985 Class 47/3, No. 47377, once common on the line, reverses to the coal staith at Drinnick to collect a wagon. *JV*

Plate 216. *(Top right)* The view down into Drinnick Mill works and at the far end Carloggas with all of the paraphernalia of an industrial complex about. This was the busiest coal train photograph secured during the two years or so that coal was delivered to Cornwall by Speedlink services. On 22nd July 1986 No.37696 seems to be getting itself in a knot with a shunting movement involving nine HEA coal wagons and an open Tiger wagon. The warnings read "BR locomotives not to enter on coal shute" and "No BR movement beyond this point except with the permission of the Shipping Captain". *JV*

Plate 217. *(Bottom right)* There is now no rail traffic at the far end of the Drinnick/Carloggas complex. In this March 1989 record the line mostly set in concrete up to Nanpean is still *in situ*. The marvellous stone ruins on the right caused much discussion with the locals who were initially undecided as to whether they were once known as North Carloggas or Drinnick No. 8 kiln. The former won the day! *JV*

Plate 215. How one of the 136-ton Class 45/0 "Peaks" with a 1 Co-Co 1 wheel arrangement ever visited the lower lines at Drinnick Mill without derailing I shall never know. Drinnick's resident shunter, Ivor Trudgeon, clings to the handrails of No. 45051 (now withdrawn) on 19th April 1985 while shunting coal wagons. At this time the coal for local distribution was new traffic for Drinnick, although many years before, a complete power station was located there. The traffic ceased during 1987 and "local" coal now comes from Exeter by road! Note the limited bridge clearance. *JV*

NO B.R. MOVEMENT BEYOND THIS POINT EXCEPT WITH THE PERMISSION OF THE SHIPPING CAPTAIN
B.P. LOCOMOTIVES NOT TO ENTER ON COAL CHUTE

Plate 218. The BR building at Drinnick Mill (main branch) from inside the "V" of the junction looking south-east. On 19th February 1982 No. 37135 faces Parkandillack with a box van and some pre-clay hood 13-ton wagons, while on the left is the Nanpean line. The old corrugated shed was probably once the lamp room. The signal box here closed on 8th May 1966. *JV*

Plate 219. The venerable Class 45 and 46 'Peaks' were once the regular motive power for the long-distance air-braked freights working to Cornwall. No sooner had they arrived from Tinsley, Bescot and Severn Tunnel Junction when they were despatched to obscure Cornish branch lines. Passing over some heavily ballasted track on departure from Drinnick Mill, No. 45051 hauling a 'Cargowaggon', two VAB vans and an HEA coal wagon, passes the site of the junction with the West of England New (or Quarry Close) siding on 19th April 1985. *JV*

Plate 220. Although there is a great deal of clutter about in clay country there are also wonderful photographic opportunities. New Railfreight liveried No. 37673 with its Cornish St Blazey lizard on the cabside passes the site of the Drinnick Mill power station which once supplied power to much of the clay industry. Photographed 5th May 1989. *JV*

Plate 221. Having just passed the sites of Luke's Old and Luke's New sidings, No. 47085 *Mammoth* approaches Slip siding on 22nd July 1986. The concrete blocks once supported a cable-hauled trolley system which carried spoil to the tips. To secure 1 ton of china clay, 4 to 5 tons of sand, 1 ton of micaeous residue and 1 ton of rock and earth must be removed. The clay hoods are bound for Treviscoe Dries. *JV*

Plate 222. A box camera negative which survived for over 50 years was printed specially for this book and shows Slip Quarry sidings in 1937. The wagons have carried coal from Cardiff but, unlike the HEA wagons in Plate 216, they do not have fitted brakes and are of wooden-bodied construction. Of special interest is the locking board on the track between the two sets of wagons which was a crude way of preventing access and runaways. *Courtesy L. Stuthridge*

Plate 223. Slip sidings referred to in the above photograph were located just to the right of the road bridge seen in the background. On the lower right was Varcoes siding and curving away to the right of this locomotive was Goonvean siding. The remaining point is the access to the closed Rostowrack siding (see Plate 225). The Goonvean & Rostowrack China Clay Company still pay BR £5 per annum to keep the point in place to facilitate reopening. No. 20904 on one end of the Chipman's weedkilling train passes by on 8th April 1989. *JV*

Plate 225. *(Below right)* The afternoon of 19th February 1982 was the only time I managed to secure a photograph of a train on the old Rostowrack siding. It was used by the Goonvean Company for the transportation of china stone (rather than the more usual china clay). Having hauled one wagon of stone up to the main branch, No. 37135 runs an empty down to the wharf. The siding closed during 1984; it saw little traffic. *JV*

Plate 224a. *(Above)* Photographs of the early days of the many clay sidings are rare. In this superb view of the West of England Company's sidings, looking south towards Drinnick Mill, wagons in the distance are being loaded with china stone. Sweeping-in on the trestle is the Hendra Tramway from the works of the same name. On the left was Snell's Stone Wharf. *Peter Bray Collection*

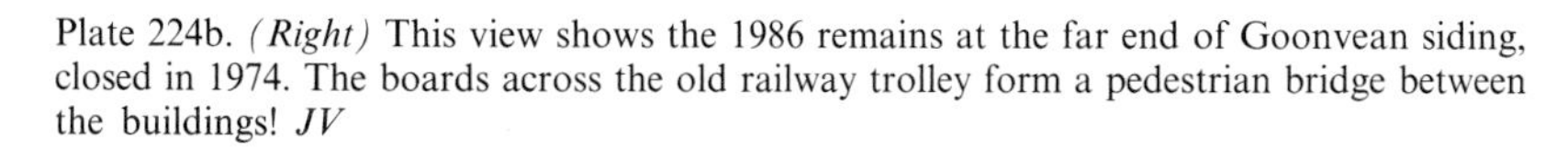

Plate 224b. *(Right)* This view shows the 1986 remains at the far end of Goonvean siding, closed in 1974. The boards across the old railway trolley form a pedestrian bridge between the buildings! *JV*

as Rostowrack, china stone was loaded at infrequent intervals until 1984. The Goonvean Company still pays for the connection and, although the lightly laid siding is covered in clay slime, the point on the branch remains *in situ*. The sidings now came thick and fast with Goonvean siding trailing on the 'down' side at 292 miles and 21 chains. This long siding, which once served the Goonvean Company's China Clay and Stone Works, was in 1895 accessed by a single 13 ft turntable from a siding adjacent to the main line but, latterly, rakes of wagons could be propelled down the siding. The former siding had been provided for Robert and John Varcoe by the GWR in 1882. Now only the remains of all these sidings can be detected in the ever-changing topography, some fifteen years after closure.

Between 292 miles 30 chains and 292 miles 38 chains was the Little Treviscoe loop on the 'up' side and off the loop was Little Treviscoe siding and, lost in the mist of time, Gear's siding. This siding was served by a narrow gauge tramway and between 1907 and 1969 (when it was removed) it was extended on more than one occasion. An early closure in 1948 was Trethosa siding which trailed in on the 'down' side at 292 miles 38 chains. Next on the 'up' side is the still used Kernick sidings, followed by Central Treviscoe. These sidings still enjoy almost daily trains but the same cannot be said of Great Treviscoe siding on the 'down' side at 292 miles 61 chains. Between the years of 1913 and 1950 there was a signal box at Kernick on the 'down' side of the line. There were extensive track layout changes at Kernick and here, as with many clay driers, much of the track in the sidings is set in concrete. The line continues to descend, as it has from the summit of the branch at Slip siding, towards Parkandillack. The line is but half a mile from the Retew branch at this point. A signal box was in operation here between 1911 and 1922.

The major clay works on the Drinnick Mill branch is undoubtedly ECC Parkandillack. This major works despatches hundreds of tons of china clay by rail every day. At least two trains per day serve the works, Monday to Friday. The leading point into the works on the 'up' side is at 293 miles 34 chains. There are sidings serving a calciner and buell drying plant. At the back of Parkandillack is, since the closure of their Carbis Wharf line in August 1989, the Goonvean & Rostowrack China Clay Company's only active railway siding – Trelavour. A wagon or two a week is loaded there but photographs are difficult to secure. The branch that once continued to St Dennis Junction now ends at stop blocks at 293 miles and 60 chains. The trackbed beyond can be traced and a derailed clay hood wagon is, at the time of writing, one of the finds (see Plate 237). The old 1852 Hendra Incline to Hendra Downs, which was removed before the First World War, can be seen on the 'up' side at the 294-mile mark. The works on the Downs are long abandoned with their spoil tips now covered in gorse.

Whitegate Crossing was to the east of St Dennis and there was once a siding there as well as a small wharf for local produce and inward coal deliveries. Passing the siding ground frame at 294 miles and 12 chains the line continued to Gothers or Pochins siding at Domellick where the 3 ft 1 in gauge line from Gothers China Clay Works transhipped its load. The substantial stone loading wharf is still much in evidence. A loop served the wharf at 295 miles and 5 chains. A final level stretch of line completed the route at St Dennis Junction.

There were once signal boxes at Burngullow, Drinnick Mill, Kernick, Parkandillack and St Dennis Junction. They closed in 1986, 1966, 1950, 1922 and 1986 respectively. Between 1950 and 1966 the branch was divided into two block sections; Burngullow to Drinnick and Drinnick to St Dennis Junction. Originally the line was worked by the CMR under the train staff and ticket system but the GWR introduced the more sophisticated electric train staff. The branch tablet instruments at the St Dennis end of the line were located at St Dennis Junction ground frame. The ground frames controlling most of the sidings were locked by an Annetts key on the train staff. Some sidings had small cast nameplates attached to the levers, while some ground frames were located in small huts. Locking bars were used on some sidings. From 1966 Burngullow signal box controlled the branch having telephone communications with Drinnick Mill. Now, the signals on the main line are under the control of Par. Extensive signalling work will be necessary if the Newquay branch trains eventually use this route.

In steam days there were always severe restrictions on motive power. With 18-chain radius curves, minor sidings and other restrictions the N&CJR was, in common with many other lines featured in this volume, restricted to small 0-6-0 pannier tanks and 2-6-2 Prairie tanks. Over the years some improvements have been made to the permanent way and most classes of diesel have worked the line. I must say the sight of a 136-ton 1 Co-Co 1 "Peak" class diesel at Nanpean Wharf was awe inspiring! In the days of non-vacuum-braked freight trains there were numerous places to pin down brakes, and double-heading or trains with even three locomotives were not uncommon. Nowadays the Class 37, 105-tonne, 1,750 hp, locomotives are the standard motive power, which regularly haul 1,000+-tonne loads! From January 1991 Class 47s and 50s were banned beyond Drinnick Mill.

Working such a multitude of sidings in the old days was a complex business, but with only two trains per day from Burngullow to Drinnick, and two from the St Dennis direction to Drinnick (one of which worked through to Burngullow), this was manageable. Towards the end of steam there was but one train per day from St Dennis towards Drinnick. By 1989 there was normally one morning and one afternoon train from Burngullow to Parkandillack calling as required at the remaining china clay driers. Occasionally there is a working just to Crugwallins. Traffic to Nanpean and Drinnick Mill is erratic but trains to Kernick, Central Treviscoe and Parkandillack are regular. Trelavour sees the odd wagon and is well served by road transport.

The N&CJR or Drinnick branch is a remarkable line. It traverses the bizarre, almost surrealistic, china clay country, passing old clay works and modern plant. There are mica dams, the old abutments of trolleyways, gorse-covered spoil tips and settling tanks. There are a few hamlets and villages and if Newquay branch trains eventually use this route platforms could be provided at Foxhole, Nanpean, Treviscoe and St Dennis. One thing for sure, passengers will enjoy a unique ride – unlike any other on the BR network.

Plate 226. *(Top right)* A personal favourite is this study taken from the top of a spoil tip, with Class 50 No. 50047 *Swiftsure* (since withdrawn) heading for St Blazey with the through brake pipe on the air-braked 'Cargowaggon' being used to control the vacuum-braked clay hoods. On this April day in 1987 St Blazey depot had been very obliging with the motive power because Class 50s, while not rare on clay trains, were still "highly required". The scene is Little Treviscoe, east of Kernick clay dries. *JV*

Plate 227. *(Bottom right)* This was the last time I was ever to see clay hoods hauled by a Class 50 – just a week before they were all withdrawn. Passing the stop block which is all that remains of Little Treviscoe siding, with the china clay making the rainwater look like milk, No. 50045 *Achilles* moves empties from Drinnick Mill to Parkandillack on 4th February 1988. Plate 226 was taken from the tip in the background. *JV*

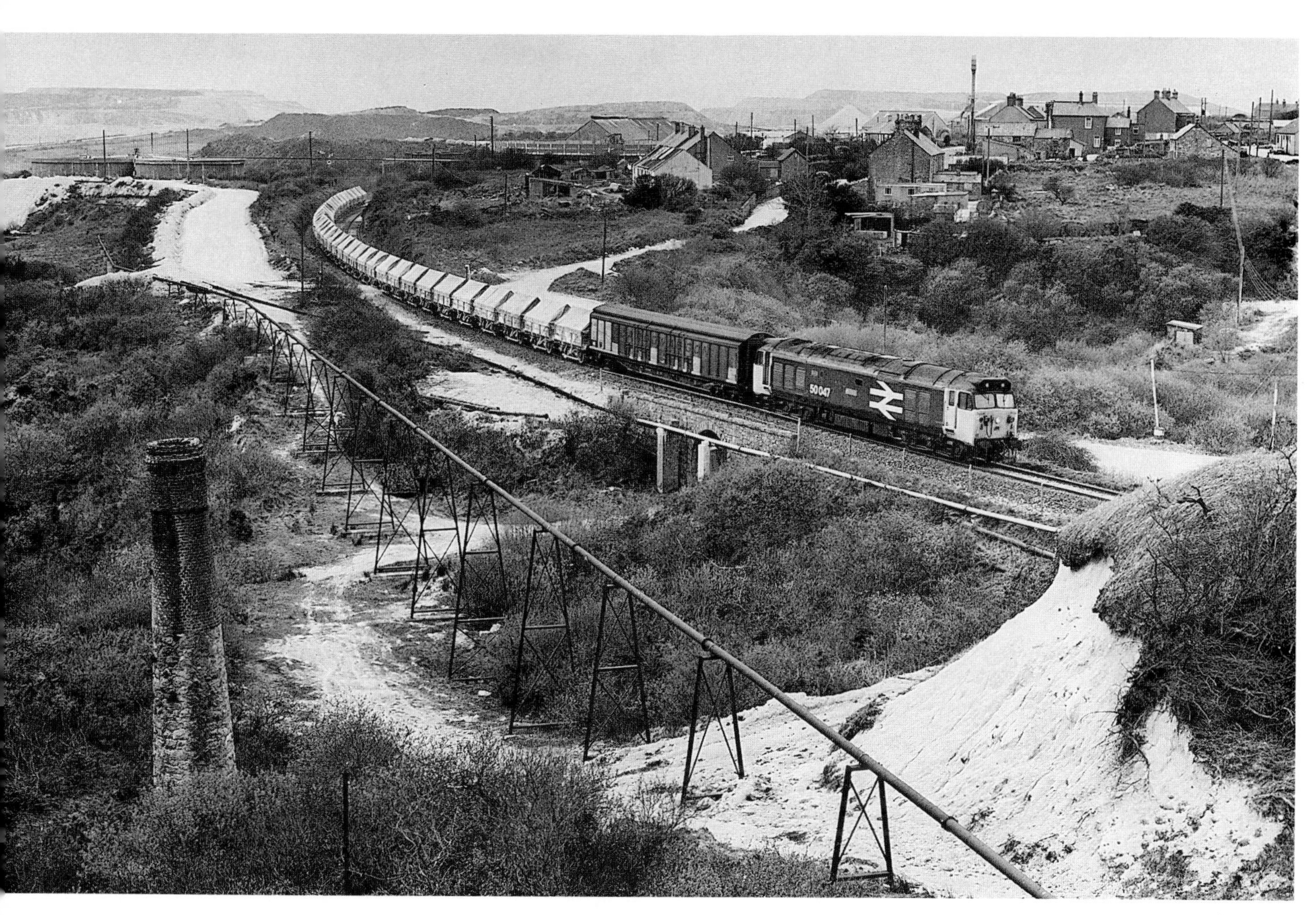
50 047

Plate 228. Having left some of their load from Parkandillack on the main branch, all blue No. 37222 and, at that time unique, Railfreight liveried No. 37196 *Tre Pol and Pen* collect additional clay hoods from Kernick Dries on 3rd October 1985. Driver Don Tregaskes then used the 3,500 hp at his disposal to take the entire load to Carne Point, Fowey. *JV*

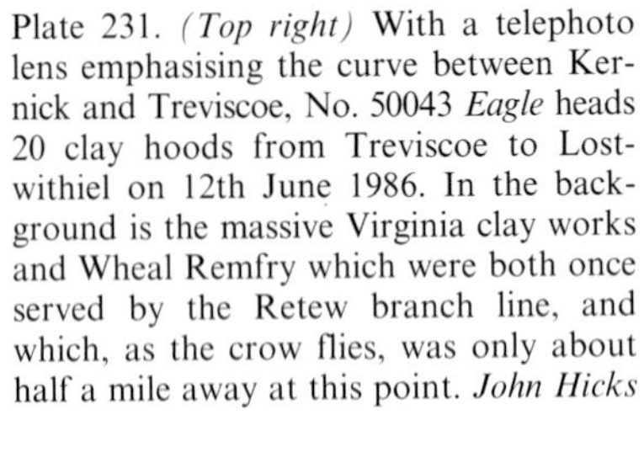

Plate 231. *(Top right)* With a telephoto lens emphasising the curve between Kernick and Treviscoe, No. 50043 *Eagle* heads 20 clay hoods from Treviscoe to Lostwithiel on 12th June 1986. In the background is the massive Virginia clay works and Wheal Remfry which were both once served by the Retew branch line, and which, as the crow flies, was only about half a mile away at this point. *John Hicks*

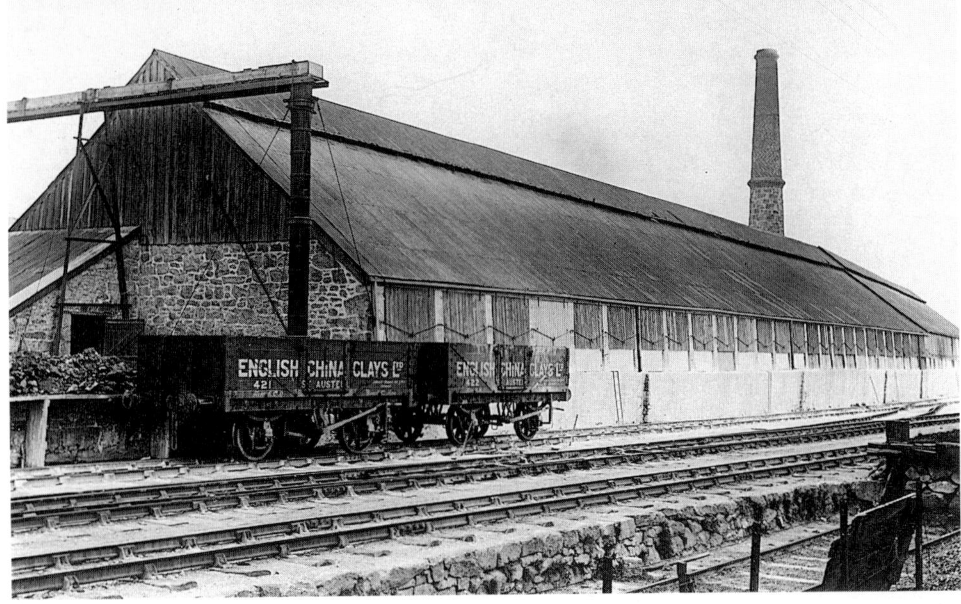

Plate 229. This vintage view taken from Great Treviscoe siding (in the foreground) shows Kernick clay dries before modernisation. The coal on the wharf, which has just arrived in ECC wagons Nos 421 and 422, will fire the kiln at one end of the dry and hot air will pass under the china clay, thereby drying it, before being emitted from the stack – which also provides the draught for the fire. *Royal Institution of Cornwall*

Plate 232. *(Bottom right)* The freight-only clay lines are always popular with railway enthusiasts and from time to time special trains are organised to accommodate their requirements. On 20th November 1983 it was BR themselves who organised a special over a number of lines. The 9-car formation has unit No. P465 leading as participants avail themselves of a photographic opportunity at Parkandillack. The gradient here is 1 in 59. *JV*

Plate 230. After passing Kernick clay dries, which once boasted a signal box but which closed on 20th December 1950, ECC Treviscoe is reached. With a Highland Terrier motif on its side, No. 37412 *Loch Lomond* enjoys some Cornish sunshine, on its very first outing after arrival from Scotland, as it reverses into the loading shed to collect a couple of Tiger wagons on 17th March 1989. *JV*

P465

Plate 233. Parkandillack is the largest clay producer on the Drinnick Mill branch and normally two trains per day serve the works. If this stretch of line carries passengers for the first time since it opened in June 1874, freight trains such as this will have to find appropriate paths for their movements. On 19th April 1985 the driver of No. 45051 opens the locomotive's large 2,500 hp Sulzer diesel engine as it departs for St Blazey. *JV*

Plate 234. A hive of activity at Parkandillack on 11th June 1987 with No. 37675 (before being named *William Cookworthy*) shunting some air-braked wagons while in the centre, Ivor Trudgeon controls by hand brake, two wagons running to the loading wharf by gravity. The line, left background, once continued through to St Dennis Junction but was closed on 6th February 1966. It was used by only one train per day. *JV*

Plate 235. Since the closure of Carbis Wharf the only loading point for railway wagons in the whole of Cornwall for Goonvean & Rostowrack China Clay Company products is Trelavour, a siding beyond Parkandillack. It is extremely difficult to photograph the siding with a train on it because of the erratic traffic pattern. The 14th March 1989 was deplorable with rain all day but spirits were raised when newly refurbished No. 37031 was photographed leaving Trelavour with a single 80-tonne Tiger wagon. *JV*

Plate 236. Modern diesel locomotives are remarkably versatile. Only two days before this photograph was taken No. 50045 *Achilles* was heading the Class 1 10.27 Penzance to Glasgow and Edinburgh express, whereas here, on 4th February 1988, it was delivering the only Goonvean Tiger to Trelavour buell drier. In a competition not many would guess the location! Note the Goonvean Company lorry on the right. *JV*

Plate 237. On the abandoned section of track beyond Parkandillack there is some rather obvious evidence of a past shunting miscalculation during a brief period when there were no stop blocks. The former trackbed is just visible in the foreground with St Dennis village visible on the hill in the right background. It takes little time for nature to restore its pre-railway environment. *JV*

Plate 240. *(Below right)* Gothers Tramway opened in 1879 to serve Higher and Lower Gothers and Wheal Frederick China Clay Works. The clay was transported on the 3 ft 1 in gauge tramway to Domellick siding on the St Dennis branch, where it was transferred to the standard gauge. Henry Davis Pochin took over the Gothers works in 1879 and the wharf was sometimes referred to in his name. The line closed in 1931 but the old wharf seen here survived in 1989. *JV*

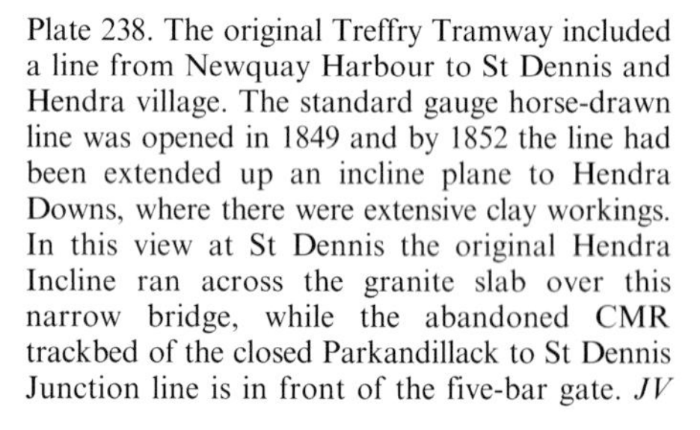

Plate 238. The original Treffry Tramway included a line from Newquay Harbour to St Dennis and Hendra village. The standard gauge horse-drawn line was opened in 1849 and by 1852 the line had been extended up an incline plane to Hendra Downs, where there were extensive clay workings. In this view at St Dennis the original Hendra Incline ran across the granite slab over this narrow bridge, while the abandoned CMR trackbed of the closed Parkandillack to St Dennis Junction line is in front of the five-bar gate. *JV*

Plate 239. Another section of the line possibly to be restored is at Whitegates. This view from the crossing looking north-west shows the site of the former Whitegates siding, on the left. The siding was used for coal traffic to St Dennis and other surrounding villages. Will High Speed IC125 Trains pass this spot on summer Saturdays in the future? *JV*

17 Gothers Tramway

Many years prior to the coming of the railway important clay works had been established on St Dennis Downs. These included Higher and Lower Gothers, and Wheal Frederick China Clay Works, the former being purchased by H. D. Pochin, one of the great names in the china clay industry, in September 1879. Pochin was well aware of the benefits of rail transport for the conveyance of coal and timber to and from his china clay works. What is curious was his decision to lay a 3 ft 1 in gauge tramway from Gothers to a siding and wharf at Domellick on the Newquay and Cornwall Junction line from Burngullow to Hendra and St Dennis Junction. One would have thought that the lower capital cost of the narrow gauge would have been less of an attraction than through workings, thus avoiding the transhipment stage.

The tramway was just over two miles long, initially travelling over the south-western edge of the bleak Goss Moor before climbing gently onto the downs near Gothers Village. Construction took but a few months and it is said that the sleepers used had come from demolition work at Devonport, near Plymouth. Originally, wagons may have been horse-drawn but certainly in the few surviving photographs of the line the small wooden wagons with their dumb buffers were hauled by small, steam tank engines. A locomotive shed was built at Gothers and there was a repair shop where work on the locomotives and wagons was undertaken.

The tramway served a total of seven clay dries at Gothers and also Dick Runnal's and Stoneman's kilns. In 1920 Pochin built a branch line from his Gothers Tramway to serve a nearby mica works owned by C. and J. Varcoe. It is thought that a single locomotive, which would have been adequate for the amount of traffic, was accommodated in the engine shed while any others were consigned to the repair shop. Although evidence is flimsy, it seems that at various times four different second-hand locomotives worked the line. They were all 0-4-0 saddle tanks and carried the names *Greenfold*, *Brooke*, *Crockfoot* and *Dinah*. There is no doubt, however, that when observed in the 1920s the line was being worked by a Hunslet 0-4-0ST (No.1423) named *Greenfold*, built in 1922.

The tramway seems to have been in decline towards the end of the 1920s and various reports show the line as closing between 1929 and 1931. In 1932 the Pochin Company was absorbed by the ECLP (later ECC) and the site still enjoys industrial use under the guise of Gothers Concrete Works.

Little remains of the tramway today. The locomotive shed walls survive in deep undergrowth and some of the old clay driers survive for storage purposes. The trackbed across Goss Moor is clearly visible beneath huge electricity pylons and the loading wharf at Domellick or Pochins siding remains.

Although there were numerous tram and wagon-ways in a large number of clay works, Gothers was worthy of specific mention because of its length and because, although the line was narrow gauge, it was significantly larger than the more usual 2 ft gauge lines which were used within the various works.

Plate 241. The Gothers Tramway was a quaint old line, some $2\frac{1}{4}$ miles long with a number of sidings at the clay works end of the line. A pair of 0-4-0 saddle tanks worked the line for a while, but in total, four locomotives seem to have appeared. The names *Brooke*, *Crockfoot*, *Greenfold* and *Dinah* were carried by the diminutive locomotives. The narrow gauge wagons were wooden with dumb buffers. Here a typical formation of the era leaves Higher Gothers. *ECC*

18 The Retew Branch

The branch was a Cornwall Minerals Railway original. In the 1873 Act their railway No. 3 was shown as the Ratew (*sic*) Branch and was described thus: "A branch railway 2 miles and 1 furlong in length, commencing in the parish of Saint Columb Major by a junction with the existing New Quay Railway at a point about 260 yards (measured along the said railway) south eastward of the turnpike road from Truro to Bodmin, passing through the parish of St Denis (*sic*), and terminating in the parish of St Enoder at or near the Melangoose Clayworks. The said railway is designated by the number 7 on the said plans."

The railway referred to was, of course, the Treffry Tramway line to Hendra and the road was the main A30 which still crosses the line at St Dennis Junction, then known as Bodmin Road Junction. Shortly after the start of the branch the line picked up the course of the infant River Fal and this facilitated the chosen alignment of the remainder of the branch, which opened on 1st June 1874.

St Dennis Junction is on the edge of Goss Moor and after passing the sidings there the line descended to the first of the crossings, Gaverigan – across the St Dennis village to Indian Queens road, and away from the moor and into the Fal Valley. At 1 mile and 55 chains the line fell at just over 1 in 200 to reach Trerice Crossing where, twice per day, gates were closed to the few vehicles using the Treviscoe to Indian Queens road. Immediately following the crossing the first siding was encountered on the 'up' side. It was known as Trerice siding and an old brickworks on the site was an early casualty amongst the twenty or so sidings which once infested the next $2\frac{1}{2}$ miles of "main" branch line. The "post-brickworks" Trerice siding closed in 1966.

A mere 16 chains further on, on the eastern ('down') side of the line, was McLarens siding, effectively a loop from McLarens North at 1 mile 62 chains to McLarens South at 1 mile 77 chains. The siding was opposite Wheal Remfry, McLarens' other name. It too succumbed in 1966. Falling still, at 1 in 149, Trerice New siding branched off at 2 miles and 4 chains on the 'down' side, formed a loop and rejoined the branch at New Trerice South, 180 yards further on. It was taken out of use in 1966. At the same point, but on the 'up' side, a siding (removed in 1972) served the Fal Valley or Retew Works. The branch and the siding crossed the third level crossing of Retew at 2 miles and 35 chains with the siding only crossing the River Fal.

Plate 242. This photograph brings the story of the Newquay branch right up to date. Between 1st December 1990 and 31st March 1991 a rake of the new CDA clay wagons was taken out to St Dennis Junction about once per week for the inner wagon coating, applied by BREL Doncaster, to be removed. This expensive exercise was to prevent the coating from flaking-off and contaminating the china and ball clay. The result for the railway enthusiast was to see the first clay wagons across Goss Moor since the end of the Retew branch in 1980. On a delightful 24th January 1991 No. 37411 propels its load of CDAs into St Dennis Junction sidings. The start of the abandoned Retew branch is on the right of the wagons. *JV*

Plate 243. The Retew branch opened from St Dennis Junction to Melangoose Mill, a distance of 2 miles 63 chains, on 1st June 1874. It was one of the original Cornwall Minerals Railway lines. The line was extended to a length of four miles in July 1912 when it reached Meledor Mill. This June 1989 view, looking south, shows the abandoned New Trerice Clay Dry which was located just over two miles along the branch. *JV*

Plate 244. It is hard to believe that within the space of only four miles there were some twenty sidings, most but not all of them for the transportation of china clay. It is equally hard to believe that this view from the north of Melangoose Mill and in the distance Grove siding was taken from a similar viewpoint to the photograph reproduced in Plate 245. The main branch was on the left and the sidings on the right. *JV*

Plate 245. At Melangoose Mill the Retew branch curves south-west towards Grove and Anchor sidings. Gradually, the clay works became worked out, were amalgamated with larger pits or had their clay transported in slurry form through pipelines to distant driers. On 11th July 1955 0-6-0PT No. 3635 was photographed delivering coal to the large Anchor Works and pan dry near Melangoose. *R. C. Riley*

Plate 246. The view a little further around the corner referred to above gives the full picture of substantial Anchor Driers and Grove sidings, leading to Virginia sidings. Part of the stack and the end access door is common to both photographs. The Retew branch is on the extreme left, while on the right, the box vans are located on a siding which descended at a 1 in 100 gradient to the back of Melangoose Mill. 31st May 1966. *Maurice Dart*

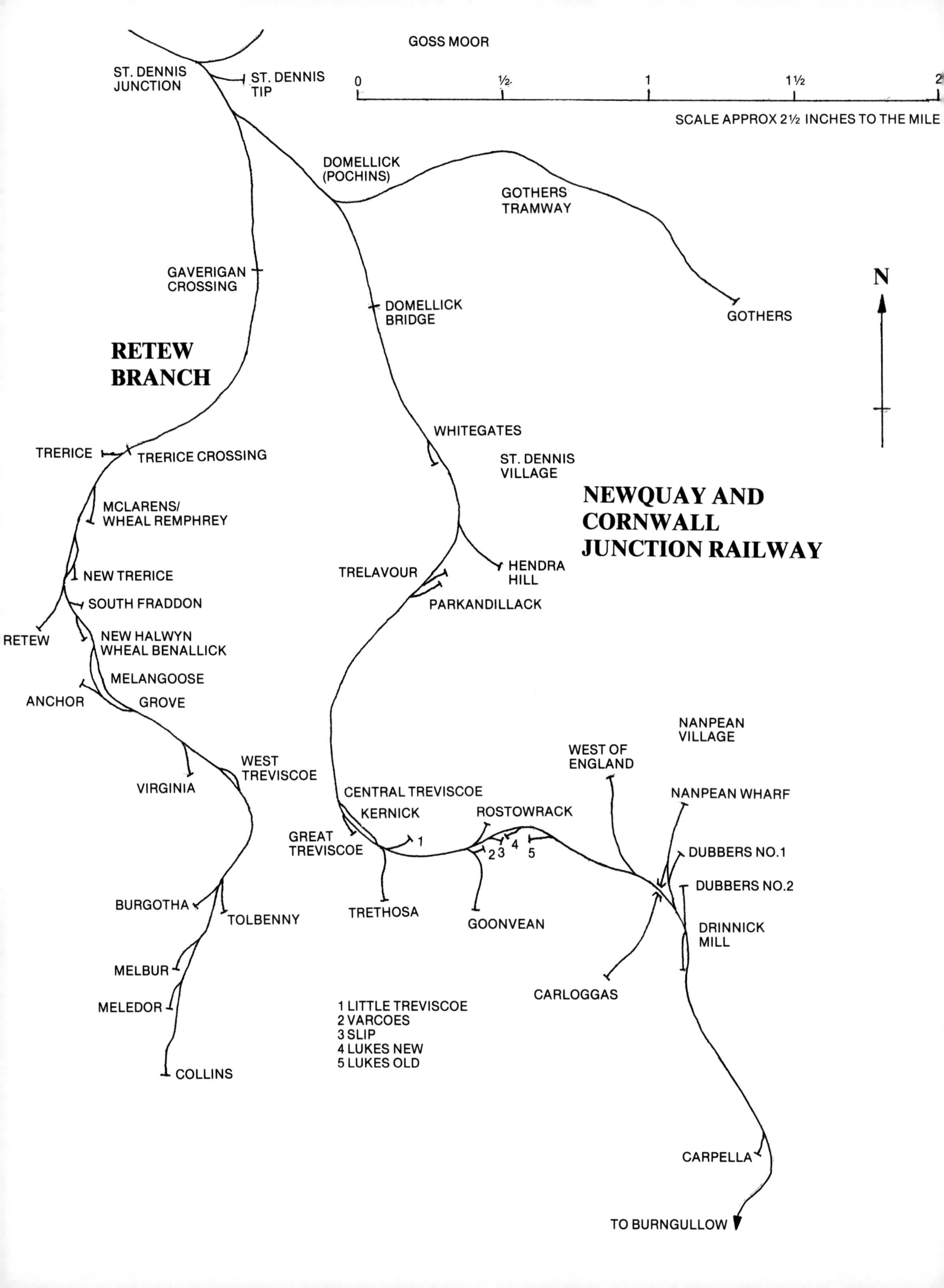
GOSS MOOR
ST. DENNIS JUNCTION
ST. DENNIS TIP
0
½
1
1½
2
SCALE APPROX 2½ INCHES TO THE MILE
DOMELLICK (POCHINS)
GOTHERS TRAMWAY
GAVERIGAN CROSSING
DOMELLICK BRIDGE
GOTHERS
N
RETEW BRANCH
WHITEGATES
TRERICE
TRERICE CROSSING
ST. DENNIS VILLAGE
MCLARENS/ WHEAL REMPHREY
NEWQUAY AND CORNWALL JUNCTION RAILWAY
NEW TRERICE
TRELAVOUR
HENDRA HILL
PARKANDILLACK
SOUTH FRADDON
RETEW
NEW HALWYN WHEAL BENALLICK
MELANGOOSE
ANCHOR
GROVE
NANPEAN VILLAGE
WEST OF ENGLAND
WEST TREVISCOE
VIRGINIA
CENTRAL TREVISCOE
NANPEAN WHARF
KERNICK
ROSTOWRACK
GREAT TREVISCOE
1
2
3
4
5
DUBBERS NO.1
DUBBERS NO.2
BURGOTHA
TOLBENNY
TRETHOSA
GOONVEAN
DRINNICK MILL
MELBUR
MELEDOR
CARLOGGAS
1 LITTLE TREVISCOE
2 VARCOES
3 SLIP
4 LUKES NEW
5 LUKES OLD
COLLINS
CARPELLA
TO BURNGULLOW

Plate 247. When photographed on 14th June 1966, two loading platforms at Meledor Mill had vacuum-braked wagons awaiting loads. Although the line was extended to this point in 1912 the line finally ended at Collins Rotary Driers a few hundred yards to the south. *Maurice Dart*

Plate 248. This scene is so typical of the Retew branch, with sidings diverging in all directions. On 19th June 1958 Prairie tank No. 5519 shunts Meledor Mill Loop North. Meledor Mill can be seen in the background; the siding on the left was known as Tolbenny siding and the spur behind the shunter went to Burgotha North. The permanent way looks in a decrepit state but, although traffic dwindled to virtually nothing in the mid-1970s, it did not close until 1982, 24 years after the date of this photograph! *C. H. A. Townley*

Plate 249. This gradient post still survives in the undergrowth between Anchor sidings and Virginia Crossing. Its survival is fortuitous in that it relates to the steepest gradient on the 15 mph restricted Retew branch. *JV*

At this point it must be said that in addition to the Retew branch and the many sidings serving various works, several clay works had their own "internal" tramway systems to move clay or waste products. Most were narrow gauge but because many faded away many years ago, and their track layout was often changed from month to month, surprisingly little has been written on the subject. It is known that two tramways were active at Wheal Remfry. Just beyond Retew Crossing a siding (opened 1939 – closed 1973) serving South Fraddon (or Great Halwyn), branched away on the 'down' side at 2 miles 25 chains while at 2 miles 27 chains there were once loops on either side of the branch; Retew Loop on the 'down' side and New Halwyn on the 'up'. They rejoined the branch at 2 miles 34 chains and 2 miles 36 chains respectively.

Another fascinating aspect of the many works in this and other areas is the precise naming of the site. Often the railway had its name for the siding, the clay company another, while in some instances local names were used – sometimes reflecting mere nicknames. There was nothing ambiguous about the once busy Wheal Benallick siding or the Melangoose Clay Works at 2 miles 36 chains. This siding made facing and trailing connections on the 'up' side of the branch, effectively forming a loop. After Melangoose Mill siding the line dropped away at a steep 1 in 40 for the short distance to Melangoose Mill Public sidings on the 'up' (west) side. Adjacent to this site, at right angles on the south side, was the large Anchor Works and siding, which with Melangoose, closed in the 1972/73 period. This location was significant in that it was the original terminus of the line. It is interesting to note that by railway milepost the distance to Melangoose is greater than that recorded in the Act. Early in the present century there was much development in this area and new clay works were opening and old ones were expanding rapidly. Accordingly, in 1912, the Great Western Railway extended the branch by just over 1½ miles to Meledor Mill.

After Melangoose the line turned quite sharply towards the south-east. One of the Melangoose Mill sidings dropped to connect into Grove sidings (closed 1963), and from there a trailing siding descended back into the rear of Melangoose Mill at 1 in 100. Apparently, a capstan was used to winch wagons back up to Grove siding. The clay driers here had deep wooden shutes which were angled down into the railway wagons for loading. At 2 miles 67 chains, and still falling at 1 in 40, the extension of Grove siding trailed in, which was immediately followed by Virginia siding which also diverged on the 'up' side. Here, the line ran through the delightful Treviscoe Wood with the massive Virginia China Clay Works to the south.

Virginia sidings were themselves something of a branch line extending over a quarter of a mile towards the clay loading point. The works also had its own tramway but there has been extensive expansion in recent years and, since closure in 1965, all trace of the sidings has gone. The River Fal was again crossed at Virginia Bridge followed by the fourth crossing. Continuing at 1 in 40 West Treviscoe siding was reached at the 3 miles 3 chains mark on the 'down' side. It was taken out of use on 5th March 1965. The line continued to follow the river in pleasant wooded country with two crossings of the Fal before Tolbenny (sometimes known as Virginia) Crossing was reached. On the 'down' side, until closed in 1972, was Tolbenny siding at the 3 miles 44 chains mark, and just beyond was the north end of Meledor Mill Loop North. Branching away from the 1 in 95 loop on the 'up' side was Burgotha siding (which had been out of use for many years before the branch closed). The River Fal was again crossed to serve Melbur Driers and Mill on the 'up' (west) side. Towards the end of the branch Meledor Mill was served on the 'up' side and the main branch ended at Meledor Crossing, 4 miles and 2 chains from the junction.

However, that was not quite the end of the story for a siding continued across the road, which was gated, to New Meledor (opened 1929 – closed 1965) and Collins Rotary Drier. At the very end the line was set in concrete, as it was in many of the driers. It should be added that a further reason for confusion over the plethora of sidings was the opening and closing dates of many. Some were closed so long ago that even railwaymen of the immediate post-war period do not remember them.

The gates at all the level crossings were worked by the train crews. Nearly all the sidings were controlled by single-lever ground frames and there were no signal boxes on the branch. In the absence of passenger trains there were no facing point locks with the sole exception of Tolbenny sidings. Tolbenny and Virginia sidings had multiple-lever ground frames. There were restrictions on motive power using the line, but St Blazey's small 0-6-0 pannier tanks and the small-wheeled Prairies presented no problems. The maximum permitted speed anywhere on the branch was 15 mph. On occasions two locomotives worked a single train onto the branch but in this event they had to be at either end of the train. Locomotives were not permitted at some sidings and so wagons could only be left or removed by means of a rake of wagons being between the engine and the relevant wagons. At some steeply graded sidings stop bars were bolted to the track to prevent runaways. With so many sidings to serve it was not surprising that only two trains a day were booked in the busiest years of the line.

With such activity it is not unreasonable to ponder over the reasons for the line's closure. In the first place most of the older driers were the classic coal-fired pan dry where a fire at one end of the long clay dry building was drawn by a tall stack at the other end, resulting in hot air passing beneath the clay which was spread over the floor (or pan) of the dry, after having surplus water removed in filter presses. Such driers were replaced by more modern methods such as rotary driers and buells, and so gradually the old inefficient, low-output pan driers were closed.

There had also been significant improvements in pipeline technology and clay in slurry form could be transported for a dozen or more miles to distant large driers, such as those at Par Harbour. Furthermore, the entire scale of the industry changed over the years and the small works were gradually swamped. Another important factor was the amalgamation and takeover of the various clay companies with, for example, English China Clays taking over control of more than 100 clay companies between 1919 and 1966. This naturally led to rationalisation in order to maximise the use of resources and eliminate duplication of effort and under-capacity.

Photographs from the 1950s show the line to be partly grass covered and in a state of decline. One by one the works closed and subsequently traffic dwindled. By the end of the 1950s only ten intermediate sidings survived. By the end of the 1960s railwaymen observed that there was little traffic but, surprisingly, clay continued to be moved from the Retew branch until the late 1970s. The last recorded traffic from Collins Driers at the end of the branch was in September 1980. The line was traversed by the annual weedkilling train in the summer of 1981 and in mid-March 1982 a locomotive and a van worked to the end of the branch and back. This was the last movement before most of the track was lifted in 1983. A few sidings remain to this day and, of course, the track set in concrete remains in places. The last recorded passenger train was an enthusiasts' special dmu in April 1977.

In addition to the china clay works, driers and sidings there were also brickworks on the line and, many years before the railway, there were a number of iron mines in the area, including Kernick and Meledor. There were also many stone quarries but, unlike the Luxulyan Valley area, their history is essentially pre-railway. Many of the waste products from the china clay producing process lend themselves to manufacture into diverse by-products, such as bricks. In fact some companies mixed titles, such as the Wheal Remfry China Clay Brick & Tile Company Limited, which was allied to H. D. Pochin & Company Limited, and which was absorbed into the ECLP and later English China Clays Group. Wheal Remfry Brick Works was at the end of Trerice sidings.

One of the operational problems concerning rail traffic on the Retew branch was the need for all trains to reverse at St Dennis Junction, and then to traverse the largely single-track line to St Blazey via Bugle. After the direct Fowey to St Blazey line closed, clay trains again had to reverse at Lostwithiel before reaching Fowey Docks. There had been plans to extend the branch by several miles following the course of the River Fal all the way to St Just Pool in Carrick Roads, virtually across the river from Falmouth but, as with the majority of these somewhat grandiose schemes, nothing came of them.

The branch is now but a memory and despite the massive Wheal Remfry, Virginia and Melbur China Clay Works, each producing thousands of tons of clay every year, not one ton now moves by railway.

Plate 250. The track at Meledor Mill, which ran towards the Melbur to Trethosa road, was not lifted following closure of the line and over the years it has gradually become more overgrown. It is now barely visible, but in July 1986 the trackwork and crossing gates looked like this. It is sad to reflect that such a busy mineral line encrusted with sidings, and where two locomotives on one train was a common sight, has now gone for ever. *JV*

19 St Dennis Junction to Tolcarn Junction

Beyond St Dennis Junction the line heads westward towards Ruthvoes. Although initially on the route of the old Treffry Tramway, at 294 miles and 55 chains, there is a significant deviation from the original line. The Treffry Tramway incorporated the 530-yard long Toldish Tunnel which was not only damp but was a mere 8 to 9 ft high, sufficient for a horse and wagon but totally inadequate for the CMR's purposes. The old route is still shown on current 1:50,000 Ordnance Survey maps, even though abandoned on 1st June 1874. The new line took a longer route to the north of Toldish Tunnel and from 1904 there was a further minor deviation from 295 miles 39 chains to 295 miles 66 chains.

Just beyond was St Columb Road station which, for the first two years of its life, was known as Halloon. The station was well over two miles from St Columb Major and in fact it was much nearer the curiously named Indian Queens. It opened in June 1876 and boasted two platforms, a passing loop and a goods yard. By 1910 the goods yard had been enlarged and a substantial loading dock was built. Between 1931 and 1933 two further extensions to the passing loop saw it lengthen by 60 yards to the west, and by 100 yards to the east. As with most other stations on the line, the service varied from three trains each way in 1888, four or five in 1910, eleven or twelve in 1938 and 1958, and six in 1989, with generally more trains on summer Saturdays, albeit not all stopping at the minor

Plate 252. *(Top right)* The passing loop at St Columb Road was taken out of use on 3rd January 1965 and the signal box closed. Entering the station on 10th June 1989 are power cars Nos 43024 and 43011, each producing 2,250 hp from their Paxman Valenta diesel engines to get the 'down' "Atlantic Coast Express" from Paddington to Newquay. The 125 mph potential train ran non-stop from Par to Newquay, 20¾ miles, in 46 minutes – an average speed of 27 mph! *JV*

Plate 253. *(Bottom right)* On its way to St Dennis Junction (and Manchester!) Class 47 No. 47459 will by-pass the old trackbed of the original Treffry Tramway which passed through the shallow and narrow Toldish Tunnel. The CMR avoided the tunnel by a lengthy deviation route. The train is the 10.05 from Newquay to Manchester of 3rd October 1987. The weather and the outlook at St Columb Road on this day were bleak. *JV*

Plate 251. *(Below)* Continuing the survey of the Newquay branch from Plate 194 featuring St Dennis Junction, this further impression shows a busy moment on 20th September 1979. With the signals 'off', No. 50030 *Repulse* makes for Newquay with the 11.00 SAGA special from Paddington. Passing on the 'up' road is Class 120 Swindon-built dmu No. 557 with the 16.15 local from Newquay. *JV*

E.M.& L.M. TAMBLIN
Wholesale Fruit & Vegetable Merchants
ST.COLUMB ROAD TEL ST. AUSTELL 860504
Beware of trains
40
InterCity 125

47 459
St Columb Road

stations such as St Columb Road.

Disaster day was, in common with so many stations on the line, 3rd January 1965 when the passing loop, goods sidings and signal box were all axed. The scene is now quite desolate, although one should be grateful that trains still call! Beyond the line reached Halloon Crossing, which even in the mid-1970s retained its crossing keeper's hut, cottage and gates across the A392 road. The line runs via White Cross over a level crossing at Coswarth before entering a deep cutting and the 31-yard long Coswarth Tunnel. After crossing under the A392 road and crossing it again on the level, Quintrel Downs is reached. This typical GWR wayside halt served a small community and was opened from 2nd October 1911. It had a pagoda hut, oil lamps, sign and a signal cabin. It had been the site of a busy siding long before the halt was built.

At the site of the halt there was once a loop and a siding, but when the platform was built the layout changed to a single branch line "main" road and two sidings. The signal box at Quintrel was closed in 1911 in favour of a gatehouse containing signals. By the early 1920s the ground frame had been removed to the platform where it remained in use until 1981 when the gates were removed, the signals uprooted and crossing keeper for 35 years, Gladys Sleeman, was retired. One of the sidings was private, owned by Martyn & Lewarnes. In addition to the 1981 carnage it was again 1965 which saw the sidings closed and removed.

Charming crossings are located at Chapel and Trencreek, 300 miles 54 chains and 301 miles 35 chains respectively, as the line drops towards Newquay. Before conversion to open crossings the former crossing keepers operated not only the gates but protective signals either side of the crossings. Just a few hundred yards beyond Trencreek was Tolcarn Junction, but over the years, the exact alignment of this large triangular junction changed and the history is best dealt with by describing each chord separately.

The junction of the west to east and west to south chords was originally known as Treloggan Junction. At the opening of the CMR it was renamed Newquay Junction and later to Tolcarn Junction. The south to east and south to west junction was known as Lane Junction but the signal box there was closed in 1888. The east to west and east to south junction was Tolcarn Junction but that box, too, closed in 1888 when the 1874 east to south curve was closed completely. In future years the entire junction complex was controlled by a single signal box which was located on the inside of the "triangle" between the "V" of the east to west and west to south chords.

It made sense for the GWR to close the direct east to south line as all traffic was either to or from Newquay. The main branch into Newquay was realigned in 1904 just prior to the opening of the Chacewater to Newquay branch throughout to passenger trains. A north chord passing loop was provided and until 1910 there was a siding made out of the abandoned east to south chord. The single track south to west chord was doubled with the coming of the passenger trains from Chacewater. The abandoned spur was relaid to single track in 1931 and a brand-new Tolcarn signal box was commissioned. The spur was provided to turn locomotives, especially tender locomotives arriving on main line trains on summer Saturdays, which were too large for the Newquay turntable. It is said that when double-headed trains with up to fifteen coaches arrived at Newquay they had to stop at the buffers, beyond the run-round loop points and accordingly it was sometimes the practice to reverse the entire formation to Tolcarn Junction for complete turning on the triangle. Generally, however, the leading locomotive was detached outside of the terminus.

With growing holiday traffic and the limited capacity of the single-track viaduct across the Trenance Valley into Newquay, a new masonry viaduct was proposed in the late 1930s providing double-track access to the seaside terminus. The viaduct was all but ready before the start of the Second World War and the double line from Tolcarn Junction was extended.

Plate 254. Although this photograph was taken 32 years after the Nationalisation of the railways, the former GWR is much in evidence with GWR station seat, pagoda hut (re-roofed) and cast-iron sign with the pretentious wording "Quintrel Down Siding East Ground Frame". In fact the correct spelling of the station's name is Quintrel Downs. Dmu set No. P470 forming the 10.10 Newquay to Par prepares to stop for six passengers and a dog on 12th June 1980. *JV*

Trains crossed the new viaduct from 27th March 1939 but the second track was not brought into use until 20th March 1946, after the end of hostilities. Additional sidings were installed on the west side of the Tolcarn triangle at the same time.

Although there was a brief period of respite in the early and mid-1950s the 1960s brought nothing but decline. The closure of the Chacewater line in February 1963 and the withdrawal of freight facilities to Trevemper siding in October 1963 resulted in the closure of both south to west and south to east chords. Furthermore, steam locomotives had disappeared from the main line scene and the diesel replacements had cabs at both ends and did not need turning. Train loads decreased and the diesels could use the run-round loops at Newquay without difficulty. On 23rd November 1964 the 1931 signal box was closed and effectively Tolcarn Junction disappeared from the railway map. Worse was to come as developers moved in and by the early 1980s an industrial and housing estate covered the entire site, with no trace whatsoever that a railway ever passed the place except, of course, for the single line of the surviving Par to Newquay branch.

Plate 255. In the past, as now, the long-distance summer Saturday trains did not stop at intermediate stations. However, a curiosity in the summer of 1976 was the rolling stock of the overnight 23.35 Paddington to Penzance which then worked empty to Par to form the 11.41 stopping service to Newquay. As "Western" Class 52 No. D1058 *Western Nobleman* stops at Quintrel Downs on 6th August 1976 a group of Air Cadets with their suitcases and kit-bags board the train on returning from camp at RAF St Mawgan. *JV*

7820
P 103

Plate 256. *(Top left)* Just before Quintrel Downs station is a cutting which contains the 44-yard Coswarth Tunnel, seen in the background of this photograph. Bustling away from the tunnel on 9th July 1960 is 'Manor' class 4-6-0 No. 7820 *Dinmore Manor* with the 11.52 am Newquay to Par local. *Peter Gray*

Plate 257. *(Bottom left)* With plenty of bovine interest – but not in the train – single power car No. 55003 slows for the approach to Chapel Crossing with the 12.45 from Newquay on 13th June 1989. The outskirts of the town can be seen on the horizon. On the right is the crossing warning light. *JV*

Plate 258. A good old Cornish stone wall protects the crossing keeper's cottage at Trencreek Crossing, just over a mile from Newquay. With warning lights flashing, Gloucester Railway Carriage & Wagon Co. Class 122 No. 55003 passes with the 11.48 Par to Newquay, also on 13th June 1989. *JV*

Plate 259. Looking like an "00" gauge model with just six ageing goods wagons and a GWR brake van, 5700 class 0-6-0PT No. 9655 arrives at Tolcarn Junction with a pick-up goods train from St Blazey on 20th July 1954. Tolcarn was called Treloggan Junction from 1849 to 1874 and Newquay Junction from 1874 to 1885. It was the junction for the East Wheal Rose branch before 1905, and for Chacewater from that year. The signal box closed on 23rd November 1964. *Les Elsey*

20 Chacewater to Newquay and Treamble

In February 1849 the first load of iron ore had been transported by rail from East Wheal Rose Mine to Newquay Harbour over the original Treffry Tramway. Subsequent developments included not only the arrival and takeover of the Treffry lines by the Cornwall Minerals Railway, the extension of the East Wheal Rose line to Treamble and Gravel Hill, the opening of the line through from Fowey to Newquay and, in 1896, the final takeover by the Great Western Railway of all the CMR, but also the arrival of the London & South Western Railway at Wadebridge via their North Cornwall line in 1895.

The LSWR had taken over responsibility for the Bodmin & Wadebridge Railway in 1846, although they did not address the parliamentary formalities until 1883. However, despite rivalries between the railway companies there had been agreement in 1888 to allow trains on the extended GWR standard gauge branch from Bodmin Road and Bodmin General, to work through to Wadebridge; the first time the isolated B&WR lines had been connected to the main railway network. The two lines joined at Boscarne Junction. However, the GWR still regarded the LSWR as a threat and in 1894 they proposed a direct line from Truro to Newquay to effectively "cut off" a LSWR proposal to open a line from Wadebridge to Truro, possibly via Newquay. This proposal was rejected by parliament.

There had been many previous schemes to link the LSWR via the Bodmin and Wadebridge lines to the CMR. In 1873 there had been a proposal to link Ruthern Bridge with the CMR at a point near Roche, a distance of only four to five miles. The reason for the proposed link was a more direct access to a port with better facilities than the restricted Wadebridge. There were other schemes outside the scope of this book but development continued with the opening of the LSWR North Cornwall line in 1895 and to Padstow in 1899.

Although there remained a competitive spirit between the GWR and the LSWR, typified by the boat train "races" from Plymouth to London on their respective routes, by the end of the 1890s the two giants had agreed to stop the fruitless competition in the County of Cornwall, even though the LSWR did run bus connections from Wadebridge to Newquay! At the end of the decade the GWR lodged their Truro and Newquay Railway Act which included a proposed route greatly different from their earlier initiatives.

The railway was to leave the main line at Chacewater, where a station had been opened as part of the West Cornwall Railway route from Truro to Penzance in August 1852. The station was about a mile north of the village it purported to serve and its importance as a junction, and also its operational inconvenience, were both recognised when, in 1912, extensive modifications including an island platform were made. The station approach and the main buildings were on the 'down' side, as was the signal box. A pair of sidings were provided at the 'down' end of the 'down' side forming a small goods yard. In fact these sidings were the last vestige of commercial activity at Chacewater which continued to be used long after the branch and the complete station were closed.

Plate 260. Chacewater station, between Truro and Redruth, was the recognised junction for Newquay via St Agnes and Perranporth, although until 1916 there was access to the branch from the west at Blackwater Junction. This photograph shows the station on 4th June 1920, which closed in October 1964 – 20 months after the branch line closed. *L. T. George Collection*

Plate 261. After closure of the main line, Chacewater station in 1964, the 'down' island platform, and much later the signal box, were demolished. However, until the contract was lost in May 1987 there was still plenty of action at the station as sometimes daily loads of cement were delivered to the Blue Circle distribution point from the works at Plymstock. On 24th July 1986 No. 47085 *Mammoth* arrived from the Plymouth area with four tanker wagons. It would take the empties all the way to St Erth, 15 miles away, to "run round". *JV*

Plate 262. From 1916 passengers would always change at Chacewater for Newquay in the 'up' direction. In the 'down' direction passengers were more likely to use Truro to change, where most Newquay trains commenced their journey. The first "station" on the branch was Mount Hawke Halt which No. 5552, on a Truro to Newquay train, is approaching on 16th July 1960. *Peter Gray*

Plate 263. The section from Chacewater to Perranporth was opened on 6th July 1903 and through to Tolcarn Junction, Newquay, on 2nd January 1905. The northern part of the branch utilised the track of the original Treffry Tramway and later the Cornwall Minerals Railway from East Wheal Rose (not to be confused with the Wheal Rose branch, near Bugle) to Tolcarn Junction. Arguably, the most distinctive structure on the line was Goonbell Viaduct and here on 11th July 1961 No. 9635 rumbles its way to Newquay with the 11.40 am from Truro. *Peter Gray*

However, the GWR did not do things by halves and in addition to the alignment from Chacewater, there was also a direct link to the branch from the Redruth direction which formed a triangular junction at Blackwater. In fact the north to west spur was very much a secondary link being used by infrequent passenger trains only between the years 1903 and 1916. It continued to be used by the occasional freight until 1919 and was closed shortly afterwards. It was not until 1924 when an independent line was provided from Blackwater Junction to Chacewater (which ran parallel with the main line) that three signal boxes – Blackwater West, North and East were finally closed. To provide the half-mile independent line the north side of the cutting to the west of Chacewater had to be widened. The evidence can still be seen as can the remains of part of the embankments forming the triangular junction at Blackwater.

Although it could never be said that the Chacewater to Newquay line had conveniently located stations for all the villages and hamlets it served, the meandering alignment clearly attempted to have regard to the local community. The only villages with a population worth mentioning were St Agnes, which had been a focal point for mining in days before the coming of the railway, and Perranporth, which subsequently owed much of its development to the railway. The latter village was the initial target of the railway builders and the Chacewater to Perranporth section opened on 6th July 1903, a distance of just over eight miles.

The railway building continued towards Shepherds, where it would form a junction with the former CMR line to Treamble. Although upgrading was necessary, the alignment from East Wheal Rose, near St Newlyn East, followed the early 1849 Treffry Tramway alignment. Even then it was 18 months later, on 2nd January 1905, before the 18-mile 49-chain branch was opened throughout. At the time of opening the only intermediate station between Perranporth and Newquay was Shepherds. Extensive modifications to track, signalling and platforms took place at Newquay during 1904/05 in anticipation of the new route to Newquay.

In the best of GWR traditions half a dozen halts were opened from 14th August 1905. These modest single-platform halts with a couple of lamps, a sign and basic pagoda hut passenger accommodation, completed the plan to provide a service for minor communities along the route. A small halt at Perranporth Beach was opened in 1931 to cater for increasing holiday traffic and trips to the seaside. St Agnes station was greatly altered in 1937 when an island platform was built and the track re-aligned. The branch had an overall speed limit of 40 mph.

The line was essentially rural in character and after leaving the embankment at Blackwater Junction it climbed for just over a mile and a half to Mount Hawke Halt. The hamlet the halt served was over a mile away and as in the case of the other halts there were no sidings. The brick-faced platform was situated in a now infilled cutting. To this day the embankment between Mount Hawke and St Agnes is visible from the B3277 road.

It must have been disappointing for the inhabitants of St Agnes when they realised that the much heralded new railway was to locate its station some three-quarters of a mile from the village centre. It could, no doubt, be argued that in 1903, as the village was the most important on the line, more money should have been spent on a more convenient alignment, but a glimpse at an Ordnance Survey map reveals that insurmountable topographical problems would have been encountered in crossing Trevellas Coombe. The red brick station initially had a single platform and boasted a Station Master. Some 34 years after opening, in 1937, a long 300 ft island platform, with passing facilities, was built and connected to the original station area by an overbridge. A 30-lever signal box was opened at the same time replacing the existing ground frame. Unlike the halts, the station had goods facilities with a goods shed, cattle pens and the usual paraphernalia.

Leaving St Agnes, 3 miles 26 chains from Chacewater, the line veered sharply eastward and a mere 45 chains from St Agnes the halt of Goonbell appeared, which like Mount Hawke, was situated in a cutting. Goonbell could perhaps have been called "south-east St Agnes", although the halt was located immediately adjacent to the few buildings which comprise the hamlet of Goonbell. The line continued across a five-arch masonry viaduct which shared the name of the previously mentioned Goonbell hamlet. At the 5-mile 46-chain mark was yet another halt called Mithian. Again, the halt was conveniently located to serve the small community.

The line then descended the Perrancombe Valley at gradients of up to 1 in 45 to within a short distance of Cornwall's north coast at Perranporth. However, from 1931 Perranporth Beach Halt was used by the bucket and spade brigade, thus saving them a quarter of a mile walk from the main Perranporth station. At Perranporth the direction of the line changed abruptly from north-north-east to south-south-east. From the date of opening Perranporth had a substantial island platform, goods shed, cattle dock, signal box and other associated railway buildings. The station was notable for its deep awnings. The resort so increased in popularity that in the 1950s there was, almost unbelievably, a through train to and from Paddington on summer Saturdays. For example, in 1958, a first and second-class, restaurant car express left Perranporth at 8.15 am, arriving in the capital 7 hours and 40 minutes later at 3.55 pm. The 'down' train ran to Perranporth and Penzance with the former portion arriving at its destination at 4.20 pm after a 7-hour 55-minute marathon.

After leaving Perranporth the railway builders again respected the terrain by running the branch line along the Bolingey Valley in a generally easterly direction, across a further viaduct to reach Goonhavern Halt at 10 miles 38 chains. Here the line crossed the main Newquay to Redruth road. The halt was easily accessible by the local inhabitants. The line curved to the north-east and through a cutting before descending to Shepherds, the junction for the freight-only line to Treamble. As distinct from Perranporth and the rebuilt St Agnes, Shepherds was built on more traditional lines with separate 'up' and 'down' platforms. It, too, had a goods depot; it was a passing loop controlled by a signal box on the 'up' platform and was 12 miles and 38 chains from Chacewater.

Plate 264. St Agnes, Perranporth and Shepherds all opened on the same day that the respective sections of track opened to passengers. However, other than for Perranporth Beach Halt which opened in 1931, all the other halts opened in August 1905. They were all of traditional GWR pattern with a lamp or two, sign and pagoda hut. In this attractive scene the 11.50 am from Newquay of 11th July 1961 headed by 4575 class Prairie tank No. 5562 seems to be assured of at least a modicum of business at Goonbell Halt. *Peter Gray*

Plate 265. There are no buildings in sight in the immediate environs of Mount Hawke Halt. In fact, although the branch meandered in its direction to serve the few settlements, this halt was well over a mile from the village it purported to serve. This photograph was taken in 1922, 17 years after the halt opened. This cutting has now been filled in. *L. T. George Collection*

Plate 266. In this period piece from the RIC Collection the names of the Station Master and the Porter on the right have survived: Mr Julian and Percival Trembath respectively. Note particularly the GWR adornments and the enamel advertisement signs. St Agnes station was also over three-quarters of a mile from the town. Although this is how it looked in 1914 the station area was completely rebuilt in 1937 when this canopy was removed and the platform seen here was demolished in favour of a new island platform. *Royal Institution of Cornwall*

Plate 267. In this view the main station building at St Agnes can be identified clearly, despite being photographed from the opposite direction to the previous illustration. This view dates from 1949, but before the war, in 1937, an island platform was built with 300 ft platform faces. The access overbridge was also erected and to control the new passing loop and altered sidings a 30-lever signal box was constructed at the southern end of the island. Note also the large goods shed which, unlike the brick station, was demolished after closure in 1963. *L. T. George Collection*

Little has been written about the Treamble branch. There had been evidence of mining to the north and west of Penhale Sands for centuries, but of primary interest was the Perran Iron Lode which ran from Holywell to the downs around Newlyn East. In the 18th and 19th centuries iron ore had been raised in the area, but due to the heavy costs incurred by the method of working, and the ore having to be carted some nine miles for shipment, few profits were made – until the railway arrived. Although there had been an application to parliament in 1865 to construct a railway from the iron lode to Newquay it was the CMR who, by virtue of their July 1873 Act, continued the old Treffry Tramway line from East Wheal Rose to Treamble.

It had been said in support of the application that there were millions of tons of ore in the lode, that it was specially adapted for making Bessemer steel, and that it needed only railway communication to develop it. The ore was near the surface but at certain points the lode was only a foot or two wide. The main mines in the area were at Gravel Hill, Duchy Peru and Deer Park. This potential was recognised by the CMR entrepreneur W. Roebuck who included in his application to parliament "Railway No. 4". It was described thus: "A railway four miles seven furlongs in length, commencing in the Parish of Newlyn by a junction with the existing tramway from New Quay (*sic*) to East Wheal Rose Mine about eight hundred yards or thereabouts from the termination thereof, and terminating in a field in the Parish of Perranzabuloe at a point one hundred and sixty yards or thereabouts to the southward of a mill known as Treamble Mill."

It was also stated, somewhat prophetically, that the success of the working would depend on the output, which would require opening up of the deposits at many more points than is done at present. In addition to the Treamble line, a 1-mile 4-chain extension from a trailing point near the terminus to Gravel Hill, at the easterly end of Perran Beach, was built with landowners' but not parliamentary authority in a period of only ten days. The line to Treamble and Gravel Hill was opened on 1st June 1874, in common with the rest of the CMR

Plate 268. Beyond Goonbell Halt and some 5½ miles from Blackwater Junction was the diminutive Mithian Halt which served a near-by hamlet. Unlike the halts on many other lines the majority of trains stopped. From an initial service in 1905 of five trains in each direction it increased to a 1939 peak of eleven 'up' and twelve 'down' trains. A single goods train traversed the line, Mondays to Fridays. A 5700 class 0-6-0PT, No. 7715, clanks its way towards the single platform with the 11 am Newquay to Truro on 11th July 1961. *Peter Gray*

Plate 269. Perranporth owes much of its present size to the railway. In 1931 a halt was built nearer to the popular beach than the main station site. The main station was large with a vast island platform, deep canopies, goods yard and shed, and a good-sized signal box at the Newquay end of the platform. It would be difficult to capture a busier scene on the branch than this; with the 4.39 pm Chacewater to Newquay headed by a brace of 4575 class Prairies, Nos 5546 and 5539, on the left with, in the distance, sister locomotive No. 5515 approaching with the 4.35 pm from Newquay. One wonders if a crew change was contemplated. The holiday crowds would be disappointed with this weather, on 3rd August 1959. *Peter Gray*

Plate 270. A much earlier view of Perranporth station, taken on 9th June 1922, gives some impression of the size of the station area. Almost half-way between Blackwater and Tolcarn junctions, Perranporth was a passing place on the branch, a distinction it shared with St Agnes and Shepherds. *L. T. George Collection*

network. Despite early optimism the mines were not efficiently worked, production slumped and following a downturn in the industry, and a slump in prices, the Cornish Consolidated Iron Mines Corporation was dissolved in 1884. The Gravel Hill extension was finally closed in 1888 and the track lifted.

Traffic was not particularly lucrative at Treamble and, despite the presence of a goods agent, the line from Shepherds closed in 1917, and in common with so many other minor lines and light railways (such as the Basingstoke and Alton) the track was lifted and used in the First World War effort. By this time Deer Park, followed by Duchy Peru and Treamble, had seen the last iron ore mined. Deer Park had its own trailing siding on the 'up' side of the line, but this was closed by the time the April 1897 GWR Service Book was issued. It seemed that after a life of 43 years a small piece of the CMR had been lost for ever.

It was therefore with some surprise that following the necessary reinstatement works, the GWR proudly announced in Notice 2131 that "The Treamble Branch which forms a junction with the Perranporth Branch at Shepherds has now been reinstated and would be opened for Goods Train traffic on Tuesday, February 16th, 1926." The $3\frac{3}{4}$-mile branch would provide accommodation for 14 trucks at the Private Siding terminus. As can be seen from the notice reproduced herein, the line was controlled by Shepherds signal box on the train staff – one engine in steam or "two coupled" principle. The wonderfully precise timings showed trains running on Tuesdays, Thursdays and Saturdays.

For the first mile the line descended at 1 in 60/88/41, followed in the second mile by the line falling at 1 in 40/100/60. At the two-mile mark the falling gradient was even more pronounced at 1 in 50/40 for over half a mile. There were similar 'ups and downs' before and after the three-mile marker. The 1926 trackwork was single from Shepherds to the loop just outside of Treamble. The loop was 276 ft long commencing at the 3-mile $1\frac{3}{4}$-chain point. The locomotive would always run round in the loop and propel wagons into the main private siding. There was a short, second siding on the 'down' side "not to be used by engines". Both sidings were beyond the "end of GWR maintenance" point at 3 miles 12 chains. There was a gate across the track just beyond the GWR boundary.

Beside the loading wharf at Treamble there was a 2 ft gauge tramway worked by a pair of diminutive 0-4-2T steam locomotives (Kerr, Stuarts 812 of 1903 and 1169 of 1911, both from Dalcoath Mine, near Camborne.) They served a quarry where gunpowder was manufactured by the C.M. Powder Co. Ltd works. The tramway was closed and lifted by 1942. Although other produce was loaded at Treamble the volume was very small and the capacity of the 13-wagon loop was never required.

Notwithstanding the steep gradients the permanent way was such that the speed limit over the entire line was a miserly 10 mph. Stop boards were fixed at 0 mile 47 chains and 2 miles 59 chains and, in accordance with incline instructions, brakes had to be picked up at 2 miles 41 chains and at Treamble Loop. Whistle boards were situated either side of the crossing near Rejerrah. Propelling along the line in either direction was not permitted.

After a handful of wartime troop trains and a few "as and when required" runs, traffic finally petered out in the summer of 1949 with closure formally posted in January 1952 and track lifting in 1956. The line can still be traced in a couple of locations but most of it is heavily overgrown, especially in the Treamble area. Curiously, British Rail still have maintenance

Plate 271. Another wayside halt on the branch was Goonhavern, which simply means the "Down" or hill of Havern. There were some quite heavy earthworks in this area and although the halt was located near the small centre of population the line had to burrow beneath three road bridges in the area. Taken on 5th June 1922 the halt would continue to eke out an existence for a further 41 years. *L. T. George Collection*

PRIVATE AND NOT FOR PUBLICATION. Notice No. 2131.

GREAT WESTERN RAILWAY.

RE-OPENING OF TREAMBLE BRANCH
SHEPHERDS.

The Treamble Branch, which forms a junction with the Perranporth Branch at Shepherds, has now been re-instated and will be opened for Goods Train traffic on **TUESDAY, FEBRUARY 16th, 1926.**

The Branch is $3\frac{1}{4}$ miles in length, terminating in a Private Siding giving accommodation for 14 trucks. Loop accommodation for 13 trucks is provided at 3m. $1\frac{3}{4}$c.

A diagram of the Branch is shewn in this notice. The method of working will be by Wooden Train Staff in accordance with the instructions shewn on Page 73 of the General Appendix, and the following addition should be made to page 22 of the Appendix to No. 6 Section of the Service Time Table:—

Working of Single Lines.

From	To	Colour and Shape of Staff.		Where Train Staff is kept.	Person at Junction responsible for exchanging Staff.	Undertaking given to Ministry of Transport as to method of working the Single Line.
		Colour.	Shape.			
Shepherds	Treamble	Black	Oblong	Shepherds Signal Box	Signalman.	Train Staff only. One engine in steam or two coupled.

The new Catch Point at Shepherds has been coupled to the Box and the points of Loop at Treamble are operated by ordinary hand levers.

TRAIN SERVICE.

R. R. train on Tuesdays, Thursdays and Saturdays only.

Truro............dep. 10 22 a.m.
Shepherds........ arr. 12 17 p.m.
" ....dep. 12 30 p.m.
Treamble Loop....arr. 12 50 p.m.
" " ...dep. 1 40 p.m.
Shepherds........ arr. 2 5 p.m.
Shepherds ....dep. 3 5 p.m.

Perranporth........ arr. 3 20 p.m.
" ....dep. x3 55 p.m.
St. Agnes ....dep. 4 20 p.m.
Chacewater........ arr. 4 35 p.m.
and coupled to 2-30 p.m. ex Carn Brea Yard, provided combined load does not exceed 25 trucks.

obligations on the line; a bridge and bridge abutments at Rejarrah, 1 mile $44\frac{1}{2}$ chains, and Treworthen, 2 miles $72\frac{3}{4}$ chains!

From Shepherds station, where in times gone by a holiday camping coach with a clerestory roof was located, the line passed Fiddlers Green before crossing Penhallow Moor. There was some difficulty in laying the original track at this point. The next halt was Mitchell and Newlyn at 13 miles 60 chains. In common with all GWR stations and halts with the words "and" or "road" in the name, it was convenient for neither Newlyn East nor Mitchell. There were no houses nearby, just the waste from the East Wheal Rose Mine which, during the 19th century, had become a legend in its time. After the CMR extension from East Wheal Rose to Treamble the mine had its own siding at a point 1 mile 57 chains from Shepherds and 4 miles 53 chains from Newquay.

Old Wheal Rose mine opened in 1814 and by 1818 it had become a major producer of lead. The price slumped in the late 1820s and it ceased production in 1831. However, in 1834 a new mining venture started at East Wheal Rose and by 1846 no less than 1,200 men, women and children were employed in the mine. Unfortunately the lode was very soft, resulting in many rock falls and the use of enormous amounts of timber. Also, at the lower levels, water infiltration was a major problem and by 1842 pumping engines were removing no less than 734 gallons per minute! In 1846 there was a terrible disaster at the mine when flash floods resulted in the loss of 39 miners who were drowned as the pumping engines failed to cope. By the time Treffry had put down his tramway to the mine it was already in decline, 1845 having been the peak year. The mine closed in August 1885.

After closure of the branch line in 1963 there were hopes of reopening part of it. But, like most projects, such hopes seemed to be more romantic notions rather than practical possibilities. In 1968 Eric Booth saw the potential for a narrow gauge steam railway running along the Lappa Valley and he commenced negotiations

Plate 272. Shepherds station was where the newly built branch line of 1905 joined up with the much earlier Treamble and Gravel Hill branch which had a chequered history. Built as an extension to the Treffry Tramway line to East Wheal Rose, the CMR's $4\frac{3}{4}$-mile line ran from there to Treamble in 1873, with an extension to Gravel Hill to exploit the Great Perran Iron Lode in 1874. The latter extension lasted only until 1888 and the branch from Treamble to Shepherds was closed and lifted in 1917, only to be relaid in February 1926, to which the above notice refers. The freight-only line closed in January 1952 but there was very little traffic after 1949. The station, loop, sidings and signal box are all visible in this 1947 view, looking south. The Treamble branch curves away to the right. *L. T. George Collection*

Plate 273. Also featured in Plate 43 – in the early days before a build-up of population, and especially in the off-season months, steam railcars were used on the branch. They were not popular and were soon displaced by traditional formations. In this Edwardian view car No. 4 pauses at Shepherds while making its ponderous way from Chacewater to Newquay. Note the quaint tail lamp half-way up the right side of the bodywork. There does not appear to be any shortage of staff! *A. Fairclough Collection*

Plate 274. Although this is as near to a comparison with Plate 272 as is now possible, the 1989 scene at Shepherds is just identifiable. The railings on the left were once on the 'up' platform, while the trackbed ahead once carried trains to Chacewater and Truro. The unusually shaped windows of the house, which curve at the top, are common to both pictures. Nature has virtually won its battle here. *JV*

with British Rail. After five years of work a 15-inch gauge line was laid from Benny Halt to the East Wheal Rose Mine, where there are many attractions for the traveller and holiday-maker. The line to this leisure area is just over a mile in length. The Lappa Valley Railway now has two steam and two diesel locomotives. This length of railway is all that remains of the railways which once ran between Tolcarn Junction and Blackwater Junction.

The final halt on the line was at Trewerry and Trerice, 16 miles and 76 chains. This halt, in common with Mitchell and Newlyn, originally had a wooden platform but in later years they were rebuilt, looking more like a Southern Railway halt with an entirely concrete structure and small basic waiting shelter. In the *Country Homes of Cornwall* publication the fine nearby Elizabethan mansion of Trerice is featured, and in the tourist season it is open to the public. A coal siding at Trewerry was closed in 1948. Early maps showed the siding just north of the level crossing as Trewerry siding or Trewerry Mill. The building by the level crossing was once a CMR crossing keeper's house. Between here and Trevemper siding the CMR line deviated slightly from Treffry's Tramway.

Trevemper siding was less than half a mile south of Tolcarn Junction. After the branch closed to passengers and freight in February 1963, just the short section from Tolcarn to Trevemper siding remained open. However, it too succumbed on 29th October 1963 and the line was lifted by January 1964. The triangular Junction at Tolcarn was the point where the branch joined the Par to Newquay branch which is described elsewhere.

When services ended in 1963 there were 24 working levers in St Agnes signal box including seven for signals, six for discs, five for points and six for facing point locks. Perranporth had twenty working levers including ten for signals, three for discs, four for points and three for facing point locks. Shepherds had just fourteen working levers including eight for signals, two for discs and four for points.

When the closure notices appeared there were rallies and protest groups fighting the closure. The typical Dr Beeching era procedures took their course with the Western National Omnibus Company Limited providing the alternative service. Except for Trevemper siding both passenger and freight services ceased on and from Monday, 4th February 1963. One curiosity on the formal closure notice read: "As an experiment a parcel depot will be maintained at Perranporth Beach Halt until the end of the 1963 Summer Season. The retention of the facility after this period will depend on the use made of it." Readers were invited to ring the Station Master, Perranporth, telephone 3211 for further information. Years later, part of the Perranporth Beach concrete platform was used in the construction of The Dell station at Falmouth.

From six trains in each direction Mondays to Fridays in April 1910, timetabled services increased on the same basis to eight in January 1927, twelve in July 1938 falling to eleven in 1958 In later years there was also a Sunday service plus seasonal adjustments. The trains varied from single-car railmotors in the early days to typical two to four-coach branch trains in the days of steam. The normal branch tank locomotives were based on Truro shed. From mid-1962 diesels took over all services and the last train on the branch was a four-car diesel multiple unit. As a means of getting to Newquay from Plymouth and London the branch was a duplication of the line from Par. But the Chacewater line always had a better service than the Par line and it was reckoned that some 600 passengers used the line daily for return journeys. However, the line lost money and against that criterion, closure was inevitable. The loss-making Par line received a subsidy in later years, a situation which prevails to this date.

Plate 275. Between Shepherds, and Mitchell, Newlyn Halt is the only sign of railway life nowadays. In 1968 Eric Booth had the vision of a narrow gauge steam railway on part of the old branch line. After protracted negotiations the 15-inch gauge Lappa Valley Railway was opened on 16th June 1974. The one-mile line runs from 'Benny Halt' south to the historic site of the East Wheal Rose mine, where a pleasure park has been designed and built. On 13th June 1989 Berwyn 0-6-0 *Muffin*, built in 1967, nears Benny Halt with a train from East Wheal Rose. *JV*

Plate 276. Tolcarn Junction was where the line from Chacewater once joined the Par to Newquay branch by a triangular connection. This early view shows Lane Junction looking north. The line on the right here, from south to east, was used in later years for turning locomotives, although for some years complete trains were turned. *L. T. George Collection*

Plate 277. Tolcarn Junction was a busy location at times. For example, on summer Saturdays there could be 25 trains in each direction to and from the Newquay terminus. In addition to these 50 movements (total for both lines) there were empty stock and light locomotive movements. At a quieter moment in 1959 2-6-2T No. 5562 takes the Chacewater line at Tolcarn with a train from Newquay. *George Hemmett*

Plate 278. An intriguing but purposeful combination for a 3-coach branch train occurred on 17th July 1954. Leaving Tolcarn Junction and having just joined the line from Par a pair of GWR Moguls, Nos 6397 and 6305, have about three-quarters of a mile to cover before reaching their Newquay destination with a well-loaded train from Chacewater. Heads peep from the carriage windows in anticipation of their arrival on the Atlantic Coast. *Les Elsey*

21 Tolcarn Junction to Newquay

Although Joseph Austen Treffry had given notice in 1835 that it was his intention to link Par and Newquay by a tramway, it was not until he had acquired Newquay Harbour in 1838 that the prospect became a reality. Following the purchase of land and the agreements from other landowners that the tramway could run across their land, work commenced on tramways from Newquay Harbour to St Dennis and Hendra in clay

Plate 279. There were once no less than seven signal boxes between Goonbarrow Junction and Newquay. The last survivor was St Dennis Junction which succumbed in December 1986. Since that date the signalman at Goonbarrow has given the branch train driver a token such as this for the journey to Newquay. *JV*

Plate 280. A sad but momentous occasion took place on 4th October 1987 when 5,400 hp of English Electric power shook the semaphore signals at Newquay on the eve of their demise. Returning to Paddington with a special, which not only commemorated the passing of regular locomotive-hauled trains to Newquay, but also the end of Newquay signal box and all terminus signalling, are Nos 50035 *Ark Royal* and 50034 *Furious* in immaculate Network SouthEast livery. The train has just crossed Trenance Viaduct at 15 mph and, as seen from the exhaust, power had been applied. *JV*

Plate 281. After rebuilding in 1873 by the CMR, in order that the viaduct could support locomotive-hauled trains, Trenance Viaduct was again rebuilt in 1937/38. The rebuild was of double-track masonry construction and the signalling was revised accordingly. Crossing the viaduct with a Bristol train, comprising maroon stock, on 11th June 1964, was Class 42 'Warship' No. D866 *Zebra*. *Les Elsey*

Plate 282. Following the visit of a special train comprising an IC125 unit in October 1987, the High Speed Train sets became regular visitors to the Newquay branch from the summer of 1988. With a power car at each end there was, of course, no need for run-round facilities at Newquay; the driver simply changed ends and returned from whence he came! This mode of working had enabled the through-train facility to continue after the abolition of the signal box. Seen through a 300 mm Nikkor lens, IC125 power car No. 43015 (with 43143 at the rear of the train) crosses Trenance Viaduct with the 14.55 Newquay to Leeds of 10th June 1989. *JV*

country and to East Wheal Rose in mining country. By 1849 the lines were ready and, following the opening of the most important structure on the line, Trenance Viaduct (according to the *Royal Cornwall Gazette*, by Treffry riding across it), on the 29th January 1849, loaded wagons found their way to Newquay. The wooden structure on part-granite piers was chosen because, at one year, the building time was only a third of that required for an all masonry example.

The tramway, having crossed the Trenance Valley, curved towards the infant town and the harbour. When the Cornwall Minerals Railway were surveying the area for their proposed Fowey to Newquay route the ideal station site was found just across the Trenance Valley, only three-quarters of a mile from Tolcarn Junction, and just a few hundred yards from the cliffs above the shore of Newquay Bay. Although the new station area was open for goods traffic from June 1874, it was 20th June 1876 when the first passenger train drew into Newquay station, having crossed the Trenance Valley on the rebuilt 1874 viaduct with stone piers and iron girders forged by William West & Sons of St Blazey.

The station had a single platform with unpretentious but permanent stone buildings on the north side of the site. A few yards outside the station was a CMR signal box and a stone locomotive shed. At a much later date a goods shed was provided. At the western, buffer stop, end of the station there was a small turntable which the CMR tank engines used to either run round their train or to visit the engine shed. There were a couple of goods sidings and the line crossed the main road to the harbour. With a service of only three or four trains per day this arrangement was to be adequate for a number of years, but with the coming of the Chacewater to Newquay branch trains, and the start of through working potential following the GWR's abandonment of the broad gauge main line in 1892, consideration was given to likely growth.

Accordingly, during the 1904/05 period, substantial changes were made. The CMR platform was extended considerably and a further island platform was built, giving three platform faces. The old CMR signal box was taken out of use and replaced by a GWR box on the opposite side of the line and to the east. The end of platform turntable was abolished and the old engine shed was razed. The goods yard was enlarged and a new locomotive shed was built, served by a new and larger turntable.

Although the old harbour branch closed in 1926 the heyday of the seaside tripper and holidaymaker was about to occur. The original platform was extended in April 1928 and lengthened again in July 1934. At the same time the crossover connections were replaced to reflect the length of platform. The engine shed closed at the beginning of the 1930s as there was no need to berth locomotives at Newquay overnight. There were water cranes at the platform ends in any event. In expectation of additional traffic and the replacement of the CMR Trenance Viaduct by a new double-track masonry viaduct, the island platform was extended in the spring of 1938 and a significant number of carriage, as distinct from freight, sidings were added.

The double-track viaduct was not fully operational until 20th March 1946 when the 1905 signal box was replaced by a later GWR model. This was to be the last of the long series of developments. After the mid-1950s peak, when 20,000 passengers would arrive at Newquay on summer Saturdays, the picture was one of decline and rationalisation. Again, it was the closure of the Chacewater to Newquay line and the general Beeching era climate which started the rot. The double-track section from Trenance Viaduct east to Tolcarn was singled on 23rd November 1964 and the goods yard was lifted shortly afterwards. One of the platform lines was shortened in 1966 and in 1968 two of the carriage sidings were removed. Two further sidings were removed in 1969, severely limiting the number of trains which could be berthed at Newquay. The old 'up' platform, which was supported on concrete stilts on the extended portion, became unsafe. The long platform awnings were severely pruned in 1964 and all the trappings of the days of steam were removed. Notes from the demolition contractor's notebook show the scale of rationalisation.

On 10th June 1964 seats were removed from platforms, the day after the roofs of platforms 2 and 3 were demolished, and the day after that, glass, wood and lead were removed from the platforms. By the 25th June 1964 lamp standards had been cut down and the wrought iron removed. On 29th June it was reported that the water column on platform 1 had been very hard to break up, "will try and finish it tomorrow". Platform 2's water column was broken up on 2nd July 1964 and that from platform 3 the day after. Two further water columns were broken up on following days. The three demolition men arrived by train at 10.15 and departed at 17.30. An amusing note on 20th June 1964 recorded that "three men commenced to cut off purlins on platforms 2 and 3 but had to stop as passengers wanted to board their train at 11.00. Started to work again at 12.30"!

Further sidings were closed in the early 1980s and platform 1 was regarded as dangerous and was no longer used. The run-round crossover had been dismantled and eventually only three trains and a dmu could be accommodated at Newquay. The final act of vandalism took place in 1987 when, at the end of the summer timetable, the last scheduled locomotive-hauled train called at Newquay; all signals were removed, the signal box closed and only a single platform was in use from Monday, 5th October. The only bright spot was the retention of through IC125 trains from distant destinations on summer Saturdays, including, in 1990, a through train to Glasgow Queen Street and the "Atlantic Coast Express" to Paddington.

The first through carriages from Paddington to Newquay were introduced from May 1906 when the journey took 7 hours 55 minutes, compared with the best "ACE" 1989 timing of 4 hours 43 minutes. Over the years Newquay has played host to an amazing variety of trains, ranging from the 4 and 6-wheelers of the early days, with their small tank locomotives of first the CMR, and later the GWR, through the Edwardian era of bogie coaches and clerestory roof lines to the non-corridor compartment coaches of the latter days of steam. Then there were the full-length holiday trains, sometimes weighing over 500 tons and hauled by two locomotives with a banker for part of the journey to and from Par, bringing a wide range of GWR and BR(WR) main line steam engines to the seaside. Diesel multiple units took over branch workings in the early 1960s and most classes of main line diesels working on the Western Region have found their way to Newquay, including those memorable 'Western' and 'Warship' diesel-hydraulics.

Unusual workings were many and varied, ranging from streamlined GWR railcars in 1932, Royal trains throughout the 1874 to 1989 period, the steam railmotors of 1905 through to the 4-wheeled railbuses of the early 1960s. There was still room for novelty in 1989 when the annual weedkilling train brought Hunslet-Barclay Class 20/9s to Newquay. Ironically, the best trains in terms of speed and comfort to visit Newquay have been the InterCity 125s and yet, it is a bleak and ravaged Newquay station that they visit. In 1989 IC125 power cars failed on two occasions and the units were assisted by Class 37 locomotives. The only saving grace in the 1990s is that at least Newquay is still served by rail!

Plate 283. A view from above Trenance Viaduct showing inside check rails on one side and an outside rail on the other, with neat point rodding on the right. Crossing the viaduct on 22nd August 1987 with the 10.40 Newquay to Paddington, comprising a grey and blue BG van and all NSE liveried stock, is No. 50021 *Rodney*. *Brian Morrison*

Plate 284. The most hectic time at Newquay has always been on summer Saturdays before the long-distance trains leave but after the overnight workings have arrived. By 1986 only three long-distance trains could be accommodated at Newquay plus the branch dmu. With manager Peter Foot having a word with the driver and with shunter Ivor Trudgeon having forsaken Drinnick Mill for a day at Newquay, Class 47 No. 47641 *Colossus* (built in 1965 as No. D1672 for work on the WR and renumbered to No. 47086 before conversion to provide electrical train heating) prepares to shunt the 10.10 Newquay to Manchester of 30th August 1986. *JV*

Passengers
must not cross
the line
P473

Plate 287. In 1964 the through service from Bodmin North to Padstow ceased and a 4-wheeled railbus was introduced to run from Bodmin North to Boscarne Junction where it would connect with Bodmin General to Padstow dmus. Just after arrival at St Blazey a rare working occurred when A.C. Cars 11-ton 150 hp 46-seat railbus No. W79977 worked to Newquay and back. The small diesel is seen at Newquay when there were still gas lamps and flower tubs on the platform. *Carey Batchelor*

Plate 285. *(Top left)* A view of Newquay signal box which was opened on 20th March 1946. This replaced a previous box which, in turn, had replaced the CMR box in 1904. Suburban unit No. P473 in all blue livery leaves the west end of Trenance Viaduct and enters Newquay with the 08.58 from Par on 12th June 1980. The signalman was the venerable Roy Stockman. *JV*

Plate 288. The classic branch terminus run round. Having arrived at Newquay at about 06.30 with an overnight train from the Midlands (which the author caught at Plymouth North Road at 04.48!) and with holidaymakers streaming off the platform with their baggage, Class 52 'Western' No. D1033 *Western Trooper* runs round its stock on 24th July 1976. The locomotive was withdrawn nine weeks later. *JV*

Plate 286. *(Bottom left)* Over the years Newquay has had its track layout modified on numerous occasions. Platforms have been extended and many additional sidings installed to accommodate the burgeoning holiday traffic. However, from the late 1960s there has been a decline starting with the withdrawal of Chacewater line trains and goods services in the 1963/64 period. By 1970 three out of seven sidings had been lifted and in this 1983 view just two sidings and three platform lines remained. Now only one line in total remains plus one refuge siding. Taken from the heights of the hospital grounds on 13th August 1983 No. 50042 *Triumph* prepares to leave with the 16.20 to Par, after bringing the eight coaches from London; the 09.47 ex-Paddington. *JV*

Plate 289. With the signal box in use as a permanent waymen's "hut" and only the single-line branch and refuge siding remaining "Bubble car" No. 55006 leaves with the 14.45 for Par on 21st October 1988. These 64-seaters are normally adequate for the traffic and on the last 'up' train in the evening the train often goes straight into St Blazey depot because there are no passengers on board. *JV*

Plate 290. A typical 1950's scene at Newquay terminus, as one of the larger 5100 class 2-6-2 Prairie tanks comes to a halt with a two-coach local from Par. A sprinklng of passengers, including men, women, a baby and dogs wander towards the station and the town. Trains no longer use this platform; the original adjoining the 1874 CMR building. *Lens of Sutton*

Plate 291. Another line-up at Newquay on a summer Saturday morning. By the time this photograph was taken on 30th August 1986 the north side platform, which was partly supported on concrete stilts, was in a state of disrepair and sported the sign "Danger Platform Unsafe". Before their decline Class 50s No.50039 (left) waited for the off with the 09.18 Newquay to Newcastle while on the right, No. 50008 was diagrammed for the 11.35 Newquay to Paddington. Unfortunately, *Implacable* was an early Class 50 casualty and the stalwart *Thunderer* was relegated to the ranks of the Departmental Civil Engineer pool. Despite the modern traction image this scene has gone for ever. *JV*

Plate 292. What must surely be the ultimate in rationalisation and a depressing scene to boot is the Newquay of the 1990s. With platform 1 track ripped up and the run-round loop removed, trains do not even reach the protective awning now. A "greenhouse" shelter (said to be vandal-proof) to the right of the dmu is the only creature comfort for would-be travellers. The once significant staff numbers have been dissipated and now only the train crew remain. For now the old station building remains, albeit not for railway use. *JV*

22 Newquay Harbour Branch

Although there is evidence that there was a small wooden quay on the site of what is now known as Newquay Harbour back in the 14th century, it was the latter part of the 16th century when records show a hamlet called "Newe Kaye". It was also included in Carew's 1602 survey of Cornwall. The hamlet comprised just a few fishermen's cottages when, in the mid-16th century, a harbour refuge was built so that in addition to the general shelter provided by the headland to the north-west, Towan Head, the small vessels of the era could shelter from inclement weather. The area grew very slowly and the primary commodity was pilchards, landed in some numbers by the locals.

The history of Newquay reflects the usual seaside story of smugglers and customs and excise men trying to outwit each other while the impoverished peasants looked on. The area was poor by any standards but the first signs of change came in 1770 when one Richard Lomax, Lord of the Manor of Towan Blistra, purchased the harbour and much of the surrounding area. Over the years from the basic activities of fishing and sheep farming, the mining industry began to influence the area. For years tin, copper and the fleeces from the sheep shearing season would be conveyed on pack mules to Penpoll Creek at Crantock for shipping. There was also a wharf at Trevemper, a mile or two south of Newquay, which was the highest point reached by tidal influence on the River Gannel.

By 1811 lead had been discovered at Wheal Rose near St Newlyn East on the land of Sir Christopher Hawkins, and also mines at Perranzabuloe were in production. Furthermore, the early days of china clay production had reached a point where transportation and shipping were high on the agenda. By 1818 Wheal Rose was a major undertaking and production from most mines and pits was on the increase. In 1821 there was an abortive survey carried out to examine the possibilities of a nine-mile canal from the inland clay country to the River Gannel at Newquay. The *West Briton* newspaper reported in 1825 that a pier had been constructed at St Columb Porth which was capable of taking schooners with an 80-ton payload potential. Again, the possibility of a canal to the port from the edge of china clay country was considered but the financial backing was not forthcoming.

The amount of produce being handled by the small harbour at Newquay continued to increase and the varieties of

Plate 293. Although undated, this interesting aerial view was probably taken in the 1930s. There are coaches with clerestory roofs in the sidings, the town still has a goods service, the Harbour Tramway has been lifted (bottom left of yard curve) but full-length awnings remain. This is the only way to comprehend just how near the station is to the cliffs and the sea. Shops and supermarkets have now gobbled up much of the land. *Woolf/Greenham Collection*

Plate 294. Plate 14 shows a typical Newquay Harbour Tramway train in the centre of the town. The standard gauge line started life in 1845 but it could not be connected to Treffry's Tramway until 1849. At the harbour end of the line there was a 1 in 4 to 1 in 6 incline which ran through a 96-yard tunnel to the harbour. These stationary winding engines/whims were used to lower and raise wagons. The cable drum can be seen in this early photograph. The long chimneys were to provide a strong draught for the fires. *Woolf/Greenham Collection*

Plate 295. This gem of a photograph shows the tunnel and incline plane to advantage. This old wooden-framed, metal-bodied GWR wagon, No. 31076 with a 4-ton 11-cwt tare, is full of coal which has just been imported, while metal water pipes rest in the next wagon. The tunnel entrance is visible today and is occupied by an aquarium. The route of the line is still easy to trace with the aid of a local map. *Woolf/Greenham Collection*

commodity included not only fish but corn, coal, iron ore, china clay, sand, manure, limestone and salt, with the ships trying to balance incoming and outgoing produce to maximise their income. After being subjected to considerable pressure, Richard Lomax embarked on a £10,000 harbour expansion scheme in 1832. The new harbour would enclose a total area of four acres. A total of 250 men were employed on building a new south quay and rebuilding and extending the north quay. The new quay at Newquay was ready for service in 1833.

In the meantime, Joseph Austin Treffry had been launching a number of schemes on the south Cornwall coast including the building of Par Harbour. Par had received its first commercial vessels only weeks after the rebuilt Newquay had reopened. In 1835 Treffry publicly announced his intention to build a tramway from Par to Newquay and it was not, therefore, a total surprise in October 1838, following the death of Lomax, that Treffry purchased Newquay Harbour and some surrounding land at auction for £7,000. Treffry's plans included a tramway from the harbour, which would rise by an incline of 1 in 4½, to run through what is now the town, to the site of the 1874 and current BR station, before crossing the Trenance Valley.

Plate 296. China clay was exported from Newquay from about 1849 until the early 1920s. In these early days loads were put into shutes manually, which then carried the clay onto small-capacity vessels of only about 50 tons. At the top of the incline and in the harbour area all wagons were horse drawn. A special central stone loading pier (seen here) was built with a wooden trestle railway connection. This Victorian view shows the loading process. *Woolf/Greenham Collection*

The Act of Parliament authorising the necessary work was passed in November 1843 and work commenced on the harbour section in the following year. The lines in the harbour ran along the quays to facilitate loading. All wagons on the quays and on the tramway itself except, of course, for the incline, were to be horse-drawn; the horses being owned and operated by the Hoytes family. By a series of points the harbour sidings converged into a single line which entered an incline tunnel which was 96 yards in length, 4 ft 6 in wide and 17 ft high at the widest and highest points. The excavations were carried out by miners from the St Dennis area who discovered some Elizabethan mining remains during construction. Initially the rope cable was connected to a whim which was horse powered but this was replaced by stationary steam engine whims which raised and lowered wagons by steel cable. The engines had particularly tall chimneys to improve the draft for the fires, the engine house being located behind Fore Street. There was a passing loop just beyond the top of the incline beyond the engine house, alongside which horses were attached/detached. The tramway then curved past the bottom of Marcus Hill via Crantock Street, Manor Road and Cliff Road and on to Island Crescent behind the Victoria Hotel. The first wagonload was conveyed along the tramway in January 1849. The tramway was standard gauge throughout, in common with all of the Treffry Tramway lines. The harbour was 303 miles and 41 chains from Paddington via Bristol with the distance from the eventual station site to the harbour being a shade under one mile.

In 1873 the Cornwall Minerals Railway built a stone jetty within the harbour to increase handling capacity, at this time Newquay shipowners possessing some 160 vessels. A wooden trestle took the single line to the jetty where it switched into two lines. However, after the jetty was built, and the through line from Newquay completed, (but more importantly the section from St Dennis Junction to Par and Fowey was opened) in 1874, most china clay headed to the southern ports. Loads to Newquay Harbour were surcharged at 2d per ton. The East Wheal Rose Mine finally closed in 1885 and towards the end of the 19th century the days of the 50-ton schooner were coming to an end. Eventually, all of the above factors combined to reduce traffic to the Harbour to a trickle, even though Newquay grew with the railway and its importance as a resort increased as passenger payloads increased every year.

It is uncertain exactly when the last wagons were drawn through the town but research shows that the last outbound cargo was in 1921 and the last incoming load was in 1922. The Great Western Railway formally closed the harbour branch in 1926. The last ever load was of agricultural fertiliser, landed from the schooner *Hobah* without ceremony. The wooden trestle was removed in the early 1950s and long after closure an aquarium was opened at the foot of the incline, inside the tunnel. During the late 1980s the tunnel mouth at the top of the incline was unearthed during excavations for a new supermarket which now occupies the site of the old winding engines.

In 1858 the horses took 2,788 tons of china clay down to the harbour at Newquay. Today there is still a handful of fishing boats using the harbour but it is now hard to imagine those heady days as the tourists stroll along the harbour where concrete covers the railway of the past. Section 60(1) of the GWR Act 1929 vested to the Newquay Urban District Council the harbour and tunnel. The tramway track from Cliff Road to Crantock Street was conveyed by the GWR to the Council on 3rd June 1931 and the whim-engine house area was purchased by the Council from the British Transport Commission on 26th May 1953.

Plate 297. A picture postcard view which shows the entire Harbour Tramway layout in the harbour area to advantage. The large building on the top of the hill beyond is the Atlantic Hotel built in 1892. With two horses visible in the photograph, two coal wagons wait to be hauled up the incline, together with two empty china clay wagons which have just discharged their load. Note the wooden trestle supports under the central pier line. *Courtesy P. Q. Treloar*

Plate 298. There is at least a period of 80 years between these two photographs but the scenes are directly comparable. The central pier is now used for lobster pot storage but the trestle railway connection was finally dismantled during 1953. The Atlantic Hotel can just be seen, top left, and the tide is in the same state in both pictures. Other than for local fishing there was little commercial trade in the harbour after the tramway was abandoned. Now the main business is catering for the holidaymakers. *JV*

23 New Route to Newquay

At the beginning of 1987 BR were asked for a statement about the future of the Newquay branch. Civil dignitaries at Newquay were alarmed at the gradual deterioration of operational flexibility of the line and the withdrawal of railway personnel from Newquay station, the loss of the parcels service, the abandonment in December 1986 of St Dennis Junction signal box and passing loop, the planned withdrawal of locomotive-hauled through trains at the end of the 1987 summer and the closure of Newquay signal box. Their obvious fear was complete closure of the branch which, in passenger terms, has been a loss-maker for decades.

Linked to their concern about the future of the railway to Newquay, Cornwall County Council had for years recognised that the railway skew bridge across the very busy A30 road in the middle of Goss Moor had been not only a hazard with its 14 ft 3 in height restriction but the road aperture was essentially "two lane", thus preventing much needed road improvements. The cost of realigning the railway or in building a new wide overbridge was prohibitive and the rail traffic over this non-freight section could never produce a sufficient return to justify expenditure of millions of pounds.

There had originally been three routes to Newquay from the Cornish main line; from Par and St Blazey via Bugle, from Burngullow via St Dennis Junction and from Chacewater via Perranporth. The 18½-mile route from Chacewater to Newquay had been lifted in 1963/64 and reinstatement was impossible, while the line from Burngullow to St Dennis Junction had been severed between Parkandillack and St Dennis Junction in 1966. This line had never had a passenger service in its 120-year history. As for the Par line – at the time of writing the present branch line – ever since the first trains of the CMR used the branch in 1874, it had always been difficult to work with long stretches of gradients up to 1 in 37, numerous speed-restricted curves and level crossings. Even in 1990 a non-stop High Speed Train takes 44 minutes for the 20¾ miles from Par to Newquay, compared with 55 minutes for a *stopping* local steam train in 1910! Although working the Par line had once been flexible with eight double-track stretches or passing loops, by 1990 the only possible passing place between St Blazey and Newquay is Goonbarrow Junction.

There was never any doubt that few passengers along the Newquay branch wanted to visit the Par area. Other than for Newquay itself, the main town for shopping in the area is St Austell and few would change trains from the Newquay branch, with inconvenient connections, in order to visit that location. Primarily, Par has been a junction station where passengers change for destinations "up country". Also it must, sadly, be said that neither Bugle nor Roche generate much passenger traffic and few customers ever stand on Luxulyan's exposed platform. All of these stations have been unmanned for years and all are shown as "request stops" in the public timetable. In the winter months loadings are almost insignificant and on many occasions there have been no passengers at all on the last train of the day from Newquay – when it runs direct to St Blazey depot without calling at its destination of Par.

At a public meeting held on 5th August 1987 BR representatives confirmed that they had given careful thought to all of the issues and produced an interesting solution to the situation. The line between Goonbarrow Junction to St Dennis Junction would close completely and be lifted. The line from St Blazey to Goonbarrow Junction, up the Luxulyan Valley, would be retained for china clay trains visiting EEC Rocks. The line from Parkandillack to St Dennis Junction would be reinstated and the entire line from Burngullow upgraded and signalled for use by passenger trains. Newquay branch passenger trains would still work to Par but via St Austell which would become the junction station for Newquay. InterCity trains would no longer call at Par which has a high stopping and starting cost, because of the gradients either side. Also, Par generates little income in its own right.

BR officials confirmed that little use was made of Luxulyan, Bugle or Roche, and indeed, the latter came in for special mention; "Roche was hardly used". On the brighter side they added that active consideration was being given to the establishment of new halts at St Dennis, Treviscoe and either Nanpean or Foxhole. According to BR, all of these villages have greater traffic potential than the stations to be closed. On the other hand, all are served by buses and the cost of construction and the effects of rail/bus competition would all need to be considered. Road users would benefit from the conversion to dual carriageway of the main A30 trunk road, with the 'down' lanes using the trackbed of the existing branch across most of Goss Moor. Rail passengers would travel direct from Newquay and stations on the branch to St Austell.

Although the old Newquay & Cornwall Junction Railway line is far from being gradient free – and indeed there is not much to choose between the Luxulyan Valley's 1 in 37 and the two miles at 1 in 48/50 from Burngullow to Drinnick Mill – the proposed "new" route is shorter and it should be quicker. It will be far more difficult for the china clay trains visiting Crugwallins, Nanpean, Drinnick Mill, Kernick, Treviscoe, Parkandillack or Trelavour to find a path on and off the branch or between the china clay loading points, but new sophisticated signalling should help.

The ride to Newquay will certainly change if the proposition comes to fruition, with the greenery of the Luxulyan Valley and the wilds of Goss Moor being traded for a china clay "moonscape", with the line meandering between old gorse-covered tips and the vast workings of the 1990s. China clay trains will continue to use the old Luxulyan route and if the line becomes freight only it will be only a matter of time before enthusiasts' specials to Goonbarrow are in demand. The new route would very sadly mean the end of both Goonbarrow and St Blazey manual signal boxes and the age of the semaphore on the Newquay branch would end; but with the march of progress it will anyway. It is hard to imagine an area like Bugle station completely devoid of trains, when in times past it was the junction for the Wheal Rose and Carbis branches, with the Goonbarrow branch "just down the road" and its own passing loop, loading wharf and goods sidings.

The positive, however, outweighs the negative and if this large investment results in the retention of a branch line to Newquay then all the better. With new generation multiple units and High Speed Trains using the line the future should be encouraging, even if the railway has been ultra-rationalised. The necessary parliamentary procedures have already been instigated and at the time of writing further updates to the total costings are being calculated. Apparently, the Department of Transport have now entered the fray and they are prepared to pay in full for the reinstatement and resignalling *less* the money that BR would have spent maintaining the abandoned stretch between Goonbarrow Junction and St Dennis Junction. Although possibly a trifle ambitious, the spring of 1993 could see passenger trains using the old N&CJR for the first time on a regular basis.

Timetables

Table 100 — TRURO, CHACEWATER, PERRANPORTH and NEWQUAY
(Second class only except where otherwise shewn)

Miles		am	am S	am E	am	am E	am S	am T	pm	pm	pm P	pm	pm E	pm S	pm T	pm S	Sun am	Sun am	Sun am T	Sun am	Sun pm	Sun pm	Sun pm	Sun pm T	Sun pm T
	Truro .. dep	6 5	7 10	717	8H45	10 8	1010	1140	1H15	2J48	3 45	4L15	5H43	6 15	7 42	910	845	9 25	1125	1155	151	.	440	542	725
5	**Chacewater**	616	7 25	729	9 15	1020	1023	1154	1 35	2 58	3 55	4 39	5 58	6 25	8 0	922	...	9 37	1140	12 6	2 2	...	451	553	736
6½	Mount Hawke Halt	521	7 30	734	9 20	..	..	1159	1 40	3 3	..	4 44	6 3	6 30	8 5	927	.	9 42	1145	1211	2 8	.	456	558	741
8¼	St. Agnes	626	7 35	739	9 25	1028	1030	12 4	1 45	3 8	4 5	4 49	6 8	6 40	8 10	932	...	9 47	1150	1216	214	...	5 1	6 4	746
9	Goonbell Halt	629	7 38	742	9 28	..	..	12 7	1 48	3 11	..	4 52	6 11	6 44	8 13	935	.	9 50	1153	1219	217	.	5 4	6 7	749
10¾	Mithian Halt	634	7 43	747	9 33	...	...	1212	1 53	3 16	...	4 57	6 16	6 49	8 18	940	...	9 55	1158	1224	222	...	5 9	612	754
13	Perranporth Beach Halt	639	7 48	752	9 38	1038	1040	1218	1 59	3 21	..	5 2	6 21	6 55	8 22	945	.	10 0	12 3	1229	227	.	513	617	759
13½	**Perranporth**	641	8F 2	8B2	9 41	1040	1044	1221	2 4	3 23	4 20	5 5	6 24	6 57	8 24	948	912	10 2	12 5	1230	230	435	515	620	8 1
15¼	Goonhavern Halt	649	8 10	810	9 49	..	..	1230	2 12	3 31	..	5 14	6 33	7 5	8 32	.	.	1010	1212	..	237	442	523	628	8 9
17¾	Shepherds	656	8 17	817	9 56	1052	...	1236	2 19	3 39	...	5 20	6 40	7 11	8 39	...	...	1018	1218	...	244	449	530	637	816
19	Mitchell and Newlyn Halt	659	8 20	820	10 0	..	..	1240	2 22	3 43	..	5 24	6 43	7 15	8 43	.	.	1022	1222	..	248	453	534	641	821
21	Trewerry and Trerice Halt	7 4	8 25	825	10 5	...	...	1245	2 27	3 48	...	5 29	6 48	7 20	8 48	...	...	1027	1227	...	253	458	539	646	826
23¼	**Newquay** .. arr	712	8 32	832	1015	11 6	..	1255	2 35	3 55	..	5 36	6 56	7 29	8 55	.	940	1035	1235	..	3 0	5 5	547	655	835

Miles		am S	am E	am K	am	am S	am ET	am	pm	pm S	pm E	pm	pm	pm	pm	Sun am	Sun am T	Sun pm	Sun pm	Sun pm	Sun pm T	Sun pm T	Sun pm
	Newquay .. dep	7 20	7 24	..	9 12	..	11 0	1150	1 35	2 55	3 20	4 35	5 52	7 55	9 15	10 0	1050	..	1 30	4 0	620	8 0	8 50
2¼	Trewerry and Trerice Halt	7 27	7 31	...	9 19	...	...	1157	1 42	3 2	3 27	4 43	5 59	8 2	9 21	10 6	...	...	1 37	4 6	626	8 6	8 56
4¼	Mitchell and Newlyn Halt	7 33	7 37	..	9 24	..	..	12 3	1 48	3 8	3 33	4 49	6 5	8 7	9 27	10 12	..	..	1 43	412	633	812	9 2
6	Shepherds	7 37	7 41	...	9 28	...	1114	12 7	1 53	3 12	3 38	4 53	6 9	8 11	9 32	10 17	11 3	...	1 47	417	637	817	9 7
8	Goonhavern Halt	7 43	7 47	..	9 33	..	1120	1212	1 58	3 17	3 43	4 59	6 14	8 16	9 37	10 22	..	..	1 52	422	642	822	9 12
10½	**Perranporth**	7 50	7 54	8 15	9 39	11 0	1125	1220	2 4	3 24	3 49	5 5	6 23	8 25	9 43	10 28	1116	1 10	1 58	428	649	828	9 18
10¾	Perranporth Beach Halt	7 51	7 55	..	9 41	11 2	1127	1222	2 5	3 25	3 51	5 7	6 25	8 26	9 47	10 30	..	1 11	2 0	.	651	830	9 20
13	Mithian Halt	7 58	8 2	...	9 48	...	...	1229	2 12	3 32	3 58	5 14	6 32	8 33	...	10 37	...	1 18	2 7	...	658	837	9 27
14¾	Goonbell Halt	8 4	8 8	..	9 54	..	..	1235	2 18	3 38	4 4	5 20	6 38	8 39	..	10 43	..	1 24	2 13	.	7 4	843	9 33
15½	St. Agnes	8 7	8 11	8 28	9 57	1114	1139	1238	2 21	3 42	4 7	5 23	6 42	8 42	9 58	10 46	1130	1 27	2 16	...	7 7	846	9 36
17	Mount Hawke Halt	8 11	8 15	..	10 1	..	..	1242	2 25	3 46	4 11	5 27	6 46	8 46	..	10 50	..	1 31	2 20	.	711	850	9 40
18¼	**Chacewater** .. arr	8 17	8 21	...	10 7	1121	1148	1248	2 31	3 52	4 17	5 33	6 52	8 53	10 9	10 56	1139	1 37	2 26	...	717	856	9 46
23¼	**Truro** .. "	8H35	8H34	8 48	10 20	1133	12 2	1H13	2Z41	4 5	4H50	5D55	7 2	9 3	1020	11 6	1150	1 48	2 36	.	730	9 6	10 0

B Arr 7 55 am
D Change at Chacewater. On Saturdays arr 5 45 pm without changing
E Except Saturdays
F Arr 7 50 am
H Change at Chacewater
J Change at Chacewater on Saturdays
K Saturdays only. First and Second class. Through Train to London (Pad.) arr 3 55 pm (Table 81)
L Change at Chacewater, dep 4 25 pm on Saturdays without changing
P Saturdays only and not after 30th Aug. First and Second class. Through Carriages from London (Pad.) dep 8 25 am (Table 81)
S Saturdays only
T Through Train from or to Falmouth (Table 101)
Z Change at Chacewater on Saturdays and arr Truro 3 5 pm

For OTHER TRAINS between Truro and Chacewater, see Table 81

Summer 1958.

(Opposite top) April 1910.

(Opposite middle) Working Timetable summer 1968.

(Opposite bottom) Summer 1989.

Table 99 — PAR, BUGLE and NEWQUAY

MONDAYS TO FRIDAYS

Miles		am	am	am	am	am	pm	pm	pm	pm	pm	pm	pm D
	Par .. dep	6 10	6 45	7 20	9 30	1034	1220	2 40	3 20	4 25	6 25	7 45	9 20
4¼	Luxulyan	...	6 59	7 34	9 44	1049	1238	2 56	3 34	4 39	6 42	7 59	9 34
6¼	Bugle	6 29	7 4	7 40	9 50	1055	1247	3 3	3 40	4 45	6 48	8 5	9 39
8¾	Roche	6 35	7 10	7 46	9 57	11 1	1254	3 10	3 46	4 50	6 54	8 11	9 43
14¼	St. Columb Road	6 50	7 24	8 0	1012	1116	1 8	3 25	4 2	5 6	7 10	8 26	9 58
18½	Quintrel Downs	...	7 33	8 9	1022	1125	1 16	3 35	4 12	5 15	7 19	...	...
20¾	**Newquay** .. arr	7 5	7 41	8 16	1030	1131	1 25	3 45	4 20	5 25	7 30	8 40	1012

SATURDAYS

	am	am	am	am	am	am H	am	am	am	pm	pm	pm	pm	pm A	pm	pm	pm	pm	pm	pm	pm
Par .. dep	4 50	5 10	6 10	6 50	7 45	8 10	9 20	10 5	1045	1225	1 35	2 5	2 40	3 10	3 25	5 30	6 12	6 50	7 30	8 15	9 20
Luxulyan	...	...	...	7 6	8 0	...	9 34	...	11 0	1239	1 53	...	2 56	...	...	5 45	6 27	...	7 44	8 31	9 34
Bugle	..	..	6 29	7 13	8 6	..	9 42	..	11 6	1246	2 0	..	3 3	..	..	5 52	6 35	..	7 50	8 38	9 39
Roche	...	...	6 35	7 19	8 13	...	9 50	...	1110	1253	2 6	...	3 10	...	...	5 58	6 42	...	7 56	8 44	9 43
St. Columb Road	5 30	5 50	6 50	7 33	8 32	9 10	1010	1042	1130	1 12	2 23	2 44	3 25	3 50	..	6 18	6 58	7 35	8 16	8 59	9 58
Quintrel Downs	...	...	...	7 42	8 42	...	1020	...	...	1 21	2 33	...	3 35	...	...	...	7 7	...	...	...	...
Newquay .. arr	5 50	6 15	7 5	7 50	8 50	9 25	1031	11 0	1146	1 30	2 40	3 0	3 45	4 5	4 30	6 35	7 15	7 50	8 32	9 13	1012

MONDAYS TO FRIDAYS

Miles		am	am	am	am	pm	pm	pm	pm	pm B	pm	pm	pm B	pm	pm G
	Newquay .. dep	8 12	9 45	1045	1130	1250	1 45	4 45	6 0	7d20	8 5	9 8	9d45	1015	10d50
2¼	Quintrel Downs	8 20	...	1051	...	1257	...	4 52	6 7	...	8 11	9 16	...	1022	...
6½	St. Columb Road	8 30	10 0	11 2	1145	1 8	2 1	5 4	6 18	..	8 24	9 27	..	1033	..
12	Roche	8 44	K	1116	1159	1 21	2 16	5 18	6 31	...	8 38	9 42	...	1047	...
14½	Bugle	8 50	1020	1123	12 5	1 27	2 22	5 24	6 37	..	8 43	9 50	..	1052	..
16½	Luxulyan	8 55	...	1129	1211	1 33	2 28	5 30	6 42	...	8 49	9 56	...	1058	...
20¾	**Par** .. arr	9 9	1040	1143	1228	1 46	2 42	5 43	6 56	8 12	9 3	10 9	1042	1111	11 40

SATURDAYS

	am	am	am	am Z	am	am	am	pm	pm	pm	pm	pm	pm	pm	pm
Newquay .. dep	7d50	8d 5	8d50	10 0	11d0	11d15	1152	1230	12d40	1 45	5 0	6 0	8 0	9 8	1015
Quintrel Downs	...	...	8d59	...	...	...	1159	...	12d48	...	5 7	6 7	8 7	9 16	1022
St Columb Road	..	8d20	9d10	10θ15	..	11d28	1210	..	1d 0	2 1	5 19	6 18	8 18	9 27	1033
Roche	...	8d35	9d24	...	...	11d42	1224	...	1d14	2 16	5 34	6 31	8 31	9 42	1047
Bugle	..	8d42	9d30	..	..	11d48	1230	..	1d20	2 22	5 40	6 37	8 37	9 50	1052
Luxulyan	...	8d48	9d38	...	...	11d54	1235	...	1d26	2 28	5 46	6 42	8 42	9 56	1058
Par .. arr	8 42	9 5	9 55	..	1147	12 9	1252	1 15	1 42	2 42	6 0	6 56	8 55	10 9	1111

SUNDAYS

	am	am	am	am	pm	pm
Par .. dep	8 35	9 30	1040	1115	5 8	7 5
Luxulyan	8 48	9 44	...	1129	5 22	7 19
Bugle	8 55	9 50	..	1134	5 28	7 25
Roche	9 1	9 56	...	1140	5 34	7 31
St. Columb Road	9 16	1012	1122	1157	5 48	7 46
Quintrel Downs	...	1021	...	...	5 58	...
Newquay .. arr	9 30	1030	1140	1210	6 8	8 0

SUNDAYS

	am	am	pm	pm	pm	pm	pm
Newquay .. dep	9 55	1110	1 50	5 17	7 5	7 20	9 5
Quintrel Downs	...	...	...	5 24	...	...	9 13
St. Columb Road	1010	1125	2 4	5 35	..	7 35	9 23
Roche	N	1140	2 19	5 49	...	7 49	9 36
Bugle	1029	1146	2 25	5 55	..	7 55	9 42
Luxulyan	...	1153	2 31	6 1	...	8 1	9 48
Par .. arr	1050	1210	2 44	6 15	7 53	8 15	10 4

A Will not run after 30th August
B Runs Fridays 1st, 8th, 15th and 22nd August only.
D Fridays only; also runs on Monday 4th August
d Passengers travelling by this train to certain stations beyond Par are required to hold Regulation Tickets (see page 30)
G Runs Fridays, 1st, 8th, 15th, 22nd and 29th August only.
H Runs 28th June to 23rd August inclusive
K Calls at 10 12 am to pick up passengers for London only on notice being given at the Station by 9 30 am
N Calls at 10 20 am to pick up passengers for London only on notice being given at the Station by 9 30 am
θ Calls to pick up passengers only
Z Restaurant Car Train to London (Paddington) arr 4 55 pm (Table 81)

Summer 1958.

TRURO, CHACEWATER, PERRANPORTH, and NEWQUAY (Motor Cars—One class only).—Great Western.

Miles	Down.	Week Days. mrn	mrn	mrn	aft	aft	aft	aft
	Truro 22 .... dep.	7 43	b9 f41	11g50	2g22	4 f25	6 10	9 0
	27 PENZANCE .... dep.	6 f35	8 45	10g35	1225	3 17	4g35	6 f20
5¼	Chacewater ¶ .... dep.	7 55	10 7	12 20	2 42	4 43	6 25	9 12
8½	St. Agnes	8 5	10 16	12 30	2 53	4 53	6 35	9 22
13¾	Perranporth .... arr.	8 18	10 30	12 43	3 5	5 4	6 48	9 35
	dep.	8 19	10 31	12 44	3 6	5 5	6 49	9 36
17¾	Shepherds..	8 32	10 44	12 56	3 18	5 17	7 2	9 50
23¾	Newquay ¶ 55 .... arr.	8 48	11 0	1 13	3 35	5 29	7 18	10 7

Saturdays only.

Miles	Up.	Week Days. mrn	mrn	mrn	aft	aft	aft	aft
	Newquay ¶ .... dep.	7 50	8 52	11 5	1 30	3 42	6 43	7 35
6	Shepherds	8 6	9 8	1121	1 46	3 57	7 1	7 49
10½	Perranporth .... arr.	8 15	9 17	1130	1 55	4 6	7 10	8 0
	dep.	8 26	9 18	1131	1 56	4 7	7 11	8 1
15½	St. Agnes	8 43	9 35	1148	2 13	4 24	7 28	8 16
18½	Chacewater ¶ 22, 27... arr.	8 53	9 45	1158	2 23	4 35	7 38	8 23
39	22 PENZANCE .... arr.	....	11g 7	1g 7	3g35	....	9g 3	11½g
23¾	Truro 27 .... arr.	9g13	10 13	1225	2 46	4 57	7 50	8 35

Saturdays only.

b Leaves at 9 50 mrn. on Mondays and Thursdays. g By Train, 1st and 3rd class.

¶ "Halts" at Mount Hawke, between Chacewater and St. Agnes; Goonbell and Mithian, between St. Agnes and Perranporth; Goonhavern, between Perranporth and Shepherds; and Mitchell and Newlyn and Trewerry and Trerice, between Shepherds and Newquay.

82 WEEKDAYS

Not Saturdays 15 June to 7 September

PAR AND NEWQUAY

SINGLE LINE.—St. Blazey to Newquay. Crossing Places, Goonbarrow Junction and St. Dennis Junction. St. Blazey Bridge Crossing is an intermediate Block Post.

Mile Post Mileage M	C	Mileage from Par M	C	DOWN	No.	Ruling Gradient 1 in	0C54 LE	2C54 07 02 Bodmin Road	2C54 08 50 Bodmin Road		2C54 10 05 Bodmin Road		2C54 11 36 Bodmin Road		3C54 13†00 Bodmin Road ECS		6C54 10 30 Truro Freight
								▽	▽		▽		▽		▽		
							FO										
281	66	—	—	**PAR** .... dep	1	—	......	07 20	09 05	......	10 21	......	11 51	......	13 10	......	13 18
—	—	—	—	St. Blazey Yard	2	—	..	..	..	..	..	..	..	..	..	..	13 25
282	22	—	36	St. Blazey	3	56F	06‖55	07 22	09X07	......	10 23	......	11 53	......	13†15	......	......
282	73	1	7	St. Blazey Bridge Crossing ...	4	96R	..	..	..	..	..	..	..	..	..	..	..
285	78	4	12	Luxulyan .... arr	5	40R	......	07 32	09 17	......	10 33	......	12 03	......	......	......	......
				... ... dep	6		..	07 32½	09 17½	..	10 33½	..	12 03½	..	..	..	..
287	40	5	54	Goonbarrow Junction ... arr	7	100R	......	......	......	......	10X37	......	12X07	......	......	......	......
				... ... dep	8		07 15	07 35½	09 20½	..	10 38	..	12 08	..	..	..	..
288	3	6	17	Bugle .... arr	9	142R	14 JUNE to 6 SEPT	07 37	09 22	......	10 40	......	12 10	......	......	......	......
				... ... dep	10			07 37½	09 22½	..	10 40½	..	12 10½	..	..	..	..
290	40	8	54	Roche .... arr	11	47R		07 43	09 28	......	10 46	......	12 16	......	......	......	......
				... ... dep	12			07 43½	09 28½	..	10 46½	..	12 16½	..	..	..	..
294	21	12	35	St. Dennis Junction ...... arr	13	40R		......	......	......	......	......	......	......	......	......	......
				... ... dep	14		07 30	07 50½	09 35½	..	10 53½	..	12 23½	..	..	..	..
296	11	14	25	St. Columb Road .... arr	15	66R	......	07 55½	09 40½	......	10 58½	......	12 28½	......	......	......	......
				... ... dep	16		..	07 56	09 41	..	10 59	..	12 29	..	..	..	..
300	16	18	30	Quintrel Downs Platform ...	17	66F	......	08a04	09a49	......	11a07	......	12a37	......	......	......	......
302	51	20	65	**NEWQUAY** ... ... arr	18	94F	07‖45	08 10	09 55	..	11 13	..	12 43	..	..	..	..

Table 142 Par — Newquay

Miles			Mondays to Fridays					A	Saturdays C 🄺	D	D	E 🄺	G 🄺	J 🄺	Sundays			
0	Par	d	07 10	09 05	11 48	14 15	17 40	19 32	06 13	08 39	10 03	13 05	15 47	17 21	09 45	11 45	14 55	18 11
4¼	Luxulyan	d	07x22	09x17	12x00	14x27	17x52	.	.	08 50	.	.	.	.	09x57	11x57	15x07	.
6¼	Bugle	d	07x27	09x22	12x05	14x32	17x57	.	.	08 57	.	.	.	.	10x02	12x02	15x12	.
8¾	Roche	d	07x32	09x27	12x10	14x37	18x02	.	.	09 02	.	.	.	.	10x07	12x07	15x17	.
14¼	St. Columb Road	d	07 43	09 38	12 21	14 48	18 13	20 04	06u43	09 14	10 39	.	.	17 54	10 18	12 18	15 28	18x43
18¼	Quintrel Downs	d	07 52	09 47	12 30	14 57	18 22	20 13	.	09 23	.	.	.	.	10 27	12 27	15 37	18x51
20¾	Newquay	a	08 00	09 55	12 38	15 05	18 30	20 20	07 00	09 31	10 55	13 49	16 33	18 10	10 35	12 35	15 45	18 59

Miles			Mondays to Fridays						Saturdays K 🄺	L 🄺	N 🄺	P 🄺	Q	Q	Sundays			
0	Newquay	d	08 05	10 00	12 45	16 35	18 43	20 25	08 20	09 50	11 25	14 55	17 01	18 50	10 42	13 40	17 05	19 02
2¼	Quintrel Downs	d	08 12	10 07	12 52	16 42	18 50	20 32	08 27	.	.	.	17 08	18 57	10 49	13 47	17 12	19 09
6¼	St. Columb Road	d	08 20	10 15	13 00	16 50	18 58	20 40	08 35	.	.	.	17 16	19 05	10 57	13 55	17 20	19 18
12	Roche	d	08x32	10x27	13x12	17x02	19x10	.	.	.	.	.	17 28	19 17	11x09	14x07	17x32	19x29
14¼	Bugle	d	08x37	10x32	13x17	17x07	19x15	.	.	.	.	.	17 33	19 22	11x14	14x12	17x37	19x34
16¼	Luxulyan	d	08x43	10x38	13x23	17x13	19x21	.	.	.	.	.	17 40	19 29	11x19	14x17	17x42	19x39
20¾	Par	a	08 55	10 50	13 35	17 25	19 34	21 13	09 10	10 34	12 09	15 39	17 50	19 39	11 32	14 30	17 55	19 52

For general notes see front of timetable

A From Falmouth Docks (Table 143)
C **InterCity Holidaymaker.** From Leeds (Table 51)
D From Plymouth (Table 135)
E **InterCity Holidaymaker.** From Manchester Piccadilly (Table 51)
G **Atlantic Coast Express. InterCity Holidaymaker.** From London Paddington (Table 135)
J **InterCity Holidaymaker.** From Glasgow Queen Street (Table 26)
K **InterCity Holidaymaker.** To Manchester Piccadilly (Table 51)
L **InterCity Holidaymaker.** To Glasgow Queen Street (Table 26)
N **Atlantic Coast Express. InterCity Holidaymaker.** To London Paddington (Table 135)
P **InterCity Holidaymaker.** To Leeds (Table 51)
Q To Plymouth (Table 135)

From time to time it is necessary to undertake extensive engineering work at weekends. This frequently affects services and passengers are advised to look for specific announcements of possible diversions and delays making a final check at stations or telephone enquiry bureaux.

Signal Boxes– Closure Dates

Plate 299. Out of the 30 sites which once had signal boxes within the geographical boundaries covered by this volume, only three, Par, St Blazey and Goonbarrow Junction, remain open. This view of St Blazey from the mid-1950s shows five of the St Blazey staff posing for the photographer. At the time of writing the station has been closed to general passengers for no less than 65 years! *R. C. Riley*

Signal box	Closed
Fowey	1968
Pinnock Tunnel	1958
Par Bridge Crossing CMR	1916
Par Bridge Crossing GWR	1968
Par	(open)
St Blazey CMR	1908
St Blazey GWR	(open)
Middleway Bridge Crossing	1981
St Blazey Bridge Crossing	1973
Luxulyan CMR	1911
Luxulyan GWR	1964
Rosevear	1893
Goonbarrow Junction	(open) (a)
Bugle CMR	1916
Bugle GWR	1964 (c)
Roche	1965
Tregoss	1965 (d)
St Dennis Junction CMR	?
St Dennis Junction GWR	1986
St Columb Road	1965
Quintrel Sidings	1911(b)
Tolcarn Junction CMR	1888
Tolcarn Junction GWR (1)	1931
Tolcarn Junction GWR (2)	1964
Newquay CMR	1905
Newquay GWR (1)	1946
Newquay GWR (2)	1987
Burngullow East	1935
Burngullow West	1986
Drinnick Mill	1966
Kernick	1950
Parkandillack	1922
Blackwater West	1924
Blackwater East	1924
Blackwater North	1924
St Agnes	1963
Perranporth	1963
Shepherds	1963
Lane Junction	1888

There were no signal boxes on the following lines:
Ponts Mill Siding
Treffry Tramways
Wheal Rose Branch
Carbis Branch
Goonbarrow Branch
Gothers Tramway
Retew Branch
Treamble Branch
Newquay Harbour Branch
All sidings had ground frames and there were many crossing keepers' signalling frames (some in huts).

Notes
(a) Built on the site of Rosevear signal box.
(b) Replaced by a ground frame – later moved – closed 1981.
(c) and (d) Reduced to groundframe status – finally closed 1973.

Plate 300. In addition to the main signal boxes there were scores of crossing keepers' huts and ground frames. In a photograph "snatched" from the front of a diesel multiple unit in June 1974 the crossing keeper at Halloon Crossing, west of St Columb Road station, stands in front of his hut, old crossing gates and gas lamps – all soon to be removed for ever. It is now an "open" crossing with audible warning signal and flashing lights. *JV*

For a picnic party there are any number of pleasant spots wherein to set up a gipsy tripod—below the viaduct is a favourite one—and at the Smithy, on the way to and near the Colkerrow Quarry, a kettle might be boiled.

The walk we describe in large type includes the best points. Those who devote a day to the excursion will easily extend it, and include the points mentioned in the small print. Perhaps the best way for a **walk of about 4 miles** (not including the disused line to the Grinding Works) is to proceed, as in large print, to the Viaduct, then from the near end to turn down, right, into the valley, and there left, under the railway and Viaduct, and 2 *min.* beyond the latter to turn up to the right. This lands us on the tram-line, where we turn to the left and proceed as given in large type (where our road is said to *cross* tram-line). In this way the return to Luxulion and Bridges would be by the small type route *viâ Mid Gready*.

Pedestrians who do not wish to return to New Quay can proceed to St. Blazey Station (for Fowey), or to Par Station on the main line without returning to Bridges Station. For this walk, see small print at the end of this excursion.

This is, we think, the best excursion from New Quay. The Luxulion Valley is a deep silvan glen of much beauty (in spite of its noisy brook being thick and white with china-clay washings), and the great tors and stupendous "perched blocks" are very striking. The Treffry Viaduct, which spans the valley, is a noble work and fine view-point.

From the up-side of the station we ascend the road for 2 *min.*, and then, from a stile, right, take the field-path, which, in 3 *min.* more, leads to Luxulion village and church (restored). There is an ancient cross in the church-yard and another dated 1687.

Go through the church-yard and a little way down the road, 3 *min.* S.E. of the church, on the left behind a pump, is an ancient **Baptistery** in good preservation. The *Colymbethra* is now dry owing to the spring which used to supply it having been drained by the railway-cutting. Down to about 1875 it was the village well. The bracket for the image still remains in the back wall of the well. Two *min.* further are five tall thin stone pillars. We return up the road to the Post Office and of course turn to the left.

Here we bear round just above the Post Office and passing the school, cross the railway by a bridge. Hence an unmistakable path leads, in 4 *min.*, down the fields to the mineral line, used for bringing the granite from the quarries, along which we turn to the left. [N.B. This is not regarded as a trespass, and no risk is involved, because the trucks conveying the stone are drawn by horses.] A walk of 6 *min.* along the line (passing an old quarry, right, and a small reservoir, left) brings us to the **Treffry Viaduct**, 657 ft. long, 90 ft. high, from which we get a lovely view up and down the glen. At the far end of the viaduct is gear belonging to a quarry, but our route lies along the line that bends back to the left.

The line straight on from the Viaduct is now disused. It passes the ruins of a waterwheel, which worked the incline, and goes through a wood. In case the leat which brings water from the far side of the main valley is not in use, a waterfall is formed nearly 200 feet high, but this is seldom running except on Sundays, when there are no trains on the railway. Further on along this tram-line are Grinding works, where the best China-stone for glazing pottery is prepared.

In 4 *min.* from the turn the line is crossed by a road, and 2 *min.* further another road crosses under the line. [The former of these we shall use presently.] Here, too, a disused branch line diverges, left, towards Luxulion. As we continue along our line, the scene on either hand is a fine combination of granite blocks, pools, and woodland, and the "perched" blocks will be noted. When the line begins to rise we may have to step aside to make way for trucks descending by gravitation. The botanist will note the sessile-fruited oak and the ordinary kind growing side by side, on the left, opposite a fine spring on the right. The former is the wood used in Westminster Hall which till recently was supposed to be chestnut. About 12 *min.* from leaving the viaduct there is a Smithy (*see above*), on the left of the line, and behind it rises the largest of all the blocks, of which only a close view will reveal the true size. To reach it, turn to the left, by the spring and over the stepping-stones in the wall, whence a track will be found through the bushes. The group of blocks consists of three, and the largest, the **Giant Block**, under which there is a considerable space, measures 49½ ft. by 27 ft., and is 72 ft. in girth.

We believe this is the largest block in Europe, larger than any of the famous boulders at the head of the Italian lakes. It may take rank with the largest known, the Agassiz blocks, in the Tijuca mountains near Rio Janeiro. The rock, which consists of large crystals of black tourmaline and pink felspar in a base of grey quartz, is called *Luxulianite*. It is only found in these blocks, and no dyke of it is known.

Returning to the line we might diverge from it nearly opposite the Smithy to Colkerrow Hill, which commands a view towards New Quay and, in the other direction, of the channel near St. Austell. If, however, we keep along the line, 5 *min.* more brings us to the Colkerrow Quarry, and a climb to the head of it is rewarded by a fine view including the Viaduct.

A path left from the quarry leads to the ancient farm-house of *Mid Gready* (look inside the court-yard and at the well), and thence an old bridle-path brings us to a lovely slope leading down to the stream and then up to *Luxulion* village, where the old Baptistery (*p.* 106) is on the right.

Our next object is to view the **Viaduct** from below, and we therefore retrace our steps along the line as far as the road which crosses it. There we turn down to the right, and in a minute or two join the road in the bottom of the valley and turn left. In 2 *min.* we are under one of the 10 arches of the viaduct. Continuing along the road in 3 *min.* more we pass under the Railway, and then, if our return is to be to Bridges Station, we turn up and back, on the right, and, with a good view of the valley, rejoin our outward route at the little reservoir near the Luxulion end of the Viaduct.

Treffry Viaduct to St. Blazey Station, 50 *min.*, or **Par Station**, 1 *hr.* A pleasant walk. After going under the Railway keep to the road, that is, do not turn as for Bridges (see above) nor left at the house just beyond. A moderate ascent brings us in 12 *min.* or less to the top of the only hill we have to mount, and when a short distance down the other side a fork is

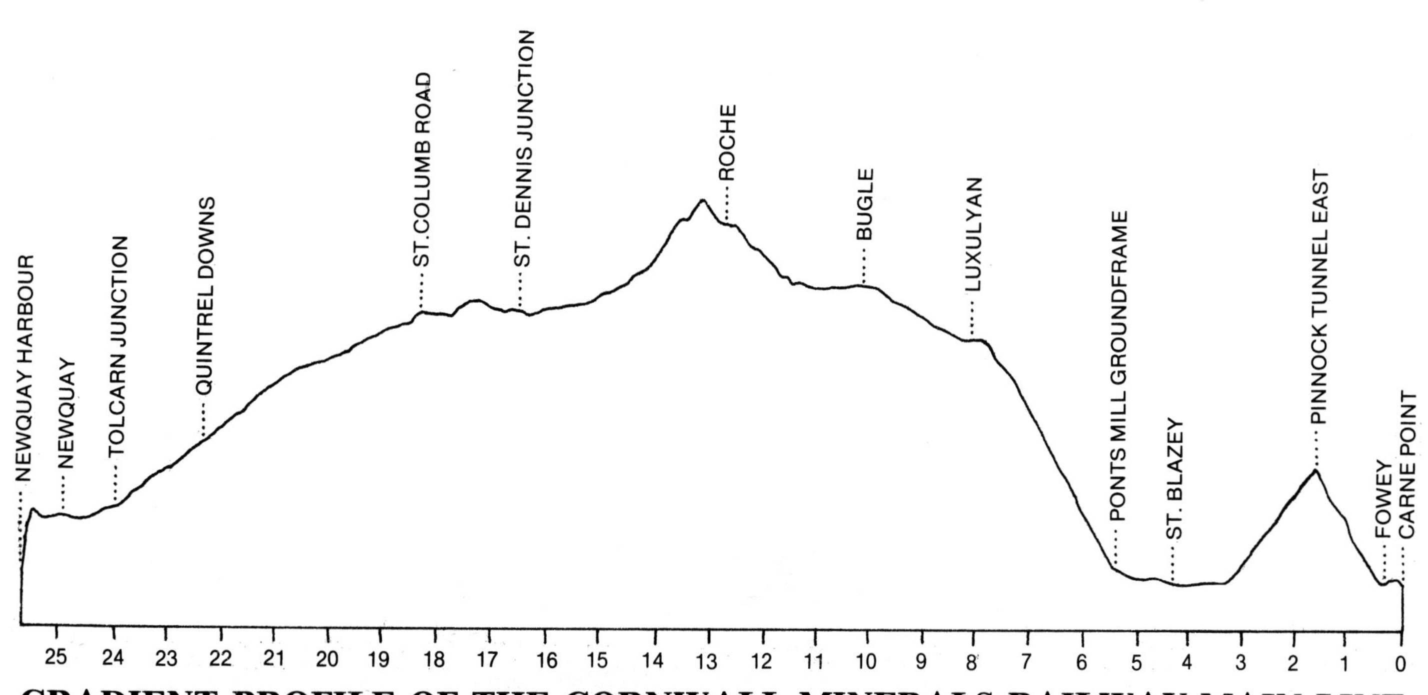

GRADIENT PROFILE OF THE CORNWALL MINERALS RAILWAY MAIN LINE

Acknowledgements

It is inevitable that when compiling a comprehensive 192-page book, which describes a series of lines which have not all been the subject of previously published histories, a large number of individuals and institutions contribute to the overall product. I wish to thank personally all of the following for their willing help and assistance, without which the compiling and writing of this book would have been far more difficult.

At the top of the long list must be railway historian and "bramble basher" Maurice Dart for his generous and invaluable assistance with a wide range of material. Also Richard Fuller of ECC who introduced me to a number of knowledgeable contacts and who willingly provided ECC photographic material. For photographs of the steam era I must sincerely thank Dick Riley, Les Elsey, Peter Treloar, Carey Batchelor – a former St Blazey driver, Peter Gray, Harry Townley, Michael Mensing, Terry Nicholls and George Hemmett. These gentlemen produced absolutely first-class material from their valuable collections. For historic photographic material I am indeed indebted to Joyce Greenham and the Newquay Old Cornwall Society, the Royal Cornwall Institute at Truro, English China Clay International, L. Stuthridge, Peter Bray, Lens of Sutton, Charlie Saundercock of Bugle and in particular Leslie T. George of Newquay. For modern material my old friends Brian Morrison and John Hicks must be thanked.

As regards general research and the supply of historical information I would like to thank S. C. May, Tom Richards, Nick Childs, the late Charles Clinker and the wonderful Brunel University Collection, Courtenay Smale of the Goonvean & Rostowrack China Clay Company, Tony Fairclough of Wadebridge, Mr Jenkins of Newquay Library and the County Records Office at Truro.

For assistance with operational matters and personal recollections my gratitude goes to Ivor Trudgeon of Drinnick Mill Goods Office, Peter Hamley – Goonbarrow signalman, Percy Wherry and Albert Hooper – St Blazey drivers, St Blazey Supervisors Norman Searle (retired), George Hemmett, Peter Bennett, John Williams and Alan Butler. BR Area Freight Manager Peter Foot supplied valuable information as did Des Arlette of Polmear, Martin Pearce of ECC and the late John Penderill-Church. Also all of the authors of the books contained in the bibliography should be thanked for their previous research into the various aspects of the railways of Cornwall. My many colleagues who, over a period of years, have travelled with me to Cornwall to pursue my railway interests in the Royal Duchy should also be recognised for their moral support including John Frith, Steve Chandler, Mike Collins, John Chalcraft, Michael Hunt, Keith Freak and Richard Cossey; the last named also for his very significant contribution and proof reading. For the freedom allowed in the design and layout of this volume I thank my publishers Haynes/OPC. Finally, my wife Carol should be recognised for her patience and understanding, especially for the author burning midnight oil regularly and doing practically no DIY about the house for some six months!

Bibliography

An Illustrated History of West Country China Clay Trains John Vaughan (OPC 1987)

Diesels in the Duchy John Vaughan (Ian Allan 1983)

The History of English China Clays Kenneth Hudson (David & Charles 1969)

The Story of Cornwall's Railways Anthony Fairclough (Bradford Barton 1970)

A History of the Cornish China Clay Industry R. M. Barton (Bradford Barton 1966)

The Branch Lines of Cornwall Lewis Reade (Atlantic Books 1984)

Cornwall's Railways – a Pictorial History Anthony Fairclough (Bradford Barton 1972)

The West Country (Regional History of Railways) David St John Thomas (David & Charles 1981)

The Cornish China Clay Traffic (TI Summer Annual) R. C. Riley (Ian Allan 1957)

Treffry's Tramways the late John Penderill-Church (ECC 1979)

The Great Western Railway in Mid Cornwall Alan Bennett (Kingfisher Railway Productions 1988)

Branch Line Memories Lewis Reade (Atlantic Books 1983)

Track Layout Diagrams – East Cornwall R. A. Cooke, School Lane, Harwell, Oxon.

Cornwall Railway Geoffrey Body (Avon Anglia Publications 1984)

The Luxulyan Valley Cornwall Archaeological Unit 1988

Cornwall Railway Heritage John Stengelhofen (Twelveheads Press 1988)

A History of the Great Western Railway E. T. McDermot (GWR 1927)

A History of the Railway Newquay to Fowey 1830–1896 S. C. May (St John's Ambulance Indian Queens 1982)

Around and About Clay Country Peter Bray (Corran Publications 1988)

Around and About St Austell Peter Bray (Corran Publications 1987)

Industrial Locomotives of South West England R. Hateley (Industrial Railway Society 1977)

Canals of South West England Charles Hadfield (David & Charles 1967)

Bradshaw's Timetables – 1888 and 1910

Various Issues – *Trains Illustrated, Railway Magazine, Railway World, West Briton, Modern Railways, Rail, Western Morning News* and *Great Western Magazine*

Other Timetables – 1878, 1958, 1968/69 and 1989

Various Papers – Clinker Collection, Brunel University (Uxbridge), County Records Office (Truro) and Cornwall Libraries